T&T Clark Studies in Systematic Theology

Edited by

John Webster
Ian A. McFarland
Ivor Davidson

Volume 16

GOD'S BEING IN RECONCILIATION

The Theological Basis of the Unity and Diversity of the Atonement in the Theology of Karl Barth

Adam J. Johnson

BLOOMSBURY
LONDON · NEW DELHI · NEW YORK · SYDNEY

Bloomsbury T&T Clark

An imprint of Bloomsbury Publishing Plc

50 Bedford Square
London
WC1B 3DP
UK

1385 Broadway
New York
NY 10018
USA

www.bloomsbury.com

Bloomsbury is a registered trade mark of Bloomsbury Publishing Plc

First published 2012
Paperback edition first published 2013

British Library Cataloguing-in-Publication Data
A catalogue record for this book is available from the British Library.

ISBN: HB: 978-0-567-63833-5
PB: 978-0-567-12345-9

Library of Congress Cataloging-in-Publication Data
A catalog record for this book is available from the Library of Congress

Typeset by Fakenham Prepress Solutions, Fakenham, Norfolk NR21 8NN

I dedicate this book to the girl with the magic markers,
whom I have liked since I was five.

CONTENTS

ACKNOWLEDGEMENTS

This book has been a longstanding collaborative effort in which different friendships, schools and churches have played a formative role. John Mark Reynolds, Fred Sanders and Paul Spears at Biola University's Torrey Honors Institute, and Gregg TenElshoff in Biola's philosophy department permanently impressed upon me a love of classic texts and vision for the role of the mind in the Christian faith. Fred in particular has proved a constant guide through the theological waters I have navigated. At Talbot Seminary, Clint Arnold and Henry Holloman helped set a foundation for my future studies in the atonement. At Princeton Seminary I greatly appreciated Daniel Migliore, George Husinger and Bruce McCormack. To the former I owe the original impetus for approaching Barth's doctrine of reconciliation as I have. My debt to Bruce McCormack is equally great; while I demur from his thesis concerning election and the doctrine of the Trinity, his command of the material and his care for his students impressed me greatly and continue to inspire me today.

At Trinity Evangelical Divinity School (TEDS), Kevin Vanhoozer, Graham Cole and Tom McCall have played significant roles as teachers and mentors. Kevin has mentored me and supervised my studies despite his recent move to Wheaton College. My time working for Graham and our discussions outside of class have been a joy. Tom has facilitated my transition from student to colleague. My thanks also to a number of fellow students at TEDS – especially Andy Abernethy, Jared Compton, Steve Garrett, Jack Gibson, James Gordon, Scott Harrower, Jonathan King, Ben Sutton and Jeremy Treat. Other friends, colleagues and mentors that have contributed to this book directly or indirectly include Greg Beale, Phil Butin, Kent Eilers, Adam Eitel, John Franke, Kevin Hector, Matt Jenson, Paul Dafydd Jones, David Lauber, Travis McMaken, Paul Molnar, Greg Peters, Robert Peterson, Rob Price, Ben Rhodes, Justin Stratis, Justyn Terry, John Webster and Stephen Williams. I would like to thank my new colleagues (and particularly my new neighbours, Ryan Peterson and Aaron James) at Cedarville University for their help and encouragement as we begin to make Ohio our new home.

Several churches have significantly helped us on our way. Blessed Sacrament (Placentia, CA) helped us discern God's call upon our lives, and the prayers of Steve and Betsy Barber have accompanied us for the better part of a decade. St Luke's (Newtown, PA) and my friendship with Fr Ernest Curtin has been greatly appreciated. Most recently the Village Church of Lincolnshire, especially our small group, has supported us in a number of ways.

Before I met any of these friends, my parents, Glen and Susie Johnson, were preparing me for these studies by investing their lives in me, teaching me to love my Lord and to love learning. My Dad is the one responsible for my first exposure to the *Church Dogmatics* – as he proudly reported to us how many pages he had read each Sunday before a well-deserved afternoon nap interrupted his efforts. He is also responsible for any 'readability' properties this book may have, having edited every research paper I have written. It has been a delight to have my theological studies bring me closer than ever to my parents.

As Barth said, '*Concentrated* theological work is a good thing ... but *exclusive* theological existence is *not* a good thing.'[1] If there has been one constant in my life ensuring that my work was concentrated, but my existence not exclusively theological, it is surely my wife and sons, though to be sure they bear the marks of my theological studies. At the ripe old age of two, my son Reuben surprised us at the dinner table by dropping one of his first theological names: Friedrich Schleiermacher (perfectly pronounced, by the way![2]). Two years later he would probe me on the way to the grocery store with questions about the relationship between the atonement and the doctrine of the Trinity. His little brother, Nathan, would carry a stack of books to his bed at naptime 'to study for my COMPS!' Only Simeon, born to us this past September, will know of these years of graduate studies only through the collective memory of the family. My wife, Katrina, bears deeper marks: the pain of interrupted friendships as we moved from seminary to seminary, and the burden of providing for our growing family through her work as a nurse. I thank her for these and other sacrifices, but far more for the great joy it has been to be her husband throughout this process. This book is a token of the work we have done together to know Jesus Christ as our Lord who frees us from every bond.

---

[1] Karl Barth, *Evangelical Theology: An Introduction*, trans. Grover Foley (London: Weidenfeld and Nicolson, 1963), 131.
[2] Cf. the dedicatory note in: Jack Forstman, *A Romantic Triangle: Schleiermacher and Early German Romanticism* (Missoula, MT: Scholars Press, 1977), vi.

ABBREVIATIONS

CD   Barth, Karl. *Church Dogmatics*. Translated by G. T. Thomson. Edited by Geoffrey Bromiley and Thomas F. Torrance. 5 vols in 14 parts (Edinburgh: T & T Clark, 1936–77).

DG   Barth, Karl. *Dogmatik im Grundriss* (Zürich: Evangelischer Verlag, 1947).

DO   Barth, Karl. *Dogmatics in Outline*. Translated by G. T. Thomson. (New York: Harper, 1959).

IJST   *International Journal of Systematic Theology*

KD   Barth, Karl. *Die kirchliche Dogmatik*. 5 vols in 14 parts (Zollikon: Evangelischer Verlag, 1932–70).

SJT   *Scottish Journal of Theology*

1

INTRODUCTION

How do we best approach the doctrine of the atonement[1] so as to have at our disposal the necessary resources to appreciate the fullness of the meaning and significance of Christ's atoning work? What Scriptural or theological framework offers the best and most comprehensive map to this terrain? And do we in fact need such a framework?[2] As Paul Fiddes notes, 'Paul, it seems, confined himself to the theme of 'Christ nailed to the cross" while visiting the church at Corinth (1 Cor. 2.2). Fiddes proceeds to explain, however, that 'this does not mean he was always repeating himself, or preaching the same sermon. The point he is making … is that he proclaimed the cross of Jesus as occupying the centre of all life'.[3] If in fact the cross of Jesus Christ decisively shapes and determines every aspect of life, as the church throughout the centuries has claimed, then it is of the utmost significance that our theological account of this event appropriate from the outset the broadest and most comprehensive framework for understanding the work of God in the life, death and resurrection of Jesus Christ, so as not prematurely to amputate whole realms of inquiry and the consideration of their implications.[4]

---

[1] 'From *at one*, as the etymologists remark, *to be at one*, is the frame as *to be in concord*.' Samuel Johnson, 'To Atone', in *A Dictionary of the English Language* (London: Times Books, 1979).

[2] One way to discover a 'unifying Christian view of Christ's saving work', according to Roger Olson, is to 'retrieve the simple faith in Christ's saving life, death and resurrection', seeking the common denominator in all (or the majority of) Christian views of Christ's work throughout history, by focusing on Jesus Christ and resisting speculation. Roger E. Olson, *The Mosaic of Christian Belief: Twenty Centuries of Unity and Diversity* (Downers Grove, IL: InterVarsity Press, 2002), 262. In response, I think that such an approach fails to embrace the powerful unity-in-diversity of Christ's work with all the resources that it contains for the life of the church.

[3] Paul S. Fiddes, *Past Event and Present Salvation: The Christian Idea of Atonement* (Louisville, KY: WJK, 1989), 3.

[4] Bernard L. Ramm, *After Fundamentalism: The Future of Evangelical Theology* (San Francisco, CA: Harper & Row, 1983), 2.

1

Recent studies of the doctrine of the atonement tend to take their cue from two related discussions: (1) non-violent critiques and constructive alternatives levied against penal substitution,[5] and (2) the heightened awareness of the multiplicity of the images, metaphors and theories of the atonement present in both Scripture and in historical and contemporary theology.[6] Those critiquing penal substitution demand the elimination of this theory altogether, or the readjustment of its status to that of one of many theories of the atonement. Unfortunately, the parties engaged in this polemic discussion emphasize biblical and historical texts that offer the strongest support for their respective positions, resulting in one-sided and overly narrow approaches to the doctrine by all the parties involved. More positively, the pressure of this discussion, combined with a host of new or reinvigorated approaches to the atonement in contemporary literature, appears to be reawakening the church to the wide array of understandings of Christ's saving work in Scripture and the history of theology.

This diversity offers the church abundant resources for proclaiming the meaning and significance of the cross in different contexts. It facilitates a multifaceted approach to the varying needs and experiences, for example, of adults whose childhood experiences consisted of a steady diet of abandonment and betrayal, communities governed by fear of a witch-doctor or inmates of an American prison. Simultaneously, it raises significant theological questions for consideration. For instance, with regard to the works by Hans Boersma, Leonardo Boff, René Girard and Denny Weaver, what criteria should the Church use to develop and test new theories of Christ's work?[7] How are we to adjudicate between sometimes

---

[5] Brad Jersak and Michael Hardin, eds, *Stricken by God? Nonviolent Identification and the Victory of Christ* (Grand Rapids, MI: Eerdmans, 2007); Marit Trelstad, *Cross Examinations: Readings on the Meaning of the Cross Today* (Minneapolis, MN: Fortress, 2006). Many of the essays in these two volumes respond to what is to date one of the best defenses of penal substitution, Hans Boersma, *Violence, Hospitality, and the Cross: Reappropriating the Atonement Tradition* (Grand Rapids, MI: Baker Academic, 2004). For a recent Evangelical interaction with many of these questions, see: Derek Tidball, David Hilborn and Justin Thacker, eds., *The Atonement Debate: Papers From the London Symposium on the Theology of Atonement* (Grand Rapids, MI: Zondervan, 2008).

[6] James K. Beilby and Paul R. Eddy, eds, *The Nature of the Atonement: Four Views* (Downers Grove, IL: IVP Academic, 2006); Stephen Finlan, *Options on Atonement in Christian Thought* (Collegeville, MN: Liturgical Press, 2007); John McIntyre, *The Shape of Soteriology: Studies in the Doctrine of the Death of Christ* (Edinburgh: T & T Clark, 1992); Scot McKnight, *A Community Called Atonement* (Nashville, TN: Abingdon Press, 2007).

[7] Hans Boersma, *Violence, Hospitality, and the Cross: Reappropriating the Atonement Tradition* (Grand Rapids, MI: Baker Academic, 2004); Leonardo Boff, *Passion of Christ, Passion of the World: The Facts, Their Interpretation, and Their Meaning Yesterday and Today* (Maryknoll, NY: Orbis, 1987); René Girard, *I See Satan Fall*

competing appeals to the authority of experience, Scripture and the historic faith of the Church in these matters?

A second major question these dynamics pose, and the focus of this book, pertains to the relationship between these diverse views or theories of Christ's saving work: what (if anything) unites the many metaphors, models and theories, such that by understanding the former we can nourish and order the Church's use of the latter in its worship, proclamation and service?[8] Henri Blocher notes the significance of this subject for the church today: 'Whether there is a unifying perspective on atonement throughout biblical [and dogmatic, I would add] writings and whether it can guide theological reflection is obviously [a question of] first rank.'[9] The Church is thus confronted with what we might call a problem of the 'one and the many' within the doctrine of the atonement: the need to discern the unity underlying the multiplicity of apparently distinct (if not diametrically opposed) understandings of Christ's saving work. What unifies this plurality, harnessing its presently diffused energy by giving it coherence and focus? What framework will form this cacophony of voices into a choir?

The Whence of Diversity

Why is there such an abundance of distinct trajectories explaining the significance of Christ's death and resurrection in contemporary theology and throughout the history of the Church, sometimes formulated as competing theories, sometimes conjoined in loosely or tightly ordered systems? Irenaeus and his hermeneutic of recapitulation,[10] Athanasius and many of the Greek fathers with their emphasis on theōsis,[11] often coincident with an account of Christ's victory over Satan (Gregory of Nyssa),[12] Anselm's

---

Like Lightning (Maryknoll, NY: Orbis, 2001); J. Denny Weaver, *The Nonviolent Atonement* (Grand Rapids, MI: Eerdmans, 2001).

[8] Brown, for instance, writes that 'preachers today must draw on a diversity of "metaphors of redemption," deployed within concrete situations, to disclose what the cross reveals about God's redemptive engagement with us.' Sally A. Brown, *Cross Talk: Preaching Redemption Here and Now* (Louisville, KY: WJK, 2008), 5–6. In full sympathy with this vision statement, my purpose is to work out the underlying foundation for this task, so as to strengthen our determination and ability to draw from this diversity.

[9] Henri Blocher, 'Atonement', in *Dictionary for Theological Interpretation of the Bible*, eds Kevin J. Vanhoozer *et al.* (Grand Rapids, MI: Baker Academic, 2005).

[10] Irenaeus, *On the Apostolic Preaching*, trans. John Behr (Crestwood, NY: St Vladimir's Seminary Press, 1997).

[11] Athanasius, *On the Incarnation*, trans. Penelope Lawson (Crestwood, NY: St Vladimir's Seminary Press, 1953), 30, 35.

[12] Gregory of Nyssa, 'An Address on Religious Instruction', in *Christology of the Later Fathers*, ed. Edward R. Hardy (Philadelphia, PA: Westminster Press, 1954), 301.

satisfaction theory[13] and Abelard's supposedly exemplarist response,[14] Thomas with his synthesis and development[15] of what was to become the penal substitution of the Reformers[16] and those who followed them,[17] John of the Cross with his account of Jesus' experience of the 'dark night,'[18] Campbell's vicarious repentance,[19] Schleiermacher's 'mystical' account,[20] Hegel's theology of reconciliation ...[21] The list goes on, without touching on the explosion of theories in the twentieth and early twenty-first centuries. Whence comes such diversity?

It is only natural that a variety of accounts of the atonement exist, we might say, when Scripture explains Christ's death and resurrection in such diverse ways as a ransom (λύτρον; Mk 10.45), seeking that which is lost (Lk. 15), defeat of Satan (Jn 12.31 and 14.30), propitiation (ἱλαστήριον; Rom. 3.25), justification of God (δικαιοσύνη; Rom. 3.25), justification of sinners (δικαίωσις; Rom. 5.18), Passover (πάσχα; 1 Cor. 5.7), redemption (ἐξαγοράζω; Gal. 4.5), reconciliation (ἀποκαταλλάσσω; Col. 1.20), payment of our debt (Col. 2.14) and sacrifice (θυσία; Heb. 10.12), to name but a few. The Old Testament likewise contributes an abundance of themes for consideration, including the Exodus, Moses' intercession (Exod. 32–3; Num. 14), the Passover (Exod. 12) and the sacrificial system in all its diversity, the scapegoat (Lev. 16), the role of kinsman redeemer (Ruth 4), and the suffering servant (Isa. 42.1–4, 49.1–6, 50.4–9 and 52.13–53.12). Many of these lines of thought are connected to other aspects of the Christian faith (such as Christology or ecclesiology), warranting sustained and relatively

---

[13] Anselm, 'Why God Became Man', in *The Major Works*, ed. Brian Davies and G. R. Evans (New York: Oxford University Press, 1998).

[14] Peter Abailard, 'Exposition of the Epistle to the Romans (An Excerpt from the Second Book)', in *A Scholastic Miscellany: Anselm to Ockham*, ed. Eugene Rathbone Fairweather (Philadelphia, PA: Westminster Press, 1956). Cf. Bernard of Clairvaux, *Some Letters of Saint Bernard, Abbot of Clairvaux*, ed. Francis Aidan Gasquet, trans. Samuel John Eales (London: John Hodges, 1904), 259–93.

[15] Thomas, *Summa Theologica*, trans. Fathers of the English Dominican Province (Westminster, MD: Christian Classics, 1981), 2258–302; 3.46–3.52.

[16] Cf. John Calvin, *Institutes of the Christian Religion* (Philadelphia, PA: Westminster Press, 1960), 464–534; II.xii–xvii.

[17] Cf. Francis Turretin, *The Atonement*, ed. C. Matthew McMahon, trans. James R. Willson (New Lenox, IL: Puritan Publications, 2005).

[18] John of the Cross, 'The Ascent of Mt Carmel', in *The Collected Works of St John of the Cross* (Washington, DC: Institute of Carmelite Studies, 1979), 172.

[19] John McLeod Campbell, *The Nature of the Atonement and Its Relation to Remission of Sins and Eternal Life* (London: Macmillan, 1869).

[20] Friedrich Schleiermacher, *The Christian Faith*, ed. H. R. Mackintosh and James Stuart Stewart (Edinburgh: T & T Clark, 1968), 425–75.

[21] G. W. F. Hegel, *Lectures on the Philosophy of Religion: The Lectures of 1827*, trans. Peter Crafts Hodgson and Robert F. Brown (New York: Clarendon Press, 2006), 452–70; 3:233–51.

independent attention for each, thereby validating to a significant extent many of the trajectories developed by the theologians mentioned above.[22]

Pointing to the diversity of the Scriptural witness, however, is not the simple solution it might at first appear to be. First, there is the rather prevalent suspicion that the Scriptural trimmings garnishing the work of many of these theologians play little or no shaping influence on what is in fact a culturally derived theology of the atonement.[23] A second difficulty is that such a solution only shifts the locus of the question at hand from the history of theology to the Bible: why are there so many different (if not contradictory) explanations of the significance of Christ's death and resurrection throughout Scripture? Furthermore, this question is no less susceptible to 'cultural' questions than the former. As Mark Baker and Joel Green put it:

> A plurality of metaphors is used [in Scripture] to draw out the significance of Jesus' death because of wider cultural considerations. If the message of salvation is universal ... and if that message is to be grasped in ever-expanding cultural circles, then that message must be articulated in culture-specific ways ... Even if they are to varying degrees transformed by their association with the crucifixion of Jesus of Nazareth, they nevertheless take their interpretive point of departure from prominent, shared, social intercourse.[24]

[22] The work of Leon Morris is of considerable value in exploring the sheer breadth and diversity of the biblical witness concerning the work of Christ. Leon Morris, *The Apostolic Preaching of the Cross* (London: Tyndale Press, 1955); Leon Morris, *The Cross in the New Testament* (Grand Rapids, MI: Eerdmans, 1965). For example, Morris anticipates a current trend by noting that Paul's 'thought [concerning the atonement] is kaleidoscopic' (Leon Morris, *The Cross in the New Testament*, 395.

[23] For example, the standard critique that Anselm's satisfaction theory owes more to the medieval feudal system than to a biblical account of God's honour and justice. Cf. Weaver, *The Nonviolent Atonement*, 192–5.

[24] Mark D. Baker and Joel B. Green, *Recovering the Scandal of the Cross: Atonement in New Testament and Contemporary Contexts* (Downers Grove, IL: InterVarsity Press, 2003), 98–9). We find a very different perspective in the thought of Kazo Kitamori, who suggests that the different aspects of the Scriptural witness are more or less discernible to cultures, such that each culture has a privileged vantage point for discerning most vividly some aspect of Christ's saving work. Kazo Kitamori, *Theology of the Pain of God* (Richmond, VA: John Knox Press, 1965), 137. Appropriating this insight, it may be that our postmodern culture is uniquely positioned so as to be able to discern most vividly the diversity of the historical and biblical account of Christ's work. As Vanhoozer notes, 'the formal challenge for atonement theory in postmodernity consists in justifying the move from many metaphors to one, and from the one metaphor to a single concept' (Kevin J. Vanhoozer, 'Atonement in Postmodernity: Guilt, Goats and Gifts', in *The Glory of the Atonement: Biblical, Historical and Practical Perspectives*, eds Charles E. Hill and Frank A. James (Downers Grove, IL:

In this model, a significant factor in the Bible's diverse witness to the saving work of Christ is a 'battle of rhetoric', a matter of shaping the metaphors available within the culture of the hearers of Scripture, so as to communicate the truth of the gospel.[25]

This approach to diversity is not altogether new, although it has taken many forms. Adolf von Harnack was particularly influential in this regard, arguing for an essence of the Christian faith which was hidden within philosophical or ethical trappings. 'The historian's task' was that 'of distinguishing between what is traditional and what is peculiar, between kernel and husk.'[26] Rudolf Bultmann, on a similar path, saw his task to be the demythologization of Scripture and therefore of the Scriptural authors' interpretation of the death and resurrection of Christ. Thanks in part to Colin Gunton's influential work on metaphor and the nature of the doctrine of the atonement, our perception of the 'husk' or 'shell' involved in our speech about Jesus and his saving work has changed considerably.[27] Whereas we discard a husk for the sake of the kernel, Gunton embraces metaphor as integral to the very structure of language, seeking to re-appropriate the traditional metaphors from the history of the church. Current discussions on the doctrine of the atonement largely presume and embrace an abundance of metaphors within Scripture concerning the work of Christ which have been variously appropriated throughout the history of theology. The primary question now is whether we ought to preserve, modify or jettison these metaphors in favour of new ones.[28]

These discussions concerning metaphors which are so prevalent today,

---

InterVarsity Press, 2004), 371). Can we listen to this challenge? Can we refrain from reductionism and honour the diversity?

[25] Baker and Green, *Recovering the Scandal*, 66.

[26] Adolf von Harnack, *What Is Christianity?* (New York: Harper, 1957), 55.

[27] Colin E. Gunton, *The Actuality of Atonement: A Study of Metaphor, Rationality, and the Christian Tradition* (Grand Rapids, MI: Eerdmans, 1989). Following Gunton, exploration of the meaning and nature of metaphor is now a standard feature of most treatments of the atonement. Cf. Baker and Green, *Recovering the Scandal*; Henri Blocher, 'Biblical Metaphors and the Doctrine of the Atonement', *Journal of the Evangelical Theological Society* 47, no. 4 (2004), 629–45; Joel B. Green, 'Kaleidoscopic View', in *The Nature of the Atonement: Four Views*, eds James K. Beilby and Paul R. Eddy (Downers Grove, IL: IVP Academic, 2006); McIntyre, *The Shape of Soteriology*; McKnight, *A Community Called Atonement*; Rachel Reesor, 'Atonement: Mystery and Metaphorical Language', *Mennonite Quarterly Review* 68, no. 2 (1994), 209–18.

[28] Many argue for the preservation of biblical metaphors, such as penal substitution. Cf. Charles E. Hill and Frank A. James (eds), *The Glory of the Atonement: Biblical, Historical and Practical Perspectives* (Downers Grove, IL: InterVarsity Press, 2004). One of the best who seek to retain these metaphors by revitalizing or modifying them is: Gunton, *The Actuality of Atonement*. For those seeking to develop new metaphors for the atonement (although not without Scriptural and historical warrant), pride of place goes to René Girard and those following him. Cf. Girard, *I See Satan*; S. Mark

however, offer little hope of addressing the unity in diversity proper to the doctrine of the atonement. The old understanding of metaphor wherein a single reality is 'dressed' up in a plurality of disposable explanatory guises clearly does not help, as it pushes past diversity to unity. The newer understanding, in which metaphor is an essential feature of language and understanding, is also insufficient for our purposes, however, for a plurality of such metaphors belies a deeper underlying plurality in the nature of the atonement itself which we are no closer to understanding. Discussions at the level of metaphor simply cannot access the deeper, underlying question of the unity and diversity proper to the atonement, the description of which is intrinsically bound up with metaphorical language. While the nature and function of metaphorical language continues to be a significant topic within the doctrine of the atonement, this discussion is not of itself sufficient to guide us to the heart of the unity and diversity of Christ's saving work.

What then of other approaches to the unity of the doctrine of the atonement? Many would elevate one aspect of the atonement, contending that it contains within itself the explanatory resources to account for the others. Such a tendency is particularly endemic among proponents of penal substitution, who argue that it offers all the benefits of an exemplarist account and the mechanism for explaining our liberation from the power of Satan.[29] Unfortunately, this approach tends to minimize the other aspects of Christ's saving work, interpreting them largely within its own categories of thought. Such a method is also vulnerable to competing alternatives that reverse the roles, such as using Christ's rescue of sinners from the power of Satan as the chief end of the atonement, arguing that penal substitution (or some variant of satisfaction theory) is simply the means thereof.[30] It is not at all clear that such a method of elevating one of the many theories over the others offers either a sufficiently strong affirmation of the aspects included within the central aspect of Christ's work, or a satisfactory account of why one particular aspect is in fact the centre or heart of Christ's death and resurrection.

Others seek to develop a conceptual scheme uniting the whole, often favouring the three-fold office of Christ (traditionally known as the *munus*

Heim, *Saved from Sacrifice: A Theology of the Cross* (Grand Rapids, MI: Eerdmans, 2006).

[29] D. A. Carson, 'The *SBJT* Forum: The Atonement Under Fire', *Southern Baptist Journal of Theology* 11, no. 2 (2007), 107; Alan Spence, *The Promise of Peace: A Unified Theory of Atonement* (New York: T & T Clark, 2006), 15; Justyn Terry, *The Justifying Judgement of God: A Reassessment of the Place of Judgment in the Saving Work of Christ* (Eugene, OR: Paternoster, 2007). For a similar critique, cf. McKnight, *A Community Called Atonement*, 43.

[30] See the fine appendix on the subject in Graham A. Cole, *God the Peacemaker* (Downers Grove, IL: InterVarsity Press, 2009), 233–42.

triplex) as a framework for understanding Christ's saving work.[31] This approach sees in Christ and his atoning work the fulfilment of Israel's theocratic offices of priest, king and prophet. While this scheme has much in its favour, claims an impressive pedigree and receives strong support today, it brings in tow considerable shortcomings. First, by emphasizing the theocratic offices of the people of Israel, it omits other aspects of the identity and history of Israel that Jesus fulfilled, such as that of the Exodus, shepherd, bridegroom and kinsman-redeemer. Second, while the *munus triplex* works quite well with Gustaf Aulén's three views of the atonement (classic, objective and subjective),[32] it does not work nearly as well when one sheds this overly rigid system of classification.[33] Theologians favouring this path tend to acknowledge that there are more than three main views of the atonement, but then baldly assert that other views can be subsumed within these three and move on with their account.

The Problem

Much more could be said both for and against these various attempts to unify the doctrine of the atonement. My purpose, however, is not to engage these approaches directly, so as to offer a final verdict, but rather to offer an altogether different theological basis for engaging the doctrine of the atonement. I note these approaches primarily to provide the context for my

---

31 Robert Sherman, *King, Priest and Prophet: A Trinitarian Theology of Atonement* (Edinburgh: T & T Clark, 2004); James Torrance, 'The Priesthood of Jesus', in *Essays in Christology for Karl Barth*, ed. T. H. L. Parker (London: Lutterworth Press, 1956). On the heritage of the *munus triplex*, see Chapter 1 of John Frederick Jansen, *Calvin's Doctrine of the Work of Christ* (London: J. Clark, 1956); Geoffrey Wainwright, *For Our Salvation: Two Approaches to the Work of Christ* (Grand Rapids, MI: Eerdmans, 1997), 99–120. Most Reformed theologians since Calvin have made at least some use of this scheme, including those of the Modern period following Schleiermacher, right on up through Brunner and Barth, and into the contemporary scene. The emphases within this scheme, of course, have varied as much as the theologies themselves. For my analysis of the role of the *munus triplex* in Barth's theology, see my forthcoming article 'The Servant Lord: A Word of Caution Regarding the *munus triplex* in Karl Barth's Theology and the Church Today', *SJT*.

32 Gustaf Aulén, *Christus Victor: An Historical Study of the Three Main Types of the Idea of Atonement*, trans. A. G. Hebert (New York: Macmillan, 1951). Aulén was exceptionally influential in ramming into the popular consciousness the unfortunate thesis that we find three main trajectories within the history of the doctrine of the atonement.

33 Paul Fiddes, for example, notes seven main trajectories in the Scriptural witness, while John McIntyre writes of 13 different models of the atonement. Fiddes, *Past Event and Present Salvation*, 4; McIntyre, *The Shape of Soteriology*, 26–52. I would be inclined to put the number even higher.

own constructive project by drawing attention to a glaring absence that they share in common. *Treatments of the doctrine of the atonement* (particularly of the unity and diversity thereof) *share a conspicuous absence of sustained theological reflection on the role of the doctrine of God as a whole (the doctrines of the Trinity, divine attributes and election) within the doctrine of the atonement.*[34] That is to say, theologians typically follow more or less in the path of Gustaf Aulén, first positing the existence of several main trajectories within the history of the doctrine, and then seeking to find a basis for unity within those trajectories, either granting preeminence to one of the theories or (more common today) exploring metaphorical/cultural issues inherent to each of the theories as a potential source of unity. Rarely does one find in these discussions sustained reflection on the God who was in Christ accomplishing atonement, using the resources provided by the doctrine of God for considering the unity of that work.

One can point, of course, to a number of books and essays on the relationship between the doctrine of the atonement and that of the Trinity, and nearly every work on the subject addresses in some depth one or more divine attributes, with love, mercy, justice, wrath and righteousness topping the charts. Unfortunately, few if any of these works step back from dealing with specific attributes to consider and develop the bearing of the doctrine of the divine attributes as a whole upon the atonement; likewise, many of these studies use the doctrine of the Trinity only as a bulwark against heresy, rather than finding in it the wellspring for constructive development of the doctrine.[35] If they do in fact go beyond this defensive measure, it

---

[34] The same is true, notes, Webster, of the doctrine of justification. John Webster, '*Rector et iudex super omnia genera doctrinarum*? The Place of the Doctrine of Justification', in *What Is Justification About? Reformed Contributions to an Ecumenical Theme*, eds Michael Weinrich and John P. Burgess (Grand Rapids, MI: Eerdmans, 2009), 42–43n2.

[35] Brümmer and Park, despite the titles of their books, offer little or no analysis on the bearing of the content of the doctrine of the Trinity upon that of the atonement. Vincent Brümmer, *Atonement, Christology and the Trinity: Making Sense of Christian Doctrine* (Burlington, VT: Ashgate, 2005); Andrew Sung Park, *Triune Atonement: Christ's Healing for Sinners, Victims, and the Whole Creation* (Louisville, KY: WJK, 2009). Ware's essay is one of the worst such instances, failing to touch on the subject at all despite its mandate. Bruce A. Ware, 'Christ's Atonement: A Work of the Trinity', in *Jesus in Trinitarian Perspective*, eds Fred Sanders and Klaus Issler (Nashville, TN: B & H Publishing Group, 2007). McFarlane fares little better in his essay: Graham McFarlane, 'Atonement, Creation and Trinity', in *The Atonement Debate: Papers From the London Symposium on the Theology of Atonement*, eds Derek Tidball, David Hilborn and Justin Thacker (Grand Rapids, MI: Zondervan, 2008). Others have sought a different path to integrating the doctrines of the Trinity and atonement, namely through the *munus triplex*: Georg Pfleiderer, 'The Atonement', in *Trinitarian Soundings in Systematic Theology*, ed. Paul Louis Metzger (New York: T & T Clark, 2005); Sherman, *King, Priest and Prophet*. Regardless of the success of aligning these doctrines in such a fashion (made somewhat questionable by the fact that more than

is only to inquire into the relationship between the Father and the Son in the death of Jesus on the cross. Furthermore, to my knowledge no one has sought to bring these considerations to bear upon the question of the unity and diversity of the doctrine of the atonement. This lacuna, I suggest, underlies many of the problems facing the doctrine of the atonement today.

Thesis: Theology Proper and the Doctrine of the Atonement

In this book I contend that developing the Theological (doctrine of God) presuppositions of the doctrine of the atonement provides a proper framework for understanding the fullness of the doctrine of the atonement (and the unity and diversity thereof).[36] Towards this end I draw on Karl Barth's integrated account of the doctrines of God and reconciliation, harnessing the resources contained within his doctrine of God to energize a properly theological account of the unity and diversity of the atonement.[37] I argue that *Barth's understanding of God's triune being-in-act in the fullness of the divine perfections, brought to bear upon our sinful condition in fulfilment of his covenantal purposes through the person and work of Jesus Christ, provides the proper theological framework for developing the doctrine of the atonement, and contains within itself the basis and the impetus for a theological explanation of the unity and diversity of Christ's atoning work.* In other words, I am contending for a radically different approach to the question of the unity of the atonement. Rather than beginning with the diversity of the atonement and then inquiring after its unity, I am beginning with the unity and diversity proper to the being of the reconciling God, establishing thereby the basis for both the unity and

---

three aspects of the atonement exist and the presence of the rule *opera ad extra sunt indivisa* lurking on the horizon), such an attempt still leaves a great deal of ground to be covered.

[36] My project is in certain significant respects a continuation and amplification of: Bruce L. McCormack, 'The Ontological Presuppositions of Barth's Doctrine of the Atonement', in *The Glory of the Atonement: Biblical, Historical and Practical Perspectives*, eds Roger R. Nicole, Charles E. Hill, and Frank A. James (Downers Grove, IL: InterVarsity Press, 2004).

Unless otherwise noted, I use 'atonement' and 'reconciliation' synonymously in reference to Barth's thought. On the relationship between reconciliation and redemption in Barth's understanding, cf. Karl Barth, *Karl Barth's Table Talk*, ed. John Drew Godsey (Edinburgh: Oliver and Boyd, 1963), 53.

[37] John Drury's presentation at the first Karl Barth Conference at Princeton Seminary, and a subsequent conversation with him and Daniel Migliore alerted me to Barth's interest in these questions.

diversity of Christ's saving work.[38] While studies of the different theories of the atonement are still of considerable value (i.e. those following more or less in the footsteps of Gustaf Aulén), the questions of our time call for an altogether different approach to the doctrine.

My goal, therefore, is to shift the fundamental framework for discussions of the doctrine of the atonement (and the unity in diversity thereof) by integrating them with the doctrine of God, using Barth's theology as my guide. Historical, biblical and cultural discussions clearly play a significant role, but properly fulfil this role only within the broader and more foundational context established by the doctrine of God. By relocating the discussion as a whole, I hope to free current discussions from a certain stalemate, relieving them of a burden they are unable to fulfil when loosed from their proper theological moorings. Apart from the doctrine of God, individual biblical texts and the Bible as a whole are disordered and ultimately unfruitful and dangerous, and the same applies to the role of cultural and historical theology studies. If we are to think properly about the doctrine of the atonement, we must do so in constant interaction with the doctrine of God which serves as its ultimate basis. This is, I suggest, the best possible framework for understanding the work of Christ in its fullness.

What then is my answer to the perennial question: why did God become man? My answer is that we could and should give any of a number of different answers, each with its respective Scriptural warrant and theological development throughout the history of the Church. The Church can and must answer this question day in and day out, and in a variety of different ways as demanded by the situation at hand. But as we answer this question, we do well to keep in mind that it was *God* who became man. It is this fact that provides us with the necessary resources to properly understand why there are and must be so many answers to the question of why he became man. My purpose is to take the needed time to reflect on the significance of the fact that it was *God* who became man, that we might use the many answers to this question all the more profitably, that we might become all the more 'adept pastoral "poets" of the cross.'[39]

At this point, a powerful counter-question may emerge for some: why not simply return to Scripture (*ad fontes!*)? Why not study the key biblical

---

[38] 'Although theology is certainly confronted with the one God, he is One in the fullness of his existence, action, and revelation. In the school of the witness theology can in no way become monolithic, monomanic, monotonous, and infallibly boring. In no way can it bind or limit itself to one special subject or another ... The eternally rich God is the content of the knowledge of evangelical theology. His unique mystery is known only in the overflowing fullness of his counsels, was and judgments' – a statement just as true of the doctrine of the atonement as it is of theology generally. Barth, *Evangelical Theology*, 33–34.

[39] I owe this beautiful phrase to Brown, *Cross Talk*, 6.

passages on the doctrine of the atonement, bypassing the various specu-lative potholes threatening our path down the bumpy road of systematic theology? After all, isn't Scripture sufficient for developing a doctrine of the atonement? In sympathy with this reaction, the purpose of this book is precisely to encourage and equip the Church to approach Scripture with a fresh and invigorated perspective, achieving thereby a fuller and more unified understanding of Christ's reconciling work. In no way do I intend to circumnavigate the scriptural witness.

Cultivating a proper perspective of the scriptural witness, however, is not simply a matter of reading the relevant passages for the fifth or fiftieth time, for the study of Scripture is itself a complex and theologically laden event.[40] The presuppositions, motives and methods informing our reading are themselves theological in nature, such that a pure or presuppositionless reading of Scripture is neither possible nor desirable. Far from circum-venting Scripture, my hope is to better inform the theological interpretation of Scripture by drawing attention to the way in which the doctrine of the atonement is rooted in the doctrine of God, thus fostering a better reading of Scripture.[41] As Vanhoozer suggests, our starting point should be a 'distinctly Christian and theological, which is to say Trinitarian, approach to biblical interpretation that begins by recognizing God as a triune communicative agent and Scripture as the written locus of God's communicative action.'[42] There is no 'simple' or a-theological return to Scripture, for our reading of Scripture is itself motivated by theological beliefs. The intent of this book is thus to offer a properly theological framework for interpreting Scripture in a manner more finely attuned to the way in which the doctrine of God informs that of the atonement – that is to say, one rooted in the doctrine of God revealed in the person and work of Jesus Christ, as opposed to one based on general or philosophical considerations.

By pursuing theological presuppositions of the doctrine of the atonement,[43]

---

[40] So argues Vanhoozer throughout much of his corpus. Cf. Kevin J. Vanhoozer, *The Drama of Doctrine: A Canonical-Linguistic Approach to Christian Theology* (Louisville, KY: WJK, 2005); Kevin J. Vanhoozer, *Is There a Meaning in this Text? The Bible, the Reader, and the Morality of Literary Knowledge* (Grand Rapids, MI: Zondervan, 1998).

[41] Like Bruce McCormack, then, in 'beginning with my dogmatic theologian', I do not intend to evade 'the exegetical task but simply' to offer 'a service in helping to *prepare* the exegete for her task'. Bruce L. McCormack, '"With Loud Cries and Tears": The Humanity of the Son in the Epistle to the Hebrews', in *The Epistle to the Hebrews and Christian Theology*, eds Richard Bauckham *et al.* (Grand Rapids, MI: Eerdmans, 2009).

[42] Kevin J. Vanhoozer, *First Theology: God, Scripture and Hermeneutics* (Downers Grove, IL: InterVarsity Press, 2002), 38.

[43] One finds a similar enterprise dealing with the doctrine of Holy Scripture in: John Webster, *Holy Scripture: A Dogmatic Sketch* (New York: Cambridge University Press, 2003).

I intend to explore the antecedent basis of this event in the being of God – in God's triune life in the fullness of his perfections and in fulfilment of his electing will. As Barth suggests, 'this action and working becomes and is significant and effective with a significance and effectiveness qualitatively different from any other action and working in virtue of the fact that it is God's action and working' (*CD* II/1, 259). The fact that it was *God*, the triune God in the fullness of the divine perfections, who was acting in Jesus Christ to reconcile the world to himself (2 Cor. 5.19) is what makes this event uniquely and decisively significant and effective.[44] To mine the implications of this great claim we must devote ourselves to considering precisely what we mean when we affirm with Paul that *God* was, in Christ, reconciling the world to himself. The resources for and the characteristics of Christ's atoning work ultimately derive from the God who willed and accomplished this event. By understanding this event in strict relationship to the God who was active in it, we avail ourselves of the best and most comprehensive framework for understanding and formulating the doctrine of the atonement.

Not that we thereby step away from Scripture in order to dwell on some abstractly derived doctrine of God! The Church has no basis for the content of its proclamation concerning the doctrine of God or any other matter apart from Scripture, the witness of God's self-revelation. As the *Barmen Declaration* states, 'Jesus Christ, as he is attested for us in *Holy Scripture*, is the one Word of God which we have to hear and which we have to trust and obey in life and in death. We reject the false doctrine, as though the Church could and would have to acknowledge as a source of its proclamation, apart from and besides this one Word of God, still other events and powers, figures and truths, as God's revelation.'[45] Developing our understanding of Scripture's witness to the doctrine of God gives us new and fuller resources with which to approach the scriptural witness concerning the meaning and efficacy of Christ's death and resurrection. The task is a circular one (although not viciously so), in which theological interpretation of Scripture (focusing on the doctrine of God) funds further theological interpretation of Scripture (concerning the atonement). At every point, therefore, the material theological claims of this book are liable to the critique of Scripture, and the success of this project will be judged in terms of its exegetical payoff in biblical studies.

A second and related concern might be whether this inquiry is not altogether too speculative. Shouldn't we simply draw on the various resources provided us by Scripture when the occasion arises? Just as we

---

[44] 'He is able to do this because he is not only man, but also *God*.' Karl Barth, *Deliverance to the Captives*, trans. Marguerite Wieser (New York: Harper & Row, 1961), 17.

[45] Arthur C. Cochrane, *Reformed Confessions of the 16th Century* (Philadelphia, PA: Westminster Press, 1966), 334.

draw upon different clubs throughout a game of golf, runs the analogy, so we draw upon different aspects of Scripture's witness to the work of Christ as needed in the course of Christian ministry.[46] Clearly the church has and will continue to utilize this method, as it applies Scripture to everyday life through a theologically attuned sense of fittingness. My interest is not to displace this practice, but rather to engage in a theological exercise that will better inform its application. For underlying the analogy from the game of golf is a sense of how the terrain, clubs, ball, rules, weather conditions, and the state and capacities of one's own body and skill level coalesce to make one or another of the clubs the best choice for the shot at hand. Equally important is the premise that the clubs in the bag are part of a complete set of clubs precisely designed by the manufacturer to provide the necessary tools to play the game in all of its varying circumstances. In other words, the 'golf' analogy does not circumvent important questions of theological unity and diversity, but rather presupposes answers to such questions.[47] The analogy would not work nearly so well for a golfer possessing neither the relevant skills, a 'sense' of which club is fitting for a specific shot, nor the proper set of clubs (but rather an arbitrarily filled bag containing a putter, broom, baseball bat and cricket wicket). The argument for practical application does not conflict with, but rather presupposes and is only strengthened by a better understanding of the theological foundation upon which it rests.

Why Barth?

Why is Barth particularly apt for such a study? Several factors would seem to mitigate this option, namely: (1) a good deal has already been written on Barth's view of the atonement, (2) questions concerning his theology as a whole abound, particularly concerning the doctrine of election and (the possibility of) its logical entailment of universalism, and (3) his consistently forensic interpretation of the cross would seem to be precisely the kind of view I want to dispute. I will address the third factor throughout the book (particularly in the fourth chapter). The first two, however, call for a more immediate response.

Concerning the publications treating Barth's doctrine of reconciliation, three major writings are currently available in English.[48] In the second

---

[46] McKnight, *A Community Called Atonement*, xiii.

[47] This is precisely McKnight's point of the golf analogy: 'the game of atonement requires that players understand the value of each club as well as the effort needed to carry a bag big enough and defined enough so that one knows where each club fits in that bag' (*Ibid.*).

[48] The following are the major works on the subject in German: Bertold Klappert, *Die Auferweckung des Gekreuzigten: der Ansatz der Christologie Karl Barths im*

half of his book *Foundation of Barth's Doctrine of Reconciliation*, David Mueller offers an extended summary of Barth's *CD* IV/1, although with relatively little critical interaction.[49] Jeannine Graham surveys *CD* IV/1–3 in a comparison of Barth with Dorothee Sölle and John Macquarrie, while providing a good deal more analysis than does Mueller.[50] Unfortunately, neither dwells on the question of the doctrinal interconnections developed by Barth in which we are interested. In a more focused work, *Barth on the Descent into Hell*, David Lauber helpfully emphasizes the role of the doctrine of the Trinity – an argument which we will both draw upon and seek to develop.[51] Also worthy of note are three unpublished dissertations on Barth's view of the atonement.[52] Apart from these major works, a number of essays offer significant insight into various aspects of Barth's theology of the atonement, treating it directly or approaching it indirectly by means of some other doctrinal locus.[53] However, only occasional attention has been devoted to the inter-relationship between the doctrine of the atonement and those of the Trinity, divine perfections and sin – an inexcusable state of affairs, given Barth's theological methodology of

Zusammenhang der Christologie der Gegenwart (Neukirchen: Neukirchener Verlag, 1974); Bertold Klappert, *Versöhnung und Befreiung: Versuche, Karl Barth kontextuell zu verstehen* (Neukirchen: Neukirchener Verlag, 1994); Ernstpeter Maurer, '"Für uns" An unserer Stelle hingerichtet: Die Herausforderung der Versöhnungslehre', *Zeitschrift für dialektissche Theologie* 18 (2002), 190–210; Raymund Schwager, 'Der Richter wird gerichtet: Zur Versöhnungslehre von Karl Barth,' 107, no. 1 (1985).

[49] David L. Mueller, *Foundation of Karl Barth's Doctrine of Reconciliation: Jesus Christ Crucified and Risen* (Lewiston, NY: Edwin Mellen, 1990).

[50] Jeannine M. Graham, *Representation and Substitution in the Atonement Theologies of Dorothee Sölle, John Macquarrie, and Karl Barth* (New York: Peter Lang, 2005).

[51] David Lauber, *Barth on the Descent into Hell: God, Atonement and the Christian Life* (Burlington, VT: Ashgate, 2004).

[52] Nathan D. Hieb, 'The Liberating Reconciliation of the Cross: Atonement for Sin and Liberation from Suffering in Karl Barth's "Theologia Crucis"' (PhD diss., Princeton Theological Seminary, 2009); Robert Clifford Shippey, 'The Suffering of God in Karl Barth's Doctrines of Election and Reconciliation' (PhD diss., Southern Baptist Theological Seminary, 1991); David Lewis Stokes, 'Barth and the Atoning Narrative: The Figure of the Cross in the Church Dogmatics' (PhD diss., Princeton Theological Seminary, 1989).

[53] Some of the more important essays include: Robert A. Bagnato, 'Karl Barth's Personalizing of "Juridical Redemption"', *Anglican Theological Review* 49, no. 1 (1967), 45–69; Pfleiderer, 'The Atonement'; John Thompson, *Christ in Perspective: Christological Perspectives in the Theology of Karl Barth* (Edinburgh: St Andrew Press, 1978); John Thompson, 'Christology and Reconciliation in the Theology of Karl Barth', in *Christ in Our Place: The Humanity of God in Christ for the Reconciliation of the World*, eds James Torrance, Trevor A. Hart and Daniel P. Thimell (Allison Park, PA: Pickwick, 1990); Williams, 'Karl Barth and the Doctrine of the Atonement'. The latter especially was helpful in its penetrating critique of Barth.

consistently and intentionally inter-relating doctrinal loci.[54] Furthermore, no work has been published that has as its central concern the question of the unity and diversity of the reconciling work of Jesus Christ, a matter called for explicitly in *CD* IV/1.[55] In short, while there is a considerable amount of interaction with Barth's doctrine of the atonement, only a fraction of this literature engages the theological presuppositions of the doctrine in the manner attempted here.

What then of the coherence of Barth's system as a whole, particularly as it bears on the doctrine of election and the logical entailment of universalism? Just as I do not intend to survey Barth's view of the atonement, neither do I seek to touch on certain points in his theology simply because they are the most controversial in the contemporary scene or are considered to be the most influential for the development of Christian doctrine.[56] While I may in fact address some of these matters at length, my primary intent is to draw on specific strengths within Barth's theology to offer a constructive approach to the doctrine of the atonement.[57] This is a constructive work within the field of Barth studies which highlights and develops certain themes (and their implications) which are largely ignored in the contemporary scene. As a result, my attention will focus much less on certain questions currently being addressed to Barth and his defenders, and which would need to be addressed directly if I were attempting a comprehensive treatment/defence of Barth's doctrine of the atonement.

---

[54] Lauber addresses the relationship between atonement and Trinity at some length, while Williams does the same in regards to the divine perfections in: Williams, 'Karl Barth and the Doctrine of the Atonement'. For the most part, however, Barth scholars share the blame with the broader theological community for insufficiently exploring the relationship between the doctrine of the atonement and other closely related doctrines. One notable exception in this area is the conjunction of the doctrines of atonement and the Church which of late has received a good deal of attention.

[55] The nearest exception is: John L. Drury, 'The Priest Sacrificed in Our Place: Barth's Use of the Cultic Imagery of Hebrews in *Church Dogmatics* IV/1, §59.2' (paper presented at the Annual Barth Conference, Princeton Theological Seminary, NJ, 21–4 May 2006).

[56] Recent works seeking to do precisely this include: Tom Greggs, *Barth, Origen, and Universal Salvation: Restoring Particularity* (Oxford: Oxford University Press, 2009); Lauber, *Barth on the Descent*; Adam Neder, *Participation in Christ: An Entry into Karl Barth's Church Dogmatics* (Louisville, KY: WJK, 2009). One would have to include as well McCormack's massive 'covenantal ontology' project as it seeks to interpret, correct and extend Barth's thought. Cf. Bruce L. McCormack, *Orthodox and Modern: Studies in the Theology of Karl Barth* (Grand Rapids, MI: Baker Academic, 2008). For more on this project, see the appendix to Chapter 2.

[57] This project is thus uniquely postmodern in its heightened awareness of the diversity of Christ's atoning work. Vanhoozer, 'Atonement in Postmodernity', 369. At the same time, of course, it is distinctively evangelical and Barthian, in that it seeks to embrace this diversity precisely within the framework of his understanding of the doctrine of God as this is rooted in the witness of Scripture.

16

Of the different contemporary hot topics which the foregoing argument touches on (implicitly or explicitly) without exploring in depth, the most important is the question of universalism. Barth himself denied *apokatastasis*: 'No such postulate can be made even though we appeal to the cross and resurrection of Jesus Christ. Even though theological consistency[58] might seem to lead our thoughts and utterances most clearly in this direction, we must not arrogate to ourselves that which can be given and received only as a free gift' (*CD* IV/3.1, 461-78, esp. 477; cf. *DO*, 136).[59] Most commentators, myself included, are not convinced, however, given the radical nature of Barth's doctrine of election (*CD* II/2).[60] At the same time, I hold that it is not necessary to engage the question of Barth's tendency towards universalism in order to profit from his work or to use it constructively, just as one need not first address the apparent logical entailment of double predestination within Calvin's thought in order to appreciate different aspects of his theology. Were I to wholly endorse Barth's theology, or seek to recapitulate his doctrine of the atonement, I would need to address this question more fully. As it stands, however, my intent is to use certain aspects of his account in order to propose a new approach to the contemporary question of the unity and diversity of Christ's reconciling work. Accordingly, I will largely leave questions such as those concerning Barth's supposed universalism to the side.

Finally, Barth is an apt choice for this project because, of the theologians I have studied, he is the one who most adroitly brings the theological task to life. Questions that I once thought arcane and scholastic (in the derogatory sense of the word) leap to life under his pen, and the questions with which I approach the text Barth either takes up and addresses or corrects me by asking better ones. In Barth I find that the theological task takes on a sense of wonder, greatness and significance that consistently compels me to further and better study. More to the point, Barth is the best I know at working out his theology in explicit relationship to the doctrine of God and the fulfilment of his covenantal purposes. 'Strictly speaking', he wrote, 'in dogmatics and in Church preaching every single statement is at once the basis and the content of all the rest' (*CD* II/1, 257),[61] and nowhere is

---

[58] On theological consistency, see: Barth, *Table Talk*, 12.

[59] See also: Karl Barth, *The Humanity of God*, trans Thomas Wieser and John N. Thomas (Richmond, VA: WJK, 1960), 61–2. For glimpses into Barth's preaching as it relates to universalism, see: Barth, *Deliverance to the Captives*, 25–6, 40–1, 46, 51, 85–92.

[60] Oliver D. Crisp, 'On Barth's Denial of Universalism', *Themelios* 29, no. 1 (2003); Greggs, *Barth, Origen, and Universal Salvation*; Tom Greggs, '"Jesus is Victor": Passing the Impasse of Barth on Universalism', *SJT* 60, no. 2 (2007), 196–212; Colin E. Gunton, *The Barth Lectures*, ed. Paul Brazier (New York: T & T Clark, 2007), 226; Ramm, *After Fundamentalism*, 165–72; Williams, 'Karl Barth and the Doctrine of the Atonement', 262–70.

[61] A claim he later makes good by affirming that in principle 'we must hold out the

this more evident than in his treatment of the doctrine of reconciliation.[62] Most theologians acknowledge this to some degree, of course, but Barth is exceptional when it comes to his heightened awareness of the role the doctrine of God plays in the constructive development of doctrine. While I could pursue my project with a number of other theologians, I find that Barth is particularly apt for this study because he makes explicit so much that other theologians only hint at. Better than anyone else I know, Barth offers an integrated vision of the atonement which is thoroughly connected to all other aspects of systematic theology, making him the ideal subject of this book.[63]

Layout of the Argument

It may help the reader to think of this book as being structured somewhat after the chiastic structure of Hebrew poetry. Chapters 1 and 7 offer an introduction and conclusion, respectively. Chapter 2 offers the most conceptually demanding and theologically abstract material (on God's being-in-act) while Chapter 6 is the most practical and concrete chapter, offering an extended test-case laden with biblical material which seeks to test the exegetical payoff of my thesis. Chapter 3 develops the Trinitarian foundation for my thesis, building towards Chapter 4 on the relationship of the atonement to the doctrine of the divine perfections, while Chapter 5 continues to play out its implications within the doctrine of sin. Chapter 4, then, is in many ways the central chapter of the book – the argument as a whole either builds towards or looks back to this primary argument.

To anticipate the content of the chapters, I begin this study (Chapter 2) by examining Barth's argument in *CD* II/1, §28.1: 'The Being of God in Act'. The purpose of this brief passage is not so much to lay out the essentials of Barth's theological ontology as it is to take a first step towards describing the nature of God, by describing him as the living God. In this section Barth

---

possibility of beginning a dogmatics with any doctrine, for instance, with the doctrine of the Church, or with the topic in Calvin's Book III: sanctification, or even a universal doctrine of the Holy Spirit. Indeed, we might even begin with the Christian man!', Barth, *Table Talk*, 13.

[62] Likewise, George Hunsinger states: 'No one ever seems to have had a stronger sense that in Christian theology every theme is connected to every other theme.' George Hunsinger, *How to Read Karl Barth: The Shape of His Theology* (Oxford: Oxford University Press, 1991), 28.

[63] One could add that some consider Barth to be the hope for the future of Evangelicalism, and is therefore all the more fitting for my task. Bernard Ramm, for example, writes that Barth 'offers to evangelical theology a paradigm of how best to come to terms with the Enlightenment' and thus to defend orthodox theology. Ramm, *After Fundamentalism*, vii.

integrates the doctrines of revelation, Trinity and election, all the while focusing on God's being as the living one. In this way he gathers together several key themes which will fund our inquiry in the ensuing chapters. With this framework in place, we will examine in turn the relationship between the doctrine of the atonement and that of the Trinity (Chapter 3), divine perfections (Chapter 4) and the doctrine of sin (Chapter 5). These three chapters constitute the core of my argument, in which I explore the determinative role of the doctrine of God within that of the atonement, and gradually unpack the implications therein for the question of the unity in diversity of Christ's saving work.

Chapter 3 explores various key aspects of Barth's Trinitarian theology, considering in turn the implications of these various aspects for the doctrine of the atonement. The emphasis here is on how the Trinity constitutes the basis for Christ's atoning act. Chapter 4 builds on this foundation, repeating the same process of exposition and development of implications, delving into the resources provided by the doctrine of the divine perfections for the unity and diversity of Christ's work – a matter which is only hinted at in the previous chapter. Chapter 5 offers an extension and recapitulation of the themes explored in the previous two chapters via an exposition and critical amplification of Barth's Christocentric understanding of sin. It also affords us a glimpse into important aspects of the theologically grounded unity and diversity of Barth's doctrine of the atonement which were muted in the sections of the *Church Dogmatics* more properly devoted to that topic.

In order to retain a proper focus on the concrete significance of the argument, I conclude Chapters 3–5 with brief test cases in which I play out the significance of its thesis with regard to some aspect of the doctrine of the atonement. Chapter 3 considers the Trinitarian basis for Barth's appropriation of a reconstituted form of exemplarism. Chapter 4 lays out a framework for a theory of the atonement rooted in the patience of God. Chapter 5 explores the possibility of a Barthian appropriation of René Girard's thought for a full understanding of the atonement. Finally, in Chapter 6 a far more extended test case is offered, in which I develop a theory of the atonement from the standpoint of the divine omnipresence – a 'Temple Theory of the Atonement'. In this chapter I pull together the various strands of my thesis, and draw on Barth's thought, a biblical theology of divine presence and omnipresence, and certain hints throughout the history of doctrine, seeking to formulate a relatively new understanding of Christ's saving work.

Aspects and Theories

While I do not focus on this particular question through the book, and my view on the subject is left largely implicit, a working definition of the terms 'aspect' and 'theory' will be helpful. An aspect of the atonement refers to the thing itself – the reality of this particular dimension of Christ's saving work. A theory of the atonement is a conceptually unified account of an aspect of Christ's death and resurrection, which explains the problem (sin), the characters (God, Christ, humankind) and an explanation of the solution by means of which to remove the problem. The biblical witness speaks diversely of each of these aspects, leading the Church to develop different theories of the atonement which draw on certain subsets of the data, and fill in missing or under-developed elements of the witness (particularly concerning causal efficacy).

Theories of the atonement are not necessarily mutually exclusive, although meta-theories necessarily become so. The criteria for an adequate theory of the atonement are that it (1) present the necessary aspects of a theory, and (2) that each of these aspects be Scripturally rooted. The 'rootedness' of these aspects in Scripture can be difficult to determine. At best, Scripture witnesses directly to each of the aspects of a given theory. Often, however, a canonical judgement is necessary to accentuate the Scriptural point that is not clearly rendered in any single passage. Less clear are those aspects of a theory of the atonement that, while themselves attested neither directly nor canonically in Scripture, are posited by theologians in order to complement other aspects of a theory that are in fact Scripturally warranted, in order to formulate a full theory of the atonement. A false theory of the atonement is one which as a whole or in one of its aspects contradicts the Scriptural witness. Those theories that as a whole or in part lack Scriptural support without contra-dicting it are tentative in nature, and must be noted and handled accordingly.

Barth himself makes this distinction – a point we will explore in some depth later in the book. He writes:

> Do not confuse my theory [*Theorie*] of the reconciliation with the thing itself [*der Sache selber*]. All theories of reconciliation can be but pointers [*Alle Versöhnungstheorien können nur Fingerzeige sein*]. (*DO*, 116; *DG*, 137)

In short, I follow the path set by Barth in this book, distinguishing between the thing itself (which I refer to as aspects of the manifold work of Christ), and the theories we develop in order to codify these different aspects.

A Final Comment

Barth once prayed in a Basel prison: 'In thy great majesty and mercy thou hast made common cause with our misery and our sin in order to lift us up. How else can we show our gratitude than by comprehending and acknowledging this mighty deed?'[64] This book is an exercise in thanksgiving, inasmuch as I seek to offer in the following chapters the proper basis for understanding the nature and extent of Christ's saving work. The success of my argument hinges therefore not solely upon my interpretation of Barth, but ultimately on the exegetical and theological fruit it bears in facilitating the church's increased comprehension of this mighty deed.

How do we best approach the doctrine of the atonement so as to have at our disposal the necessary resources to appreciate the fullness of the meaning and significance of Christ's atoning work? My thesis is that we best approach Christ's saving work by listening to the witness of Scripture to this event (and the history of interpretation thereof) in light of Scripture's understanding of the God incarnate in Christ – the triune God in the fullness of the divine perfections. It is only as we consistently keep before us and develop the implications of God's triunity and the divine perfections proper to the being and life of God that we can understand both Christ's saving work in his life, death and resurrection, and its distinctive unity and diversity. The exegetical, theological and pastoral payoff of such an approach, I suggest, is immense.

[64] Barth, *Deliverance to the Captives*, 75.

2

GOD'S BEING IN ACT AND THE DOCTRINE OF THE ATONEMENT

According to Barth, the key to the doctrine of the atonement is that the death and resurrection of Jesus Christ was an event in the life of God. The history of Israel and its expectations for a Messiah, the role of the Romans in the crucifixion of Jesus, the faith Christians have in Jesus Christ and his resurrection from the dead by the Father ... these and other important aspects of the doctrine of the atonement have their role to play only within the context and framework provided by the decisive fact that in this event, in the death and resurrection of Jesus Christ, God brought the resources of his own being and life as the triune God in the fullness of the divine perfections to bear upon our fallen condition so as to save us, bringing us to fellowship with himself. The meaning and significance of these other aspects of Jesus' Passion are irrevocably and irremediably altered by the exclusion or minimization of the fact that this was an event in the life of God.

Barth's first and most general description of 'the whole complex of Christian understanding and doctrine which here confronts us' in the doctrine of reconciliation is the statement 'God with Us' (*CD* IV/1, 4). The doctrine of the atonement, in short, is 'primarily ... a statement about God: that it is He who is with [us] as God' in this way, in Jesus Christ (*CD* IV/1, 4). To adapt an earlier statement of Barth's: 'as the Subject of [this work] God is so decisively characteristic for [its] nature and understanding that without this Subject [it] would be something quite different from what [it is] in accordance with God's Word, and on the basis of the Word of God we can necessarily recognise and understand [it] only together with this [its] Subject' (*CD* II/1, 260). That God was in Christ, and in this specific way reconciling all things to himself, is the decisive and pre-eminent foundation for understanding the work of Jesus Christ. 'While much depends upon [our] coming to see that [Christ's work] applies to [us] ... everything depends upon [our] coming to see that it all has to do with God; that it is God who is with [us] as God' (*CD* IV/1, 4).

Building on this thesis, the purpose of this book is to explore the way in which the atonement receives its unique shape and significance from the subject whose act it is (the triune God in the fullness of the divine perfections), taking Karl Barth as our guide due to the consistency and rigour with which he upholds this conviction.[1] To prepare ourselves for this venture, however, we will be well served by exerting some patience, seeking first to understand the theological commitments informing the intensity and consistency with which Barth binds together the doctrine of God and the work of Christ. Such a move affords us the opportunity to understand with greater clarity: (1) why it is so vital that we ask questions concerning the being of God when we could simply dwell on the benefits we receive from him as attested in Scripture, (2) why it is so significant that we see the fullness of God's being in Christ, and (3) why we must focus on Jesus Christ in particular, as opposed to other significant revelatory events in the economy of salvation. In short, taking this route offers us a firm and energizing basis from which to begin our inquiry, by means of which we will gather momentum for the work ahead. If the doctrine of God is in fact the broadest and strongest platform for appreciating the fullness of what God accomplished in the death and resurrection of Jesus Christ, we will do well to ensure that we have a proper understanding of the theological commitments motivating this approach.

We find the roots of Barth's commitment to this project developed in an earlier volume of the *Church Dogmatics* (CD II/1, §28.1), in which he explores at some length the notion of God's life or livingness (cf. *CD* II/1, 299) in light of the synonymous concepts of God's 'being in act' and 'being in person'. Barth draws on this passage from the very beginning of *CD* IV/1, when he develops his claim that the atonement is 'primarily a statement about God and only then and for that reason a statement about us men' (*CD* IV/1, 5). He writes: 'our starting-point is that this 'God with us' at the heart of the Christian message is the description of an act of God, or better, of God Himself in this act of His' (*CD* IV/1, 6). But what does it mean to affirm 'God Himself in this act of His'? In this chapter I offer a close reading of this passage (*CD* II/1, §28.1), as it offers the foundation for the key themes of the first few pages of *CD* IV/1, and therefore an excellent platform from which to appreciate Barth's unremitting focus on the being of God in Jesus Christ.

While this passage offers considerable theological payoff, it also calls for a good deal of caution.[2] Barth warns us in the next section (§28.2) that 'it

---

[1] Thomas W. Currie III, 'The Being and Act of God', in *Theology Beyond Christendom: Essays on the Centenary of the Birth of Karl Barth, May 10, 1886*, ed. John Thompson (Allison Park, PA: Pickwick, 1986), 10.

[2] That is, apart from discussions revolving around Bruce McCormack's recent and highly contested thesis that make interpreting this passage all the more difficult. I offer

would be dangerous and ambiguous if we tried to prolong the definition of the divine essence as His being in act generally' (*CD* II/1, 272); and in §28.3 he again reminds us of this danger, writing that 'only in preparation ... only in development of the prior logical assertion that God is an acting Subject, did we linger for a moment (but in fact only for a moment) to reflect upon God's being in act' (*CD* II/1, 299). In this passage Barth takes a first step towards describing the being or essence of God by means of a general exposition of God's livingness. While this may sound innocuous enough, the danger Barth senses is that 'livingness' [*Gottes Sein Leben ist*] or God's 'being in act' [*Sein in der Tat*] or 'being in person' [*Sein in Person*] as he also calls it (Barth uses these three notions synonymously), has a rather general feel to it which is difficult to develop properly apart from a massive account of the concrete way in which God is the living one. We might get caught up in this first and general statement, forgetting that it is meant more as a first step than as some sort of foundation, in which it is the living God who determines the meaning of the various concepts Barth uses.

Its purpose is thus not to explain and defend Barth's actualistic ontology[3] or his basic ontological commitments, but rather to gather together some of the key themes from earlier volumes of the *Church Dogmatics* while anticipating others yet to come, and thus set the stage for the exposition of the divine perfections by emphasizing the unity of God's being and activity as the living one. As Jüngel puts it, Barth offers in this passage a demanding but rewarding first step towards describing the being of God, in which he attempts 'to think theologically in what way God is *the living one* ... to think God's livingness'[4] – a series of reflections which have great

---

a brief explanation of my stance towards McCormack's thesis in an appendix at the end of this chapter.

[3] As Adam Neder notes, 'Barth's Christology is not the outworking of a commitment to a preconceived actualistic ontology, but rather an attempt to offer a fitting description of the living Lord Jesus Christ himself, as attested by Holy Scripture'. Neder, *Participation in Christ*, 61. Barth's intent in §28.1 is to pay particularly close attention to the word 'living' as an introduction or first step towards a fuller exposition of the 'living' God's divine perfections.

[4] Eberhard Jüngel, *God's Being is in Becoming: The Trinitarian Being of God in the Theology of Karl Barth*, trans. J. B. Webster (Grand Rapids, MI: Eerdmans, 2001), xxv. Jüngel offers us two more options, which mean essentially the same thing. First, he uses the expression: 'God's being is in becoming.' He explains: "'Becoming' ... indicates the manner *in* which God's being exists, and in this respect can be understood as the ontological place of the being of God.' Jüngel, *God's Being is in Becoming*, xxv. Second, he speaks of the 'historical being' of God: 'Does not the *being* of God which becomes manifest in and as history compel us to think of God's being, in its power which makes revelation possible, as *already* historical being?' Jüngel, *God's Being is in Becoming*, 6. Act, history, becoming, and relation: each of these terms strives to capture the life proper to the being of God in himself. While each offers a unique perspective, I use these terms synonymously, speaking primarily in terms of God's act.

significance for our project as it is precisely this being of God which is in Christ, working for us and for our salvation.[5]

I will not delve into those developments preceding Barth which contributed to his understanding of God's being in act. Jürgen Moltmann offers some guidance in this direction, tracing some of the history relevant to certain aspects of Barth's thought in: *The Trinity and the Kingdom: The Doctrine of God*, trans. Margaret Kohl (San Francisco, CA: Harper & Row, 1981), 11–15. Of the various relevant sources, Hegel is likely the deepest influence, with his actualistic/historicist understanding of the being of God. Barth himself notes this connection, writing that 'theology in particular was and is reminded by Hegel of the possibility that the truth might be history, event; that it might always be recognized and discovered in actuality and not otherwise'. Karl Barth, *Protestant Theology in the Nineteenth Century: Its Background and History*, trans. Brian Cozens and John Bowden (Grand Rapids, MI: Eerdmans, 2002), 401. It is important to note, however, that while Barth's understanding of God's being in act has both a theological and philosophical pedigree, its basis in his thought comes from strictly theological concerns; specifically, God's self-revelation in the incarnation of Jesus Christ. See: Bruce L. McCormack, 'The Being of Holy Scripture is in Becoming', in *Evangelicals and Scripture: Tradition, Authority, and Hermeneutics*, ed. Vincent Bacote, Laura C. Miguélez and Dennis L. Okholm (Downers Grove, IL: InterVarsity Press, 2004), 74.

[5] At the broadest level, Barth's theology of being in act, or actualism, refers to his 'think[ing] primarily in terms of events and relationships rather than monadic or self-contained substances' (Hunsinger, *How to Read*, 30). More specifically, actualism has to do with the nature of personhood, both divine and human. As Bruce McCormack puts it, Barth's is a '"historicized" ontology', a 'historical mode of thinking in accordance with which the 'essence' of God is constituted through his sovereign and free act of Self-determination in eternity'. McCormack, 'Ontological Presuppositions', 359–60. This is opposed to 'substantialist forms of ancient metaphysics', where 'what a person "is"' is something that is complete in and for itself, apart from and prior to all the decisions, acts, and relations that make up the sum total of the lived existence of the person in question' (*McCormack, Orthodox and Modern*, 211. Cf. Neder, *Participation in Christ*, 32–5).

Whether Barth's actualism constitutes a radical innovation in the history of theology is open to question, and not essential to my thesis. It is interesting to note, however, the work of W. Norris Clarke, who suggests that Thomas Aquinas understands substance to be an 'abiding center of activity, naturally oriented towards self-fulfillment through activity', while attributing to 'modern philosophers after Descartes and Locke' the 'so-called "classical" notion of substance' (W. Norris Clarke, *Explorations in Metaphysics: Being – God – Person* (Notre Dame, IN: University of Notre Dame Press, 1994), 62). In a chapter provocatively titled 'To Be is to Be Substance-in-Relation', Clarke states that his project is to use Thomas to 'retrieve the classical (pre-Cartesian) notion of substance as dynamic, as an active nature, i.e., an abiding center of acting and being acted upon …; and secondly, to integrate it more closely with the notion of relation as an intrinsic dimension of being' (Clarke, *Explorations in Metaphysics*, 102). To be sure, Clarke notes that 'the full implications of his own metaphysics of existence as act had not yet been drawn fully into the light by Thomas himself, nor perhaps fully even by his followers to this day' (Clarke, *Explorations in Metaphysics*, 104; cf. p. 109). A more recent contribution to this discussion is: Bruce D. Marshall,

For Barth, God is 'not only to be found alone in His act' but, more specifically, God is to be found in His act alone because as the living one 'alone in His act He is who He is' (*CD* II/1, 272). The purpose of this chapter to explore the meaning of this claim, in order to grasp the underlying reasons fuelling the intensity with which Barth integrates the doctrines of God and Reconciliation, and in turn fuels my own constructive project.[6] We will explore this thesis in two main sections, each put in the form of a response to a question. First, why should we ask questions concerning theological ontology? Why not simply remain content exploring the biblical witness to the benefits we receive from Christ, avoiding dogmatic theology's speculative and scholastic pitfalls? Second, why should we focus on the death and resurrection of Jesus Christ? Doesn't such an emphasis occur at the expense of the whole spectrum of God's self-revealing work? What of God's self

'The Dereliction of Christ and the Impassibility of God', in *Divine Impassibility and the Mystery of Human Suffering*, eds James Keating and Thomas Joseph White (Grand Rapids, MI: Eerdmans, 2009).

[6] I qualify this investigation with a note of caution derived from the work of George Hunsinger, who explores the 'shape of Barth's theology' through an analysis of what he finds to be the most significant motifs in Barth's *Church Dogmatics*. He offers his work in contrast to a litany of unsuccessful attempts to find 'a single overriding conception that would serve as a key to reading Barth', Hunsinger, *How to Read*, 3. Given his purpose, Hunsinger notes the multiplicity of concepts necessary for understanding Barth's thought, and would challenge Barth's readers not to over-emphasize the concept of actualism. Simply put, in exploring this very significant concept we must not presume to possess the key to Barth's theology. The point is well made, and I do not presume to elevate God's being in act over other of Barth's motifs or simply to deduce my conclusions from an analysis of this motif. However, it must also be said that this particular concept or motif is so pervasive in Barth's thought that Hunsinger himself suggests that it could serve to describe the whole of his theology (Hunsinger, *How to Read*, 30). In a bolder statement, Roberts suggests that 'the doctrine of God's being-in-act is the ontological *fundamentum* of the *Church Dogmatics*' (Richard H. Roberts, *A Theology on its Way? Essays on Karl Barth* (Edinburgh: T & T Clark, 1991), 20).
Furthermore, while 'actualism' is indeed a motif in Barth's thought, I am not concerned in this book with a motif as such (cf. Paul T. Nimmo, *Being in Action: The Theological Shape of Barth's Ethical Vision*, 7). My interest is with God's being in act inasmuch as this is a concrete theological commitment with decisive material consequences for Barth's theology, such that I am more interested in material content than formal patterns (a point consistent with Hunsinger's work: Hunsinger, *How to Read*, 271). Nevertheless, I recognize that just as the motifs Hunsinger considers bear upon each other and function cohesively, Barth's notion of God's being in act emerges from and remains in vital relationship with the doctrines of revelation, Trinity, the Perfections and Election. While my treatment can only develop some of these relationships in detail, I recognize that being in act as such (that is, as a general or philosophical concept derived independently of material theological concerns) has no particular meaning or explanatory value within Barth's thought.

revelation to Moses on Mount Sinai? Is God less himself in this event; is it an instance of incomplete revelation and therefore no revelation at all?

Theological Ontology

Should we seek to know the God who accomplished our salvation in Jesus Christ? Are we not pushing beyond our limits, probing where we shouldn't, risking the confusion, conflict and error attending idle speculation? Do not questions about the Trinity and divine attributes, themselves complicated and arcane subjects, only serve to complicate matters? How could the doctrine of the Trinity possibly make *anything* simpler to understand?[7] Along these lines, Barth asks: 'Should we not be content with the definition of [God] which we make when we adopt the statements which according to the Word of God are necessary for the description of the action and working of this subject?' (*CD* II/1, 259). On what basis, Barth wonders, do we go beyond mere description of God's acts as revealed in Scripture (and their benefit to us) to speak of God's being? What impels us to seek to 'define the subject' of these acts, to speak of God's being?

The Stakes

Barth's first move is to point out just how much is at stake in this matter. 'If the Word of God forbids the question of God's being as a particular question, or leaves us in doubt about this particular question, it means that it gives us no real revelation of God' (*CD* II/1, 259). Without knowledge of God's being, there is no real revelation – there is no knowledge of God, for a chasm has been opened between God's act toward us (*ad extra*) and God's own proper being and life (*ad intra*), such that we may possibly be able to know the former but certainly not the latter. But even this is questionable, for without revelation in the sense of knowledge of God's being, we cannot know whether a given act is God's and the extent to which it is so. Remember Descartes: what is to distinguish the providence of a sycophant from that of a compassionate redeemer? Knowledge of the being of God is essential to knowledge of his acts *ad extra* (and vice versa), much as we must know someone to discern between jokes and threats, between love and treachery.

---

[7] Noting how counter-intuitive such a claim is, Webster insists: 'the setting of a Christian theology of salvation is not in anthropology, but in the works of God *ad extra*; those works, in turn, have their setting in and refer back to the *opera Dei immanentia* as their condition and ground' (Webster, '*Rector et iudex*', 39).

While it might seem to be the case that we could appreciate God's acts without knowing his being, this ultimately undermines any possibility of our knowledge of those benefits we thought it so simple to appreciate.

> If the Word of God … gives us no real revelation of God … It keeps from us, and therefore does not reveal, the fact that [an act] is, and how far it is, the action and working of God. This action and working becomes and is significant and effective with a significance and effectiveness qualitatively different from any other action and working in virtue of the fact that it is God's action and working. It is not because it is proclaimed and believed in itself, not because there is proclaimed and believed a creation, reconciliation, and redemption, but because the whole is proclaimed and believed as God's action and working. (CD II/1, 259)

The decisive events of Scripture, Barth suggests, matter not simply because we believe in them, or even because they are 'very significant and effective' (CD II/1, 259) events, which speak even of our salvation.[8] Rather, this action and working derives its unique significance from the fact that it is the action of God. Without this knowledge we cannot know the ultimate meaning and significance of these acts. If these events are not anchored in the very being and will of God and granted their significance by him, who is to say that they will not be surpassed or qualified by yet further acts? What significance or permanence do they have in the grand scheme of things given that the flow of history is sure to sweep past them just as it does every other event, swallowing them up in its path? How can we discern whether Jesus' resurrection wasn't simply a mysterious event, or even if caused by God, of no more significance to us than Elisha raising the Shunammite's son (2 Kgs 4.34–5)? The being of God is the decisive element in these events, and the

---

[8] 'If Christ has not been raised, then our preaching is in vain and your faith is in vain. We are even found to be misrepresenting God … If Christ has not been raised, your faith is futile and you are still in your sins' (1 Cor. 15.14–17). Faith and belief concerning salvation matter only because Christ was raised. And the passive form of this statement (was raised) is significant, because it binds God to this act (as the one who raised him) such that the apostolic preaching about the resurrection, should it be false, is a misrepresentation of God! God is the one raising Christ, 'putting all things in subjection under his feet' (v. 27), that he 'may be all in all' (v. 28). Our thanks are 'to God, who gives us victory through our Lord Jesus Christ,' and we are to abound 'in the work of the Lord, knowing that in the Lord [our] labor is not in vain' (vv. 57–8). Faith is of no significance apart from the resurrection of Christ, and the decisive significance of the resurrection is that it is God's work, as God raises Christ and gives us victory through him. Apart from the knowledge that this was the work of God in giving us victory, our faith is of no more significance than the belief Martha and Mary in Lazarus' resurrection.

hermeneutical key for our interpretation thereof: 'Without this Subject they would be something quite different from what they are in accordance with God's word' (*CD* II/1, 260).

As Jüngel puts it, 'the being of God *goes before* all theological questioning in such a way that in its movement it paves the way for questioning, leading the questioning for the first time onto the path of thinking'.[9] The being of God in God's act, his manifest presence within his acts, is precisely that which paves the way to our understanding of the meaning and significance of his acts. Deprived of this, 'we are of all people most to be pitied' (1 Cor. 15.19). If the scriptural witness to God's acts does not reveal to us God's being in these acts, not only do we not know God, we also lack the basis for understanding these acts which are supposedly God's – whether and to what extent they are in fact God's acts. In short, without knowledge of God's being, we cannot know his benefits: 'the *beneficia Christi* cannot be properly investigated if some consideration of the *mysteria divinitatis* as such has not been undertaken in its proper place' (*CD* II/1, 259).[10] To put this point in the terms of my thesis: the doctrines of the Trinity, divine perfections and the electing will of God (in short, the *mysteria divinitatis*) play an essential and therefore indispensable role in a proper and full understanding of the meaning and significance of Christ's death and resurrection (the *beneficia Christi*).

Scripture's Affirmation

Thus far Barth's point is to indicate what is at stake in this question, and the stakes are indeed high. His primary concern, however, is to note the decisive fact that '[Holy Scripture] does not remain silent on the particular question of God's being ... It authorizes us and commands us quietly and candidly to halt at this point and to consider specifically what we are saying when we make this hardest and most comprehensive statement that God is,' instead of hurrying on to the saving work of Christ (*CD* II/1, 259).[11] Barth's first

---

[9] Jüngel, *God's Being is in Becoming*, 9.

[10] Cf. Webster's claim that 'God's being is indeed being in act; but by "act" here we do not restrict ourselves to those acts whereby God establishes, preserves, redeems and perfects creatures, for we also – primarily – refer to the infinite underivative movement of God in himself, which is the founding condition of the economy. We do not understand the economy unless we take time to consider God who is, though creatures might not have been' (John Webster, 'Trinity and Creation', *IJST* 12, no. 1 (2010): 7.

[11] 'The Word became flesh and lived among us, and we have seen his glory' (Jn. 1.14); 'Whoever has seen me has seen the Father' (Jn. 14.9); 'This is eternal life, that they may know you, the only true God, and Jesus Christ whom you have sent' (Jn. 17.3); 'Let the same mind be in you that was in Christ Jesus, who, though he was in the form of God, did not regard equality with God as something to be exploited' (Phil. 2.5–6);

move in his account of God's being in act is thus to emphasize the demand which the event of God's self-revelation places upon us to attend not only to the working of God, but to the God whose working this is. The knowledge of the being of God made known to us thereby provides the context for properly understanding God's works.[12]

We can understand God's act in its depth and seriousness only by halting at this point and attending specifically to the being of God which is in this act. Only by knowing the being of God in his works can we understand his works: 'what first gives its significance to the humiliation and abandonment of this man is the fact that this man is God's Son, and it is none other than God Himself who humbles and surrenders Himself in Him' (DO, 115). Our belief in the death and resurrection of Jesus, our faith in him as our saviour, the ethical imperative derived from his life: these and similar pillars of the Christian faith are frail and impotent vessels apart from the underlying reality of God's being and will decisively shaping and characterizing these events. For instance, the claim that 'we know love by this, that [Jesus Christ] laid down his life for us – and we ought to lay down our lives for one another' (1 Jn. 3.16) has meaning only because of the underlying belief that Jesus Christ is the Word of God become flesh (Jn. 1.14), and that in doing so he reveals God's love for the world (Jn. 3.16), a love which ultimately rests in the very being of God himself: 'God is love' (1 Jn. 4.7). The core of the Christian faith rests on its claim to know God, to know his being – in this act.

Barth's next step is to advance the argument beyond the claim that we can only properly understand God's act in connection with the being of God, exploring the definitive relationship between God's act and his being. 'God is who He is in His works ... In the light of what He is in His works it is no longer an open question what He is in Himself ... [in them] He is Himself revealed as the One He is' (CD II/1, 260). We have already seen that Jesus' death and resurrection derive their unique and decisive significance precisely from the fact that these were events in the life of the incarnate Son of God, and not simply the life of any man; but beyond that, Barth adds that the passion of Jesus is something that God does precisely

---

'Whoever knows God listens to us, and whoever is not from God does not listen to us. From this we know the spirit of truth and the spirit of error. Beloved, let us love one another, because love is from God; everyone who loves is born of God and knows God. Whoever does not love does not know God, for God is love' (1 Jn. 4.6–8). These and hosts of similar passages presume either that we know God or root the decisive events of the Christian faith in the being and work of God, demanding that we consider the works of God in light of his being.

[12] 'Who and what God is – this is what in particular we have to learn better and with more precision in the new change of direction in the thinking and speaking of evangelical theology ... But the question must be, who and what is God in Jesus Christ, if we here today would push forward a better answer' (Barth, The Humanity of God, 47).

because this is who God is – God is precisely who he is in the self-revealing and therefore saving work of Jesus Christ. That is to say, God reveals himself fully and finally in the person and work of Jesus Christ. It is here, in this event, that we know the being of God, full stop. In order to better appreciate the nature of Barth's argument, we must attend to the role of the doctrine of the Trinity, which Barth has had firmly in mind throughout his treatment of God's being in act.[13]

Trinity and Theological Ontology

As he writes in the summary statement (*Leitsatz*) for *CD* II/1, §28, without and apart from us God 'has His life from Himself' as 'Father, Son and Holy Spirit', and shares this life with us by seeking and creating fellowship 'in the act of His revelation'; and in this act of revelation 'God is who He is' (*CD* II/1, 257). Attending to the role of the Trinity within this argument allows us to better understand Barth's thesis. God reveals himself by means of himself, such that the very possibility of the theological task, the event of God's self-revelation, is rooted not only in an event which somehow relates to God's being, but in an event which is precisely that of God's own triune life shared with us.[14] That God's being is in act thus means that God shares his being with us by enacting his already living and active being in a new direction (namely, toward his creatures).[15]

Alan Torrance captures this point beautifully, writing that for Barth 'the doctrine of the Trinity is ... not 'read off' the information content of revelation independently of its givenness. Rather, there is an absolute integration of form and content in this revelation, every facet of which requires to be expressed in terms of the divine Triunity.'[16] In Barth's words, 'God is He who in this event [of revelation] is subject, predicate and object;

---

[13] As a sign that we are taking the proper interpretative steps, this is precisely what Jüngel does, delving into the doctrines of the Trinity and election in order to develop Barth's account of God's being in act. Jüngel, *God's Being is in Becoming*.

[14] As Wood notes, 'revelation is not a matter of propositions or objective events; it is exclusively the selfhood of God as he discloses Himself. Hence historical events and the words of the Bible are not the revelation of God. Rather, the revelation of God is *God Himself*' (Laurence W. Wood, 'Defining the Modern Concept of Self-Revelation: Toward a Synthesis of Barth and Pannenberg,' 41, no. 2 (1986), 85).

[15] The 'sharing' in question is not a matter of ontological deification. Rather, it is a matter of God bringing us into fellowship with himself, such that we share in the divine life. This line of thought has everything to do with Barth's emphasis that God's being is living being. To share such a being is to share the life in which it consists through fellowship. Cf. Neder, *Participation in Christ*.

[16] Alan J. Torrance, *Persons in Communion: An Essay on Trinitarian Description and Human Participation, with Special Reference to Volume One of Karl Barth's* Church Dogmatics (Edinburgh: T & T Clark, 1996), 101.

the revealer, the act of revelation, the revealed; Father, Son and Holy Spirit' (*CD* II/1, 262–3). God enacts his own proper being with us as Father, Son and Holy Spirit through the incarnation such that the being of God is identical with the event in which he reveals himself and the content of that revelation: Jesus Christ.[17] There is thus no division between the content of revelation, the event in which it takes place and the being of God. That 'God is who He is in the act of His revelation' (*CD* II/1, 262) is true because revelation, to be true revelation and therefore self-revelation, is simply a matter of God being who he is a second time, under new circumstances: with us in the person and work of Jesus Christ.

God gives himself to us in the full and genuine sense of self-revelation by means of an act which is itself not foreign to God because he is the living and active one from eternity as the triune God (regardless of his determination to be with and for us). Antecedently, the being of God is in act as he lives out his triune being. 'As and before God seeks and creates fellowship with us, He wills and completes this fellowship in Himself. In Himself He does not will to exist for Himself, to exist alone. On the contrary, He is Father, Son and Holy Spirit and therefore alive in His unique being with and for and in another' (*CD* II/1, 276).[18] In God's self-revelation and therefore in God himself, being and act are thus inseparable, for the being in question is the living being of God's act, an act which God repeats with us: 'what He seeks and creates between Himself and us is in fact nothing else but what He wills and completes and therefore is in Himself' (*CD* II/1, 275).[19] For this reason, 'we have to take revelation with such utter seriousness that in it as God's act we must directly see God's being too' (*CD* I/1, 428).[20]

---

[17] For Barth the root of the doctrine of the Trinity is the fact that God reveals himself to us as Lord, and this takes up within itself the biblical testimony of God as Father, Son and Holy Spirit. The Bible's explicit reference to the Father, Son and Holy Spirit (*CD* I/1, 314) thus 'prefigures' the 'problems that developed later in the doctrine of the Trinity'. It is important for Barth, however, that even the doctrine of the Trinity is not simply or even primarily content given to us about God through Scripture, but rather an analysis of the event in which God makes himself known to us.

[18] George Hunsinger writes: 'God's being correlates with God's vitality. As the living God, God's being is in the process of becoming. This life process occurs independently of any relationship that God may have with the world. The triune God does not need the world for the sake of self-actualization, for this God is always already totally actual in the *hypostases* and perfections of his eternal life' (George Hunsinger, *Disruptive Grace: Studies in the Theology of Karl Barth* (Grand Rapids, MI: Eerdmans, 2000), 196).

[19] Although Barth does not himself often use such terminology, it may be helpful to think of this in terms of God repeating the life he has with himself (his immanent life in eternity) with us in the economy. The economic Trinity and its actions, in other words, is a free repetition of the life of the immanent Trinity.

[20] This raises the question of whether our knowledge of God can be partial, for, after all, 'God is One ... He Himself does not consist of quantities' or parts, we might add, 'for

This bond between God's being and his act is so intimate that they are, in fact, identical. Barth writes: 'God's essence and work are not twofold but one. God's work is His essence in its relation to the reality which is distinct from Him' (*CD* I/1, 371). That is to say, God's essence is his life as the triune God, and his work is the event of sharing his life as the triune God with his creatures in seeking and creating fellowship with them; therefore God's work is a matter of sharing his divine essence, his divine life. The 'oneness' in question is a unity of repetition or overflowing: 'It implies so to speak an overflow [Überfluß] of His essence that He turns to us. We must certainly regard this overflow as itself matching His essence, belonging to His essence. But it is an overflow which is not demanded or presupposed ...' (*CD* II/1, 273; *KD*, 307).[21] Synonymous with 'overflow,' Barth refers to God 'sharing',[22] 'confirm[ing] and display[ing]'[23] or 'repeating [*Wiederholung*]' the divine life,[24] or of a 'temporal analogue [*zeitliche ... Analogon*], taking place outside God, of that event in God Himself by which God is the Father of the Son' (*DO*, 52; *DG*, 59). These images coalesce to make the point that God's essence is his life, and that his work towards us is the event in which he shares his life and therefore his essence with us.[25]

For Barth, God's intervention within the created order is not simply a matter of making certain content about himself known or remedying the

---

the parts under consideration here are ... the one, entire and indivisible being of God, who has unreservedly made Himself accessible ... to us' (*CD* II/1, 234). Briefly, our knowledge can be partial, but that which we know (the object itself) cannot. God's self-revelation is not partial, but our grasp of it is. I disagree with Colin Gunton's interpretation when he suggests that 'the more God reveals, at the same time the more there is the hidden mystery that is not made known ... God makes certain things about his character, his being, made known to certain people. But this is by no means to say that he lets us in for the whole' (Gunton, *The Barth Lectures*, 81).

[21] Elsewhere, with regard to 'overflow', Barth writes: 'The fact that God makes this movement, the institution of the covenant, the primal decision "in Jesus Christ," which is the basis and goal of all His works – that is grace. Speaking generally, it is the demonstration, the overflowing of the love which is the being of God, that He who is entirely self-sufficient, who even within Himself cannot know isolation, willed even in all His divine glory to share His life with another, and to have that other as the witness of His glory' (*CD* II/2, 9–10). Cf. *CD* II/2, 121, 169, 175, 412; *CD* IV/1, 52, 201; *CD* IV/2, 346, 352.

[22] 'We are given a 'share' in 'God's Godhead', through 'the event of His action [*an welchem wir in Gottes Offenbarung beteiligt werden*]' (*CD* II/1, 263; *KD*, 294).

[23] Barth, *Evangelical Theology*, 11.

[24] 'So no more and no less than a repetition of the divine life, a repetition which we do not bring about and which we cannot take from ourselves, but which it is God's will to allow in the creaturely realm – this is, outside the Godhead' (*DO*, 45; *DG*, 50).

[25] Webster writes that 'God – Father, Son and Holy Spirit – is life in himself', and uses the following list of terms to capture the idea of God overflowing his life/essence towards us: 'purposive turning', 'further movement', 'stretch[ing] forth', 'repeat[ing] his self-realized life', and 'bodying forth' (Webster, '*Rector et iudex*', 36–40).

disastrous condition of fallen creation. While such claims are not false, they fail to acknowledge the completeness with which God gives himself to his creation (gives himself as the God he is and therefore without giving himself away, or losing himself), and thus in effect suggest far too great a gap between God and his creation in the incarnation. God intends to share with us his life, his being: 'To its very deepest depths God's Godhead consists in the fact that it is an event ... the event of His action, in which we have a share in God's revelation [*an welchem wir in Gottes Offenbarung beteiligt werden*]' (*CD* II/1, 263; *KD*, 294).[26] God shares with us his own proper life in the event of his working in, with and among us, in the event of creation, revelation, reconciliation and redemption. He does this by overflowing or repeating with us that which he has within himself from eternity, such that this event is a genuine sharing, a true and complete gift. In this actualization of God's living being by which God makes his being known to us, we are given a share in God's being.[27]

In the next section we will consider the precise location of this encounter (where God deals with us as Lord and Saviour). For the time being, however, we simply note the force and depth of Barth's claim: by God's grace we encounter and know 'what God is as God, the divine individuality and characteristics, the *essentia* or "essence" of God', for he 'has not withheld Himself from men as true being, but ... has given no less than Himself to men as the overcoming of their need ... Himself as the Father in His own Son by the Holy Spirit' (*CD* II/1, 262). In Jesus Christ God gives us his whole undivided being as the triune God in the fullness of the divine perfections.[28] As Hunsinger notes, 'Nothing essential of God's identity ever

---

[26] Barth writes that 'Only God is eternal; only His love in all its inner and outer, positive and negative forms – except that in the act of His love God exalts something else to share in His eternity, so that there is now and for this reason an eternal life of which even we may live in hope and an eternal fire which even we have to fear' (*CD* II/1, 609). In this we see an example of just how radically Barth understands this sharing, this overflow.

[27] Again, I recommend the reader to: Neder, *Participation in Christ*. McKnight makes a similar point, while talking of the doctrine of perichoresis: 'Genuine, final reality for humans is to participate in the reciprocal interiority of the Trinity in Christ through the Spirit, and to extend this interiority to others as an approximation of that *perichoresis*' (McKnight, *A Community Called Atonement*, 16).

[28] As Barth writes, 'God exists in this entirety of His being and therefore not in any kind of parts ... At no time or place does He exist in only one of His modes of existence, or in only one sphere of His proclamation or action, or in only one particle of his lordship. A separable being of this kind or one part of such a separable being would have nothing whatever to do with the being of God' (*CD* II/1, 52). Barth extends this unity to his treatment of the divine perfections: 'Our doctrine therefore means that every individual perfection in God is nothing but God Himself and therefore nothing but every other divine perfection ... and that each individual perfection is identical with every other and with the fullness of them all' (*CD* II/1, 333). The unity of God is

34

needs to be sought elsewhere, Barth argued, than in Jesus Christ, God's definitive, final and binding act of self-revelation ... In Jesus Christ, God's being is present in its unity and entirety.'[29] Barth thus firmly establishes the ontological depth of revelation by emphasizing that we know God in his saving activity, but, more precisely, we know therein 'what God is as God', the 'essence of God' himself. The act of God has its basis in and is itself the living essence of God, and for this reason and this reason alone God is no other than the one who meets us in fellowship in his works.

In this section we have seen just how strongly Barth integrates the being of God and his works – for God's work is simply God's ineradicable decision to be the God he is, with us. Concerning our thesis, this section explains why we must interpret the work of Christ in light of the being of God in order to understand it properly: because the work of Christ is the being of God repeated for us. But why this specific event – why the death and resurrection of Jesus Christ – among all the events of God's economy? What of other revelatory events throughout the Old Testament? In the next section we see that Barth refuses to leave the meaning of God's 'act' or 'work' unspecified. He explains why we encounter the essence of God 'at the place where God deals with us as Lord and Saviour, or not at all' (*CD* II/1, 261). A proper exposition of this statement, according to Barth, calls for a treatment of the doctrine of election as it bears on God's being in act.

Election and Being in Act

Given that Scripture demands that we know the benefits we receive from God only in light of who he is, why is Barth so concerned that we focus on the person and work of Jesus Christ? What of God's self-revealing work throughout the economy of his saving history with Israel and the church? Are God's acts in the Old Testament less than revelatory? To answer such questions, we turn to Barth's doctrine of election (and its Christological specification characteristic of his mature thought in *CD* II/2), which he anticipates in a crucial part of his exposition of God's being in act.[30]

the unity of his perfections, such that as God meets us in his self-revelation, he meets us in the fullness of his divine perfections.

[29] Hunsinger, *How to Read*, 37.

[30] Bruce L. McCormack, *Karl Barth's Critically Realistic Dialectical Theology: Its Genesis and Development, 1909–1936* (New York: Oxford University Press, 1995). McCormack later notes that Barth took some time to consistently incorporate the Christological reorientation of his thought. McCormack, *Orthodox and Modern*, 262–4.

It is important, however, not to overstress the significance of Barth's development. As Justin Stratis notes, 'it may indeed be the case that *CD* II/2 represents a new material insight, but reading the prior volumes may not require as much revision as McCormack thinks' (Justin Stratis, 'Speculating About Divinity? God's Immanent Life

In his doctrine of election (*CD* II/2) Barth dramatically re-orients the traditional Reformed understanding of the doctrine of election, such that election first and foremost pertains to God's unreserved entanglement in world history:[31]

> In the beginning ... before there was any reality distinct from God which could be the object of the love of God or the setting for His acts of freedom, God anticipated and determined within Himself ... that the goal and meaning of all His dealings with the as yet non-existent universe should be the fact that in His Son He would be gracious towards man, uniting Himself with him. (*CD* II/2, 101)

The beginning of all God's outward or creative acts (*ad extra*), and therefore of all reality *ad extra*, is the decision of God to become man in the person of the Son, and thus to unite himself with humankind.[32] Specifying the nature of this union, Barth adds: 'As the subject and object of this choice, Jesus Christ was at the beginning' (*CD* II/2, 102). The beginning of God's creative ways was the determination to be our God, to be Jesus Christ, and in this sense Jesus Christ is the object of God's election. In so far as Jesus Christ is the incarnate Son of God, the subject willing this self-determination, Jesus Christ is said to be the subject of election.[33]

This passage goes beyond establishing the foundation of God's ways *ad extra*, which of itself would not provide Barth's grounds for locating the doctrine of election within the doctrine of God. The crucial point is that this event is a matter of divine self-determination: 'it is ... a decision which

and Actualistic Ontology', *IJST* 12, no. 1 (2010), 20–32). Barth himself was capable of some ambivalence with regard to the increased Christological emphasis characteristic of his later work. Responding to a question suggesting a more Christological emphasis to *CD* I/1, Barth responded: 'That would be an improvement. The Christological character of the *Church Dogmatics* is perhaps not so clear in Volume I as it should be! But pedagogically, there is a certain advantage in beginning with hesitation and then ending with equation' (Barth, *Table Talk*, 30). That Barth refers to a relative lack of clarity rather than something stronger, such as an omission, indicates that he thinks that the early volumes of the *Church Dogmatics* do in fact have a Christological character, even if that character was somewhat tentative and unclear at times.

[31] Maurer, '"Für uns" An unserer Stelle hingerichtet', 191.

[32] Justin Stratis offers a helpful explanation of the context of Barth's point concerning the divine decision [*Entscheidung*], thus establishing an interpretative framework for understanding the relationship between *CD* II/1 and II/2 which diverges significantly from that of Bruce McCormack (Stratis, 'Speculating About Divinity', 7–9).

[33] Bruce McCormack understands this statement to 'mean that the historical man Jesus of Nazareth is himself the electing God', while I, along with Kevin Hector and several others, understand it 'in terms of the notions of antecedence and repetition' (Kevin W. Hector, 'Immutability, Necessity, and Triunity: Towards a Resolution of the Trinity and Election Controversy,' *Scottish Journal of Theology* 65:1, pp. 64–81).

affects God himself … in a fundamental way [such that] it is dogmatically consistent to treat the doctrine of predestination as a part of the *doctrine of God*.'[34] The act of election is God's 'free, subjective self-determination', an 'act of unconditional self-determination' in which God ordained 'Himself the bearer of this name' and 'determined Himself …[and] put Himself under an obligation to man' (CD II/2, 100–1). Barth locates the doctrine of election within the doctrine of God, rather than at the beginning of God's creative acts, because first and foremost election is a self-determination, a specification and commitment on God's part to be the God he always was and always will be, though in a new way and in a particular relationship: to be the God of humankind in Jesus Christ. As a result of God's determination to be this God, 'in no depth of the Godhead shall we encounter any other but him' (CD II/2, 115). That is, in the act of election God determined or specified the particular way in which he would be God with an ontological and eternal significance. According to Barth, subsequent to this event there is no God who has not bound himself to humankind through his electing self-determination.

Within his treatment of God's being in act (CD II/1, 257, 260) and throughout his treatment of the doctrine of election, Barth establishes that this act of self-determination in which 'God tied Himself to the universe' (CD II/2, 155) was a free act. God is who He is in His works toward us, but this is because 'He is the same even in Himself, even before and after and over His works, and without them' (CD II/1, 260; cf. CD II/2, 121).[35] Because God is in himself what he reveals to us, and is so prior to and without us, God has the freedom, the possibility within himself to be what he is for us in Jesus Christ. As Colin Gunton notes,

> It is the Trinitarian grounding of the divine freedom that enables Barth to conceive as a unity the acts of love and freedom in which God relates himself to what is not himself, and yet in doing so remains free. The essential unity of the two is seen to derive from the fact that God *is* his act, his becoming.[36]

The doctrine of the immanent Trinity (God's eternal life as Father, Son and Holy Spirit) provides the antecedent basis within God for his relation

---

[34] Jüngel, *God's Being is in Becoming*, 84.

[35] Among Barth scholars, Paul Molnar stands out as one particularly sensitive to the role of freedom in Barth's thought. Cf. Paul D. Molnar, *Divine Freedom and the Doctrine of the Immanent Trinity: In Dialogue with Karl Barth and Contemporary Theology* (New York: T & T Clark, 2005).

[36] Colin E. Gunton, *Becoming and Being: The Doctrine of God in Charles Hartshorne and Karl Barth* (Oxford: Oxford University Press, 1978). Both Gunton and Jüngel use the phrase 'God's being is in becoming' in a sense synonymous with 'God's being in act' as used in this book. Cf. Jüngel, *God's Being is in Becoming*.

to creation (economic Trinity), thus grounding the divine freedom.[37] It does so precisely by being the eternal act of God which serves as the precondition for the possibility and actuality of his outward acts (cf. the overflow or repetition mentioned earlier). As Jüngel puts it, 'precedence of God in his primal decision shows that God's being not only "proceeds" on the way into the far country but that God's being is *in movement* from eternity' – an eternal movement within God which has taken this new and definitive form.[38] God can elect to be a living and active triune God for us because in himself and apart from us he already is this living and active triune God.[39]

Central to our concern is the fact that in this act of election God determines himself to be the man Jesus Christ. That is to say, he determines for himself a human history, the life of an Israelite.[40] On this basis, all of reality has its origin and goal in the life and work of Jesus Christ, as the first and decisive act of self-determination is God's decision to become Jesus Christ in the person of the Son. Returning to our analysis of *CD* §28.1, we can see more clearly why Barth claims that in God's revelation we have to do with 'an event which is in no sense to be transcended' (*CD* II/1, 262). This event, Barth specifies, 'is always the birth, death and resurrection of Jesus Christ, always His justification of faith, always His lordship in the Church, always His coming again, and therefore Himself as our hope', in short, the event of the history of Jesus Christ (*CD* II/1, 262). It is this event, and above all

---

[37] Why refer to the God '*extra nos*' when the Church's sole knowledge of God is rooted in his activity '*pro nobis*'? Because God's election is gracious. 'If that is so, if reconciliation is based on the free, gracious election of God, then we must accept in the living God no external necessity' (Barth, *Table Talk*, 14). While God can and does bind himself, talk of God '*extra nos*' is essential, as Barth understands it, for properly safeguarding the freedom and grace of God in turning to us.

[38] Jüngel, *God's Being Is in Becoming*, 14.

[39] As Jüngel notes: 'Barth places the doctrine of the Trinity at the beginning of his *Dogmatics* in order that 'its content be decisive and controlling for the whole of dogmatics (*CD* I/1, 303)' (*ibid.*, 16). Cf. Barth's claim in 1968 that 'behind the doctrine of election stands the doctrine of the Trinity. That is the order [*Reihenfolge*]. The doctrine of the Trinity, election, and then sanctification, and so forth' (quoted in: George Hunsinger, 'Election and the Trinity: Twenty-Five Theses on the Theology of Karl Barth', *Modern Theology* 24, no. 2 (2008), 182.

[40] Particularly important for Barth is Ephesians 1.3–6: 'Blessed be the God and Father of our Lord Jesus Christ, who has blessed us in Christ with every spiritual blessing in the heavenly places, even as he chose us in him before the foundation of the world, that we should be holy and blameless before him. In love he predestined us for adoption as sons through Jesus Christ, according to the purpose of his will, to the praise of his glorious grace, with which he has blessed us in the Beloved.' The same might be said for Rev. 13.8, which speaks of the lamb who was slain before the foundation of the world: τοῦ ἀρνίου τοῦ ἐσφαγμένου ἀπὸ καταβολῆς κόσμου, which is a key biblical support for Barth's position.

the death and resurrection which forms the centre of that history, that we are confronted most starkly with the being of God, for as a result of God's election 'to its very deepest depths God's Godhead consists in' this specific event, Jesus Christ – 'the event of His action, in which we have a share in God's revelation' (*CD* II/1, 263).[41]

While God acts and reveals Himself throughout his history with Israel and the Church,[42] God chose for his interactions with his creatures to head towards and look back upon a concrete centre: the person and work of Jesus Christ.[43] All of God's acts, all the events in which God reveals himself throughout the Old Testament[44] find their completion and ultimate meaning and relevance within the sphere of Christ's work,[45] just as the acts of God following Christ's ascension look back to his life, death and resurrection for their significance. Just as we do not identify God with 'a sum or content of event, act, or life generally' (*CD* II/1, 264), neither do we identify him with the whole of his acts generally or with any one act chosen at random: 'God's revelation is a particular event … It is a definite happening within general happening' (*CD* II/1, 264). To return to a passage cited earlier, 'What God is as God … is something which we shall encounter either at the place where God deals with us as Lord and Saviour, or not at all' (*CD* II/1, 261). The making of the covenants, the exodus from Egypt, the giving of the law, the building of the temple and its filling by the presence of God, the gathering of the church … these and other decisive events within the history of Israel and the church have their proper interpretative context, their fulfilment and basis only within the person and work of Jesus Christ, the creator incarnate in whom all things hold together and through whom all things are being reconciled (Col. 1.15–20; cf. Eph. 1.3–10).

Why then do we focus on the death and resurrection of Jesus Christ, among all the events of God's economy? What sense does it make to suggest

---

[41] As Webster notes, however, 'even that moment which of all others has a special claim to supremacy – the incarnation of the divine Word – is only the center of this history because around it other moments are ranged' (Webster, '*Rector et iudex*', 41).

[42] The book of Exodus comes quickly to mind, particularly Exodus 34: Graham A. Cole, 'Exodus 34, the Middoth and the Doctrine of God: The Importance of Biblical Theology to Evangelical Systematic Theology', *Southern Baptist Journal of Theology* 12, no. 3 (2008), 24–36.

[43] Wood, therefore, is not quite correct when he suggests that from his view of self-revelation 'Barth properly draws the logical deduction that only in one event can God be revealed, namely, in the Christ event' (Wood, 'Defining the Modern Concept of Self-Revelation', 86. Barth is interested not so much in a deduction as he is in thinking through the reality of God's self-revelation which has as a matter of fact this centre in the person and work of Jesus Christ.

[44] 'God is He who is to be found in the book of the Old and New Testaments, which speaks of Him' (*DO*, 37).

[45] And vice versa: God's relationship with Israel is the external basis of the life and work of Jesus Christ, while the latter is the internal basis of the former.

that there is a centre within the acts of God? The answer has to do with the act of election. In this event God chooses to be himself in a new way, with us, but to be with us in a history which has an event, a person and work, at its centre. In other words, God wills to repeat himself in such a way that his self-repetition reaches completion only in Jesus Christ, although anticipated and prepared for before-hand.[46] While God revealed himself to his people prior to this, the revelation was incomplete, replete with questions and awaiting fulfilment. While for his part God was fully present and active, he did so in such a way that his self-revelation, while true, was veiled by the fact that the fullness of time had not yet come for the event in which his self-revelation would be complete and the meaning of the whole would become apparent. In other words, God's being was hidden behind a double veil: the veil behind which all of God's acts are hidden (*CD* II/1, 16: God is not objective to us 'directly but indirectly, not in the naked sense but clothed under the sign and veil of other objects different from Himself'), and a second veil consisting of the incompleteness, the promise, the waiting for fulfilment characteristic of his acts in the Old Testament.

For this reason we focus on the death and resurrection of Jesus Christ, because here God's being is fully present in the fulfilment of his electing will. To properly understand the doctrine of the atonement we must see its relationship to the being of God because precisely here we find God's being as specified by God's freely electing will in the event of self-fulfilment.[47]

Being in Person

But what, on Barth's account, differentiates one act of God from another? This brings us to Barth's affirmation that God's being is 'being in person [*Sein in Person*]' (*CD* II/1, 268; *KD*, 300). With this concept, however, it is important to understand that we are not departing from or adding to Barth's earlier treatment of God's 'being in act' – for God's 'being in act'

---

[46] The self-fulfilment in question has to do with God fulfiling the purposes or promises to which he bound himself with covenantal and therefore ontological force.

[47] It might be important to distinguish Barth from Hegel on this point. 'In contra-distinction to a Hegelian understanding, wherein God comes to the world and in coming to the world realizes himself as God, God is neither *constrained* by nor in need of that which is outside himself in order to be God. Rather, God's liveliness *in se* is what grounds and establishes genuine creaturely reality. And because God is free in relation to what is outside him – precisely because God is free in relation to himself – Barth does not define God in opposition to creaturely reality' (Christopher R. J. Holmes, *Revisiting the Doctrine of the Divine Attributes: In Dialogue with Karl Barth, Eberhard Jüngel and Wolf Krötke* (New York: Peter Lang, 2007), 44. All that to say, the self-fulfilment in question is a matter of God's free self-repetition rooted in the fullness and freedom of God's own being.

is not itself an independent concept in Barth's thought with any unique explanatory power. Rather, 'being in act', 'livingness' and 'being in person' are all synonymous concepts by means of which Barth elaborates the conviction that when we think of God's being we must not think first of being itself and only later of act or life, but rather from the very start think of God's being as an intrinsically, necessarily and to its deepest depths living, active and personal being. That God's 'being is in becoming,' writes Jüngel (and here we could insert 'being in act' or 'livingness'), means 'first of all, that God in his being is indeed to be thought of as subject, but subject in no other sense than as *active* subject. God *is* active'.[48] The vitality of Barth's notion of God's being in act as the living God emerges precisely from the union of the emphases on both being and act in specific reference to the one living and personal God. The concept of God's 'being in person' simply gets at God's 'being in act' from another angle – from that of the personal God.

God is 'event, act and life in His own way, as distinct from everything that He is not Himself' (*CD* II/1, 264). God's event, act and life is the 'free event, free act and free life' of the divine person, such that God is distinct from every other act and event even while he is in relation to it. Exploring the basis of this freedom, Barth makes the surprising claim that the event or act in which God is who he is occurs 'in the unity of spirit and nature' (*CD* II/1, 268). That God is spirit means that he has the 'freedom of a knowing and willing I, an I which itself distinguishes itself from what it is not, and what is not from itself, an I which controls nature' (*CD* II/1, 267). That God has a nature means that there is that in God which is directed by God's spirit.[49] In the inseparable unity of these two, God's being is 'being in person' (*CD* II/1, 268), on which basis God intends, purposes, decides and works – in short, has a real history with real doings.

Barth takes this history and the reality of God's actions and decisions with utmost seriousness. In his treatment of the divine patience, for instance, he writes:

> God is not more powerful in His action than in His forbearance from action. Indeed there is no antithesis here: God's forbearance is only a specific form of His always powerful doing and being. God is therefore no less effective in His patience than in His grace and mercy, than in His holy and just wrath which includes His grace and mercy. (*CD* II/1, 410)

[48] Jüngel, *God's Being is in Becoming*, 78.

[49] As Cole puts it, 'the God of biblical revelation has a character. Divine action flows from that character' (Cole, *God the Peacemaker*, 52).

On the basis of Barth's affirmation that God is the unity of his spirit and nature, I wonder whether McCormack over-emphasizes Barth's actualism in such a way as to minimize the substantial or natural aspect of that which is active, such as when he writes that 'essences are, for Barth, relations with an event-character' in McCormack, 'The Being of Holy Scripture', 69.

This passage brings home the full significance of Barth's further specification of God's being in act as being in person, through the unity of spirit and nature in which God lives from eternity. God's act is not a force, not a constant and monotonous overflow from the divine being resulting in an unchanging act in relation to creation like the rays of the sun; he is not 'bound to be and say and do only one and the same thing, so that all the distinctions of His being, speaking and acting are only a semblance' (CD II/1, 496). Rather, God's act is the consequence of his intentional or personal will and movement.[50] His being is personal, in that he has control over his nature such that his act can take different forms of action according to his purposes. For instance, it can take the form of forbearance – an active, intentional, powerful and effective refraining-from-activity. And because God can actively exercise forbearance, he can order his acts toward a centre, both acting and exercising patience so as to guide things towards their ultimate fulfilment at the proper time.

God, whose active being consists in the fact that God is person, has control over his own nature, choosing and determining now to act, now to refrain from action, all the while doing so as the one who exists fully in this act. Taking this point to the extreme, Barth affirms that God can and 'does in fact repent of having promised, threatened or even done something, and in a sense retracts either once or many times, and sometimes goes on to retract His retraction, returning to what He had originally said and done' (CD II/1, 496).[51] According to Barth, Scripture witnesses to the fact that God can and does change, although to be sure he is constant: 'His constancy consists in the fact that He is always the same *in every change*' (CD II/1, 496, emphasis added).[52]

---

[50] Barth specifies that in fact God is the only one of whom the term 'person' can properly be used (CD II/1, 271).

[51] Barth goes on to cite a number of Scriptural instances of such retractions, including Genesis 6 and 18, Exodus 32, Amos 7 and Jeremiah 18. On the apparent proximity of Barth to Open-Theism in this passage, cf. Bruce L. McCormack, 'The Actuality of God: Karl Barth in Conversation with Open Theism,' in *Engaging the Doctrine of God: Contemporary Protestant Perspectives*, ed. Bruce L. McCormack (Grand Rapids, MI: Baker Academic, 2008).

[52] McCormack suggests that 'the red thread that runs throughout the whole of Barth's theology – and that gives to his theological ontology its character as relational and actualistic – is the strictly theological problem of the meaning of divine immutability in relation to the fact of the incarnation ... God's self-revelation in time' (McCormack, 'The Being of Holy Scripture', 74). Cf. John Webster's similar point in the introduction to: Jüngel, *God's Being is in Becoming*, xvii. Barth writes, for example: 'In biblical thinking God is certainly the immutable, but as the immutable He is the living God and he possesses a mobility and elasticity which is no less divine than His perseverance, and which actually and necessarily confirms the divinity of His perseverance no less than its own divinity naturally requires confirmation by His divine presence' (CD II/1, 494–6).

The net gain from Barth's point that the being of God is personal, that God is an ordered unity of spirit and nature, lies in his account of the ways in which God can and does act. There is a 'true, real history of His doings', there are 'decisions and working of God', there is 'reconciliation and revelation ... creation and redemption as happening and decision' (CD II/1, 267). God is neither 'the formless, motionless being of a spirit' or 'accident or necessity', but the 'freedom of a knowing and willing I, an I which itself distinguishes itself from what it is not, and what it is not from itself, an I which controls nature' (CD II/1, 267), an I which controls itself. God's being is at God's disposal, knowing, deciding and moving itself. To be more precise, God's being not only moves itself (something true of human persons as well) – it is self-moved being: 'the movement of nature and spirit, which occurs in His revelation and is effected by it, does not lead back to any self-movement of man' (CD II/1, 270). The motives and resources for God's acts and history have their sole source in God's own proper being, such that he is not moved by that which is outside of him.[53] But because God's being is personal, because he has control over his own nature, and thus purposes and acts or refrains from acting according to his will, God's acts and history are diverse and can be ordered towards a centre if God so chooses.

To return to our question, God's history with us can and does have a centre because God can and does order his being and acts in such a way as to be wholly who he is in each of his acts and yet order those acts such as to have their meaning and centre not within themselves as such, but in the person and work of Jesus Christ. In this way, while the various acts are revelatory, for they are the acts of God, they are nevertheless veiled until seen in light of their ultimate goal – for the form of God's self-revelation in any given act may be that of self-restraint and forbearance, and thus a veiled form of self-revelation. Accordingly, each of God's acts is not equally revealing of his being, for the acts are ordered towards an event which is itself (according to God's election) the centre and therefore the decisive hermeneutical basis for the entire history of God's acts and our understanding of God's being. The 'order' in question has to do with God's control over his nature as he works in creation, bringing it to the fulfilment of his electing purposes. It is for this reason that we encounter the essence of God 'at the place where God deals with us as Lord and Saviour, or not at all' (CD II/1, 261).

With regard to our thesis, this section explains all the more why we must interpret the work of Christ (and specifically this work) in light of the being

---

[53] That is to say, while God can and does choose to respond to his creatures and in this sense is moved by them, he is not moved by anything outside of himself in the sense that nothing outside of God has a claim on God, deserves anything from him, or has some basis upon which to bring God to action apart from God's own gift and internal self-movement towards the creature.

of God, in order to understand it properly. The reason is that God's being is a personal being – God is spirit, and has control over his own nature – such that even though his being is fully present in all his acts, he can order his acts such that they aim towards and work out from a centre, that centre being the person and work of Jesus Christ as determined by God in the free event of self-determination. We cannot understand the atonement apart from the being of God because God, whose being is personal being, ordered his acts to have a centre in Jesus Christ, such that neither his own being nor the history of his acts can be understood apart from this centre.

Christology

We have seen how Barth develops the understanding of God's being as living being, and how as a consequence of the way in which God has elected to live with us, we must focus on the person and work of Jesus Christ in order to know God and thereby to understand the true meaning and signifi- cance of Christ's work. It will be helpful at this point to briefly consider Barth's Christology, as it recapitulates some of these key themes, providing precisely the integration of the self-determining being of God and the life of Jesus Christ which we would expect. Even a modest survey of Barth's Christology is out of the question in the present work, however,[54] so I limit myself to the key commitments underlying Barth's Christology, as they bear on the integration of the being of God and the doctrine of the atonement.[55]

---

[54] For an introduction to the topic, see: George Hunsinger, 'Karl Barth's Christology: Its Basic Chalcedonian Character,' in *The Cambridge Companion to Karl Barth*, ed. J. B. Webster (New York: Cambridge University Press, 2000). A recent treatment which offers a comprehensive examination of the topic while paying close attention to the humanity of Jesus Christ is: Paul Dafydd Jones, *The Humanity of Christ: Christology in Karl Barth's* Church Dogmatics (New York: T & T Clark, 2008). The most provocative work on the subject is that of Bruce McCormack, as seen, for example, in Part 3 of McCormack, *Orthodox and Modern*.

[55] In other words, I draw out the impetus for what we might loosely refer to as the 'Alexandrian' element in Barth's thought. Cf. Hunsinger, 'Karl Barth's Christology'. On whether this is a particularly helpful label for Barth's theology, see Bruce L. McCormack, 'Karl Barth's Historicized Christology: Just How "Chalcedonian" is it?', in *Orthodox and Modern: Studies in the Theology of Karl Barth* (Grand Rapids, MI: Baker Academic, 2008). I fully recognize that such an approach fails to do justice to Barth's Christology as a whole. For those interested in more thorough treatments of this doctrine, I commend the works of those cited in this section, particularly those of George Hunsinger, Bruce McCormack and Paul Dafydd Jones. The work of the latter in particular (emphasizing the humanity of Jesus Christ) offers a helpful balance to my own emphasis in this book.

As my purpose is not to offer a comprehensive overview of Barth's thought, however, I hold such imbalance to be an acceptable aspect of a specific and limited theological

In the fulfilment of the covenant in Christ's atoning work we have to do 'with the heart of the message received by and laid upon the Christian community and therefore with the heart of the Church's dogmatics': That God is with us (*Gott mit uns*), 'that it is He who is with [us] as God … Everything depends upon [our] coming to see that it all has to do with God; that it is God who is with [us] as God' (*CD* IV/1, 3–4). But God's 'being with us' is not an idea, a general truth or reality, but rather a history that has to do with the concrete name of Jesus Christ, in whom and through whom God is with us (*CD* IV/1, 16–20).[56] Barth's fundamental concern underlying his Christology (at least in *CD* IV/1)[57] is that in the fully integrated person and work of Jesus Christ[58] the living God is present and active among us.

We see this clearly in one of those passages which for Barth 'in a classic way encompass the whole of [reconciliation as the fulfilment of the covenant]' (*CD* IV/1, 70): 2 Cor. 5.19. "God was in Christ reconciling …': It is God Himself who intervened to act and work and reveal' (*CD* IV/1, 74). Returning to explore the significance of this verse in the next part-volume of the *Church Dogmatics*, Barth asks: 'What does it mean that "God was in Christ" (2 Cor. 5.19)?[59] It obviously means that all that God is, without either needing or being subject to any change or diminution or increase, is characterized by the fact that He is everything divine, not for Himself only, but also, in His Son, for the sake of man and for him' (*CD* IV/2, 86). Appealing to Col. 2.9 for further support, Barth emphasizes 'the totality of the divine' that is present in Christ: 'Is not each perfection of God itself the perfection of His whole essence, and therefore in any modification the sum and substance of all others? How can some of these perfections be separated off from others? Would it be the divine essence of the Father, Son and Holy Spirit if such separations were to take place in it?' (*CD* IV/2, 86).[60]

---

exercise, as long as I acknowledge it as such without any pretense of offering a complete Christology, and do not ossify my interpretation into a rejection of the other aspects of Christology which Barth 'juxtaposes' throughout the *Church Dogmatics* (Hunsinger, 'Karl Barth's Christology', 130–1).

[56] Hartmut Ruddies, 'Christologie und Versöhnungslehre bei Karl Barth', *Zeitschrift für dialektische Theologie* 18 (2002), 177.

[57] This is true in *CD* IV/1 which focuses on the doctrines of the atonement and justification. When Barth turns in *CD* IV/2–3 to other related topics, he juxtaposes this concern with others – particularly the humanity of Jesus Christ.

[58] Klappert, *Die Auferweckung*, 90.

[59] 'Jesus' sufferings were but the outward and visible sign of an inward event. Through the visible suffering and death of this man Jesus an invisible event took place … A man like us, yet at the same time different from us because in him God himself was present and at work' (Barth, *Deliverance to the Captives*, 79).

[60] To step back for a moment, it would may be helpful to sum up Barth's understanding of God's being in act by suggesting that Barth is in effect offering an extended theological interpretation of Col. 1.19 and 2.9: 'For in him all the fullness of God [τὸ πλήρωμα] was pleased to dwell' and 'in him the whole fullness of deity [τὸ πλήρωμα

Barth's Christology is equally concerned to affirm that in Jesus Christ we are confronted with the elect man: that 'this One exists, not only in His divine, but also in human being and essence, in our nature and kind' (*CD* IV/2, 50).[61] For our purposes, however, the vital point Barth makes is that:

> All that characterizes divine essence in distinction from human or any other – the height of freedom and the depth of love actual in God the Father, Son and Holy Ghost; each perfection of true Godhead, holiness or mercy or wisdom, omnipresence, or omnipotence or eternity – all this is unlimitedly and unreservedly proper to the One who as Son of God became also Son of Man. (*CD* IV/2, 73)[62]

Barth's Christology resolutely affirms the full being of God present and active in the person and work of Jesus Christ, drawing repeatedly on these resources to give a full account of the person and work of Christ. To be sure,

---

τῆς θεότητοσ] dwells bodily'. As N. T. Wright explains, 'there is no word for "God" in the original of verse 19, but the grammatical subject ("fullness") must be a circumlocution for "God in all his fullness" (see 2.9). It is appropriate that Christ should hold pre-eminence, because God in all his fullness was pleased to take up permanent residence (this is the best way of taking the Greek verb) in him' (N. T. Wright, *The Epistles of Paul to the Colossians and to Philemon: An Introduction and Commentary* (Grand Rapids, MI: Eerdmans, 1988), 75).

New Testament commentators offer warrant for seeing in this passage the force Barth senses. Lightfoot writes that 'an absolute and unique position is claimed for Him, because in Him resides "all the plerome", i.e. the full complement, the aggregate of the Divine attributes, virtues, energies. This is another way of expressing the fact that He is the Logos, for the Logos is the synthesis of all the various *dunameis*, in and by which God manifests Himself whether in the kingdom of nature or in the kingdom of grace' (J. B. Lightfoot, *Saint Paul's Epistles to the Colossians and to Philemon* (London: Macmillan, 1916), 262. Wright reinforces his statement from the note above by suggesting that 'The "knowledge of God's will" [1.9] is more than simply an insight into how God wants his people to behave: it is an understanding of God's whole saving purpose in Christ, and hence (as in v. 10b) a knowledge of God himself (Wright, *Colossians and to Philemon*, 57.

61 Again, and more extensively, Barth writes: 'All that characterizes human essence in distinction from divine or any other – its littleness and greatness in creation, its distinctive qualities, its capacity and limitations, its historicity and therefore temporality, its humanity as fellow-humanity, its responsibility before God and determination for Him, its susceptibility to temptation and suffering, its mortality, and more than this, its qualification by the aberration of man and all men, its consequent eternal jeopardy, its abandonment to nothingness, its character as "flesh" – all this is unlimitedly and unreservedly proper to the One who as Son of God became also Son of Man' (*CD* IV/2, 73).

62 The standard English translation is here revised to account for a translation error rendering '*Alles, was das göttliche Wesen ... ausmacht*' as 'all that characterizes human essence' (*CD* IV/2, 73; *KD*, 79).

it is only the Son who becomes incarnate (an act of humility which 'corresponds' [*entspricht*] to his particular mode of being), and not the Father and Spirit; but the incarnation itself is an event based in 'the intra-trinitarian life of God Himself', a 'work of the whole Holy Trinity'. Accordingly, it is not an act of the Son in which the Father and Spirit happen to be involved, but rather an incarnation of God himself through the differentiated act of God's triune being. The significant point is that in the incarnation of the Son, the full and uncompromised essence of God is living and active in Jesus Christ and his life, death and resurrection for us (*CD* IV/2, 43–4).

The doctrine of God and that of the atonement thus come together in Barth's theology, via the doctrine of election, such that neither can be understood apart from the other. The salvation of humankind in the person and work of Jesus Christ is precisely the centre of God's economic self-fulfilment according to his electing purposes. The atonement is thus the decisive basis from which to develop our doctrine of God. Simultaneously, and more to the point of our thesis, the doctrine of God is the key for properly understanding Christ's reconciling work – for the reconciliation is accomplished precisely by God bringing himself to bear upon our situation, that he might have fellowship with us.

An Actualistic Overwhelming of Reality?
The Question of Time

To wrap up this argument, we turn to a prevalent apprehension regarding Barth's theology (he himself felt its prick) which bears directly on our thesis, affording an excellent opportunity to sum up certain key points of Barth's position. The concern is that God, in bringing his being to bear upon our situation in Christ, might be unbearably intense and overwhelming.[63] Does Barth's notion of 'God with us' allow for an 'us with God'? 'What is left to us? … In what sense is the history of the acts of God at this centre and end our history? Are we not without history?' (*CD* IV/1, 14). Does not God's being overwhelm our lives such that all of history is swallowed up and determined in the life, death and resurrection of Jesus Christ? Or at another level, is God's act of election in eternity so decisive that everything subsequent, including our own experience, follows simply as a matter of course? Does 'time itself in its duration, and human life in time with its responsibilities, problems and possibilities, [come] to have the position of a kind of appendix, though one that [is] expressed with force' (*CD* II/1, 632)?[64]

---

[63] Cf. Maurer, '"Für uns" An unserer Stelle hingerichtet', 118.

[64] These related questions are perennial issues in Barth's theology. See, for example, Richard H. Roberts, ed. S. W. Sykes, 'Barth's Doctrine of Time: Its Nature and Implications', in *Karl Barth* (Ithaca, NY: Clarendon, 1979).

This concern regards the whole of Barth's theology and bears significantly on our understanding of Barth's doctrine of God's being in act. To narrow the scope of the issues involved, I will offer a brief response within the parameters of the question of time and eternity, an issue Barth raises within his treatment of God's being in act (*CD* II/1, 262–3) and is therefore particularly suitable for our inquiry.[65] In this way I hope to sketch a response to this concern which could be filled out in more detail.[66]

Early in his treatment of God's being in act, Barth writes that God's revelation 'is now a past fact of history ... it is also an event happening in the present, here and now ... but it is also an event that took place once for all and an accomplished fact. And it is also future – the event which lies completely and wholly in front of us, which has not yet happened, but which comes upon us' (*CD* II/1, 262). This and similar passages raise the question of whether Barth in fact has the resources within his understanding of God's eternity to account for a real history of God with us. Is our time simply overwhelmed by the presence and activity of eternity within it? How is it that God's revelation, centred as it is upon the work of Christ, can be simultaneously past, present and future? Does not each of these necessarily vie for pre-eminence at the exclusion of the others?

Barth's fundamental concern in his treatment of God's eternity is to explore the essence of the living God as the readiness of God for his time with us. That is, the living God has in himself that which is the constitutive basis for that which he does outwardly; namely, to be in time. God's eternity, therefore, has nothing to do with a negation of time according to Barth. 'Time ... is the formal principle of His free activity outwards. Eternity is the principle of His freedom inwards' (*CD* II/1, 609). God's eternity, his 'pure duration [*reine Dauer*]' (*CD* II/1, 608; *KD*, 685), 'is the principle of the divine constancy, of the unchangeableness and therefore the reliability of the divine being ... Because and as God has and is this duration, eternity, He can and will be true to Himself, and we can and may put our trust in him' (*CD* II/1, 609). God's pure duration is the principle of

---

[65] Although his critique of Barth is harsh and seems to rest largely upon a confusion of epistemological and ontological categories in Barth's thought (taking a denial of natural theology to imply in some way a denial of or incompatibility with 'mundane, empirical reality'), Richard Roberts' essay is helpful in that it shows just how pervasive the treatment and implications of the doctrine of time/eternity are within Barth's thought, as well as how related these are to the doctrine of God's being in act, thus calling for this particular section in the midst of my argument. Roberts, *A Theology On its Way*, 19–20, 37, 44, 56–8. George Hunsinger similarly notes Roberts' view as being 'severe', critiquing Roberts for failing 'almost entirely to take its Trinitarian structure into account (Hunsinger, *Disruptive Grace*, 197n14).

[66] Other facets of this question include the objective/subjective work of Christ, God's election of us that we might elect him in return, and the relationship between the divine and human freedom.

divine constancy because it provides the stage within the being of God for a genuine movement from beginning to middle to end within God's own life in which God himself can and does remain constant in all his 'difference, movement, will, decision, action, becoming old and becoming new [*Alt- und Neu-werdens*]' (*CD* II/1, 492; *KD*, 553).[67] This duration within the being of God then serves as the internal basis for his creation of creaturely time ('Time … is in a sense the special creation of the "eternal" God' [*CD* II/1, 609]), providing the external basis for God's constancy with us.

These statements offer a helpful context for understanding Barth's claim that 'eternity is God in the sense in which in Himself and in all things God is simultaneous [*einmal und zugleich*], i.e. beginning and middle as well as end, without separation, distance or contradiction [*ohne Trennung, Ferne und Widerspruch*]' (*CD* II/1, 608; *KD*, 685). The simultaneity of God does not trump his pure duration; God's simultaneity is not one in which his beginning and end collapse into the middle, in which there is no movement or change, for 'His constancy consists in the fact that He is always the same in every change' (*CD* II/1, 496). It is not as though God has simultaneously before him his own past, present and future, standing apart and gazing at it, or that these distinctions (between beginning, middle and end) do not really obtain in God who is and always has been all that he ever will be such that there is no movement within God. God's eternal life, his simultaneity, moves from a beginning, is a middle and heads toward an end. As the living God, 'there is in Him no opposition or competition or conflict, but peace between origin, movement and goal, between present, past and future … It is not the case, then, that in eternity all these distinctions do not exist' (*CD* II/1, 612).

The separation, distance and contradiction of time have nothing to do with God, but 'God has time because and as He has eternity' (*CD* II/1, 611).[68] The decisive point for our concern is that God shares this time with us on the basis of his own proper time: eternity. 'Only God is eternal … except that in the act of His love God exalts something else to share in His eternity, so that there is now and for this reason an eternal life of which even we may live in hope and an eternal fire which even we have to fear' (*CD* II/1, 609). God has time for us: 'He himself is time for us. For His revelation as Jesus Christ is really God Himself' (*CD* II/1, 612). Because God has his own proper time, he can and does give us time, a gift in which God shares himself and therefore his eternity.

---

[67] The standard English translation is here lightly revised, exchanging 'degeneration and rejuvenation' for 'becoming old and becoming new'. As Robert Jenson notes, this is one of the worst translated volumes of the *Church Dogmatics*. Robert W. Jenson, *Alpha and Omega: A Study in the Theology of Karl Barth* (New York: Nelson, 1963), 69n1.

[68] For clarification of Barth's potentially ambiguous use of the word 'time', see Hunsinger, *Disruptive Grace*, 189ff.

But this brings us back to our question: does God's sharing of his being with us, and in this particular case his exalting us to share in His eternity, overwhelm us and do away with our own proper reality?[69] This overwhelming can be perceived to occur at two different levels.[70] First, it can occur within eternity itself, such that the act of election is one that is so decisive that our own perceived reality is simply the playing-out of God's eternal decree, depriving our own experience of its meaning and significance. On this view, election, rather than the death and resurrection of Jesus Christ, could be said to be the Gospel. Barth's response to this concern would be to point out that with regards to time, God's eternity is the basis within God for his gift of time to us, and similarly, election is the basis within God of his gift of being and purpose to us: being God's fellows, as God's covenant partners who by God's election are given the freedom to elect him in return.[71] Election is an act within eternity which constitutes the beginning of all things outside of God, but it is an act which includes within itself a beginning, middle and end. Election thus sweeps us up into a truly meaningful history; a history in which God shares his own proper being with us through his presence with us as the triune God.

But addressing this concern also addresses the concern at the second level – that the invasion of our reality by God in the incarnation is so complete and decisive that there is no meaning or significance left to our own place within this history. Barth is emphatic that this is a genuine sharing, a genuine fellowship that God seeks with us, and therefore a fellowship and sharing to which we are called and to which we must respond (although one in which God clearly and necessarily retains the priority and initiative). God in his eternity gives us the gift of time, and then heals our time and exalts us to share in his eternity (CD II/1, 609). In entering our time he heals and restores our time for the sake of our fellowship with God. The decisive and objective invasion of God into our time is ordered towards the

---

[69] This touches on the question of divinization in Barth's theology. A majority of Barth scholars contend for a participation in Christ which does not entail divinization in the sense of our becoming God or gods. Cf. Bruce L. McCormack, 'Participation in God, Yes; Deification, No: Two Modern Protestant Responses to an Ancient Question', in *Orthodox and Modern: Studies in the Theology of Karl Barth* (Grand Rapids, MI: Baker Academic, 2008); Neder, *Participation in Christ*, 65–9; Nimmo, *Being in Action*, 176–9. To balance this critique, however, it is worth noting Colin Gunton's statement that 'the more and more I read this IV/1 the more and more I realize how Patristic it is [in the way that it defines salvation as a sharing or participation]' (Gunton, *The Barth Lectures*, 152).

[70] As a preliminary comment, we should be careful about the way in which we cling to 'our own proper reality', for it is precisely by God's grace that Jesus dealt with our sinful reality so as to do away with it for our benefit and salvation.

[71] 'The electing God creates for Himself as such man over against Himself. And this means that for his part man can and actually does elect God, thus attesting and activating himself as elected man' (CD II/2, 177). Cf. Barth, *The Humanity of God*, 79.

subjective realization and fulfilment of this reality in the form of union and fellowship with Christ.[72] This subjective element is no mere after-thought, but weaves its way through the whole of the *Church Dogmatics* and is a vital part of Barth's theology.[73]

Conclusion: The Fullness of God's Living Being in Jesus Christ

Barth's exposition of God's being in act is a theological exercise designed to prepare us for contemplating God's history with us by first dwelling on the more general fact that God is a living God. That is to say, God reveals himself by means of his act, by means of repeating his own proper (immanent) triune life in his (economic) saving fellowship with us. The event of God's activity and fellowship with us is not foreign or accidental to his own proper being, but is rather a repetition or overflowing of the life he enjoys within himself as Father, Son and Holy Spirit in the fullness of the divine perfections. The life that God shares with us, however, is not equally manifest in all of God's acts because God has elected that the history of his relationship with us (and therefore the fulfilment of the repetition of his being as self-determined by his election) have a centre: namely, Jesus Christ. The person and work of Jesus Christ, and particularly his death and resurrection, form the concentrated point at which God brings his own living essence to bear upon our sinful condition so as to restore us to fellowship with himself in fulfilment of his covenantal purposes.

Because God's triune being in the fullness of the divine perfections is concentrated precisely on the fulfilment of his election in the death and resurrection of Jesus Christ, we properly understand that decisive event only in light of the fullness of God's being or essence acting in that event. It is only as we think of the events of Good Friday, Holy Saturday and Easter Sunday as the being in act of the triune God in the living fullness of the divine perfections that we can grasp the full meaning of this event. Only through the doctrine of the Trinity can we understand Christ's passion, only by means of sustained integration of the doctrine of the divine perfections with that of reconciliation can we comprehend the meaning and significance of Christ's work on the cross. Apart from such doctrinal interconnections, without a robust affirmation of God's being in act precisely at

---

[72] Or as Adam Neder puts it, our *de jure* participation in Christ is ordered toward our *de facto* participation in him. Neder writes, 'Salvation is not first of all a question posed to humanity. It is a truth proclaimed to humanity. But this truth itself poses a question that demands an answer from humanity' (Neder, *Participation in Christ*, 46).

[73] This is the burden of Neder's recent book.

this crucial point, we deprive ourselves of the most vital resources at our disposal to truly appreciate the meaning and significance of Christ's death and resurrection: the event by which God decisively dealt with our sin and its consequences, reconciling all things to Himself. Apart from the *mysteria divinitatis* (divine mystery) there can be no proper investigation of the *beneficia Christi* (benefits of Christ) (*CD* II/1, 259): the key to the doctrine of the atonement is reading the events of Christ's passion in light of the doctrine of God.

APPENDIX TO CHAPTER 2

Excursus on Trinity and Election

Before proceeding with my argument, it will be helpful to engage with a thesis within Barth studies which is so far-reaching as to impinge upon nearly every aspect of this book, and in the immediate context concerns the order and the content of my exposition of Barth's notion of God's being in act. In the last decade Bruce McCormack has advanced a thesis which offers a 'critical correction' of Barth's theology, suggesting that after a certain point in Barth's development 'we see the triunity of God, logically, as a function of divine election'.[1] According to McCormack, the act of election is a self-constituting act in which God gives himself his triune being as the basis for his covenantal relationship with us in Jesus Christ.[2] That God's being is in his act thus means that act is so constitutive of being that it logically precedes it: act precedes and constitutes being. McCormack thus further specifies Barth's actualism as 'covenant ontology', since God's decision to enter into covenant with us is the logically prior ontological basis for the being which God gives to himself.[3] On this basis, McCormack suggests that we revise certain aspects of Barth's theology, particularly the doctrines of the Trinity and divine perfections, in light of Barth's mature thought in *CD* II/2.[4]

While the literature specific to this debate might still be said to be manageable in scope, the issues raised therein are so far-reaching as to defy quickly-won verdicts.[5] The various trajectories within the debate include:

---

[1] McCormack, *Orthodox and Modern*, 193.

[2] Hunsinger's alternative is to distinguish between self-constitution and self-determination, wherein God self-determines his necessarily pre-existent Triune being to 'also exist for the sake of the world'. Hunsinger, 'Election and the Trinity', 193. When Barth writes that: 'He is God as He takes part in the event which constitutes the divine being [*Er ist es, indem er an diesem Geschehen teilnimmt, das das göttliche Sein ausmacht*]' (*CD* IV/1, 129; *KD* 141), Hunsinger interprets such statements to refer to the specification of the pre-existent Triune being of God to be this God in this particular way.

[3] McCormack, *Orthodox and Modern*, 190.

[4] *Ibid.*, 192–6. McCormack engages more fully in this revisionary project in McCormack, 'The Actuality of God'.

[5] The bulk of McCormack's argument is now consolidated in: McCormack, *Orthodox and*

(1) Barth's theological development, particularly as it pertains to the doctrine of election, (2) the interpretation of the relevant passages spanning the Barthian corpus (extending far beyond the *Church Dogmatics*), (3) the context of Barth's thought as it relates both to Modern theology and Barth's contemporary interlocutors, and (4) general theological implications of the specifically Barthian thesis in question. In short, this debate demands a mastery of Barth's theology and its development and historical context, not to mention questions of a more general theological nature independent of Barth interpretation.

Given the scope of the argument, my present purpose is simply to state my position and offer a brief defence, without seeking to advance the argument beyond its present state. In my view, McCormack interprets Barth's claim that 'Jesus is the subject of election' in a manner divergent from Barth's own understanding. The interpretative question at hand can be clearly seen in the following claim made by Paul Nimmo: 'For Barth, the beginning of all the ways and works of God, *and therefore of the identity of God,* is the self-giving of God in Jesus Christ.'[6] The question is whether this second clause, pertaining to the identity of God, is in fact an accurate interpretation of Barth's thought: does the self-giving of God in Jesus Christ constitute the identity of God (with regards to the modes of God's being or his perfections), or does it simply specify his being and life in a new direction? Throughout his work Barth relies upon the being of God prior to the act of election which functions as its antecedent basis. In the face of repeated claims by the 'mature' Barth that God would be triune without us, combined with the lack of a textual basis for affirming McCormack's thesis that act is constitutive of being in the specific sense that act logically precedes being, I demur that Barth should have affirmed that God's election logically precedes his triunity, and revised his theology accordingly. With Kevin Hector, I affirm that 'trinity and election are both necessary to God,

---

Modern. His latest contributions are: Bruce L. McCormack, 'Election and the Trinity: Theses in Response to George Hunsinger,' *SJT* 63, no. 2 (2010); Bruce L. McCormack, 'God *Is* His Decision: The Jüngel–Gollwitzer "Debate" Revisited', in *Theology as Conversation: The Significance of Dialogue in Historical and Contemporary Theology*, eds Daniel L. Migliore, Bruce L. McCormack and Kimlyn J. Bender (Grand Rapids, MI: Eerdmans, 2009). A sampling of those who disagree with him includes: Kevin W. Hector, 'Election and the Trinity: How My Mind Has Changed', paper presented at the American Academy of Religion, Chicago, IL, 31 October 2008); Hunsinger, 'Election and the Trinity'; Paul D. Molnar, 'Can the Electing God be God Without Us? Some Implications of Bruce McCormack's Understanding of Barth's Doctrine of Election for the Doctrine of the Trinity', *Neue Zeitschrift für Systematische Theologie und Religionsphilosophie* 49, no. 2 (2007), 199–122; Webster, 'Trinity and Creation', 11.

[6] Nimmo, *Being in Action*, 8 (emphasis added). While Nimmo supports McCormack in this work, it is not clear to me that McCormack's specific understanding of Barth's actualism is in fact essential to Nimmo's own position.

though not in the same respect'; namely, while God's triunity is absolutely necessary to God, election is the event in which God made something to be freely necessary to himself, or what Hector labels *volitionally* necessary'.[7]

The central interpretative issue regards Barth's claim that Jesus is the subject of election. Concerning this matter, Barth writes:

> As the subject and object of this choice [election], Jesus Christ was at the beginning. He was not at the beginning of God, for God has indeed no beginning. But He was at the beginning of all things, at the beginning of God's dealings with the reality which is distinct from Himself. Jesus Christ was the choice or election of God in respect of this reality. (*CD* II/2, 102)[8]

> *Und als Subjekt und Gegenstand dieser Wahl war Jesus Christus am Anfang. Er war nicht am Anfang Gottes: Gott hat ja keinen Anfang. Er war aber am Anfang aller Dinge, am Anfang alles Handelns Gottes mit der von ihm verschiedenen Wirklichkeit. Jesus Christus war Gottes Wahl hinsichtlich dieser Wirklichkeit.* (*KD* II/2, 109)

The election of Jesus Christ is not the beginning of God's being and therefore his being as Father, Son and Holy Spirit, but the beginning of the triune God's interaction with all that is not God.[9] Election is thus an act of God in which God specifies how he will be who he is, which is to say: given that God was the triune God from all eternity, he chooses to be Himself with and for us in the person of Jesus Christ. The act of election is the act of God at the beginning of all things (*ad extra*) by a God who Himself has no beginning – and the nature of this act is first and foremost with regards to himself by willing to become Jesus Christ.

While some passages appear to support McCormack's interpretation, and his genetic-historical interpretation of Barth makes for a formidable argument, Barth repeats his fundamental standpoint throughout the *Church Dogmatics* and his other works (namely, that God's triune being preceded the event of election) with a consistency which in my opinion makes McCormack's interpretation untenable.[10] The role of such statements is to

---

[7] Hector, cf. 'Immutability, Necessity, and the Limits of Inference'.

[8] For a more in-depth analysis of this passage, see: Molnar, 'Can the Electing God be God Without Us', 206–8.

[9] In a similar vein, Jüngel writing that 'God's election of grace is the beginning of 'all the ways and works of God (*CD* II/2, 3),'' and continues: 'In speaking of a beginning of these ways and works, we mean a relation of God to that which he is not. For God himself 'has indeed no beginning' (*CD* II/2, 202).' Jüngel, *God's Being Is in Becoming*, 83.

[10] Some of those passages which I find to be most decisive include: 'This is what we can call a decree ...: God's free election of grace, in which even in His eternity before all

guarantee the freedom of God, specifying the nature of the ontological force with which the act of election affects the being of God, while simultaneously allowing us to affirm that God's act *ad extra* is in fact a genuine sharing and therefore an act of love, of grace.[11] On this basis I proceed along the lines of a more traditional interpretation of Barth's thought, although still drawing on McCormack's significant contributions to Barth scholarship in areas unrelated to his specific thesis (concerning the logical relationship between Trinity and election). I understand, however, that I have in no way offered a sufficient argument to rebut McCormack's position – my purpose is simply to state my rejection of McCormack's thesis with a brief explanation, so as to proceed with my own constructive project.

---

time and the foundation of the world, He is no longer alone by Himself, He does not rest content with Himself, He will not restrict Himself to the wealth of His perfections and His own inner life as Father, Son and Holy Spirit [*sich ... schon nicht mehr auf sein inneres Leben als Vater, Sohn und Heiliger Geist beschränken will*] ... In this free act ... the Son of the Father is no longer just the eternal Logos, but as such, as very God from all eternity He is also the very God and very man He will become in time' (*CD* IV/1, 66; *KD*, 70); 'The true humanity of Jesus Christ, as the humanity of the Son, was and is and will be the primary content of God's eternal election of grace, i.e., of the divine decision and action which are not preceded by any higher apart from the Trinitarian happening of the life of God [*der außer dem trinitarischen Geschehen des inneren Lebens Gottes keine höhere vorangeht*], but which all other divine decisions and actions follow, and to which they are subordinated' (*CD* IV/2, 31; *KD*, 33); 'The triune life of God ... is the basis of His whole will and action even *ad extra* [*In dem dreieinigen Leben Gottes ... ist ja als sein uns zugewendeter Lebensakt sein ganzes Wollen und Tun auch nach Außen ... begründet*], as the living act which He directs to us ... [and] of the relationships which He has determined and established with a reality which is distinct from Himself' (*CD* IV/2, 345; *KD*, 386); and 'In His life as Father, Son and Holy Spirit He would in truth be no lonesome, no egotistical God even without man, yes, even without the whole created universe' (Barth, *The Humanity of God*, 50).

11 Stratis, 'Speculating About Divinity', 9–11.

3

TRINITY AND ATONEMENT

My purpose in this book is to explore the theological framework provided by the doctrine of God for a full and proper understanding of Christ's atoning work. Within Barth's theology, the best dogmatic locus from which to begin this venture is that of the Trinity, for Barth was convinced from his first years in Göttingen that the history of God with us in his self-revealing and reconciling activity is characterized at every moment by the fact that it is this subject with us, the living God who is inalienably himself as Father, Son and Holy Spirit.[1] Our understanding of the reconciliation accomplished in Jesus Christ depends at every point and is ultimately unintelligible apart from the subject of this act: the triune God.[2] We must attend to Christ's passion as the triune God's response to human sin, willing this reconciliatory event and bringing it to fulfilment in Himself.

As we saw in the previous chapter, the action and working of God 'becomes and is significant and effective with a significance and effectiveness qualitatively different from any other action and working in virtue of the fact that it is God's action and working' (*CD* II/1, 259). To hone in on one aspect of this claim, the death and resurrection of Christ, derives absolute and unique significance from the fact that they are events in the life of the triune God as he brings his immanent life to bear upon our situation in the economy.[3] The benefits we receive from Christ are inseparable from the mystery of

---

[1] Karl Barth and Eduard Thurneysen, *Revolutionary Theology in the Making: Barth–Thurneysen Correspondence, 1914–1925*, trans. Geoffrey W. Bromiley (Richmond, VA: WJK, 1964), 185.

[2] Vanhoozer, *The Drama of Doctrine*, 43.

[3] As Sanders argues, 'the economic-immanent axis is indeed a central element of all Barth's theology', providing the resources for safeguarding both the freedom of God (and his 'immanent objective otherness from us') and the 'actual history of God with us'Fred Sanders, *The Image of the Immanent Trinity: Rahner's Rule and the Theological Interpretation of Scripture* (New York: Peter Lang, 2005), 154–5. The point of this 'axis' is to secure the power and completeness with which God has given himself to us, once the reality of 'God in himself' has been established as the basis from which this movement occurs. But the movement is vital, as I attempted to show

God's triune being. Because 'the Trinity itself is the authentic power-house of theology from which radiates the true energy of Christian revelation',[4] it is only by harnessing the energy within this doctrine that we position ourselves to bring the understanding of Christ's work to its full potential.

Thus, by way of the doctrine of the Trinity, we begin to develop the thesis that *Barth's understanding of God's triune being in act in the fullness of the divine perfections, brought to bear upon our sinful condition in fulfilment of his covenantal purposes through the person and work of Jesus Christ, provides the proper theological framework for developing the doctrine of the atonement.* This chapter will also introduce a key theme that subsequent chapters will greatly develop, indicating how Barth's view *contains within itself the basis and the impetus for a theological explanation of the unity and diversity of Christ's atoning work.*

The Problem

The difficulty, of course, is to honour the vitality of the relationship between the doctrines of the Trinity and atonement with more than lip-service.[5]

in the previous chapter. God is a living God, for whom there are events, decisions and movements, both in eternity and in creation.

[4] Roberts, *A Theology On its Way*, 81.
[5] Much of the literature on the relationship between the doctrines of the Trinity and atonement disappoints. Bruce Ware, in a chapter on the subject, focuses mostly on Christological issues rather than dealing explicitly with the atonement, circumventing the subject matter of the essay: Ware, 'Christ's Atonement'. Robert Sherman's work correlating the *munus triplex* and doctrine of the Trinity offers good biblical reflection on the former topic, but surprisingly little theological connection to the doctrine of the Trinity in support of its thesis: Sherman, *King, Priest and Prophet*. Colin Gunton's chapter titled 'The Atonement and the Triune God' offers little more than the affirmation that 'the purpose of the Father achieved by the ... incarnate Son has its basis in the creation by which the world took shape, and will find its completion in the work of the Spirit who brings the Son's work to perfection' (Gunton, *The Actuality of Atonement*, 154; cf. 61). Although Vincent Brümmer's section on 'Atonement and the Trinity' concludes by noting that 'God's activity in reconciling us with himself is Trinitarian in the sense that it involves the creativity of the Father, the revelation of the Son and the illumination and inspiration of the Spirit', the bulk of the section concerns anthropological questions revolving around forms of freedom and religious experience. Brümmer, *Atonement, Christology and the Trinity*, 93–7. Graham McFarlane's essay states that it is the 'doctrine of creation that provides the backdrop against which our thinking of the cross and the Trinity must be developed' but relegates his consideration of the Trinity to a single paragraph at the end of the argument (McFarlane, 'Atonement, Creation and Trinity', 205. Unfortunately the word 'triune' often seems to function as an appellative for the Christian God rather than indicating a commitment to explore the role of God's triune being in Christ's reconciling work.
To be sure, a number of theologians argue against various prevalent abuses of

As Karl Rahner lamented decades ago, 'one has the feeling that, for the catechism of head and heart (as contrasted with the printed catechism), the Christian's idea of the incarnation', and of the atonement, we might add, 'would not have to change at all if there were no Trinity'.[6] The situation has improved since Rahner wrote these words, but not as dramatically as one might hope. Like Augustine's vision in book VII of the *Confessions*, our glimpse of this vista remains unattainable in the distance.

Karl Barth offers great promise in regard to this lacuna. As Fred Sanders writes, 'it would be difficult to overestimate [Barth's] impact on the revival of Trinitarian theology in the twentieth century', largely due to the fact that in his thought 'trinitarianism stops being a rarified riddle and becomes instead the hermeneutical key for opening up questions in all theological loci'.[7] Berthold Klappert notes that for Barth the function of the doctrine of the Trinity was to uncover the inner depths of the doctrine of reconciliation.[8] This was Barth's intent even early in his theological career, as evidenced in a letter to Eduard Thurneysen: 'A Trinity of *being*, not just an economic Trinity! At all costs the doctrine of the Trinity! If I could get the right key in my hand there, then everything would come out right'[9] – particularly, we might add, everything would come out right in the doctrine of the atonement.[10]

---

the Trinity within the doctrine of the atonement, contending against 'polarizing the persons of the Trinity' and playing off 'one person of the Trinity over against the other' (McKnight, *A Community Called Atonement*, 42). While such defensive measures are sorely needed, surely there is more to the relationship between these doctrines than a mere defensive measure against straw-man formulations of penal substitution.

6 Karl Rahner, *The Trinity*, trans. Joseph Donceel (New York: Herder and Herder, 1970), 11.

7 Sanders, *The Image of the Immanent Trinity*, 50–52. George Hunsinger more broadly states that 'No one ever seems to have had a stronger sense that in Christian theology every theme is connected to every other theme' (Hunsinger, *How to Read*, 28).

8 Klappert, *Die Auferweckung*, 188.

9 Barth and Thurneysen, *Revolutionary Theology*, 176.

10 Barth is not the only candidate for such a project. Jürgen Moltmann, for instance, has written extensively on the relationship of the Trinity and the atonement. Cf. Jürgen Moltmann, *The Crucified God: The Cross of Christ as the Foundation and Criticism of Christian Theology* (Minneapolis: Fortress, 1993). Hans Urs von Balthasar has also contributed greatly to this topic, especially with his work on Holy Saturday. Hans Urs von Balthasar, *Mysterium Paschale: The Mystery of Easter*, trans. Aidan Nichols (San Francisco, CA: Ignatius Press, 1990). T. F. Torrance also offers in his work an excellent and sustained reflection along the lines pursued here. Thomas F. Torrance, *Atonement: The Person and Work of Christ*, ed. Robert Walker (Downers Grove, IL: InterVarsity Press, 2009); Thomas F. Torrance, *The Mediation of Christ* (Colorado Springs, CO: Helmers & Howard, 1992). Hunsinger notes that the latter two theologians 'seem to bring out more clearly than does Barth the Trinitarian context of the cross that he surely presupposed but left more implicit' (Hunsinger, *Disruptive Grace*, 34–5). I choose Barth over these other theologians largely because he was a major

One might expect that Barth's interpreters would offer substantial analysis of the bearing of the doctrine of the Trinity upon the atonement. Colin Gunton suggests as much in an essay on Barth's soteriology, but ironically the promised treatment fails to materialize apart from his critique of Barth's use of the Trinity![11] Georg Pfleiderer's essay on Colin Gunton and Karl Barth is more promising, but falls short of an adequate treatment, in that the possibilities for correlating the doctrine of the Trinity with the *munus triplex* (Christ's threefold office of prophet, priest and king) at best only scratch the surface of this topic.[12] Bruce McCormack's essay on the ontological presuppositions of the atonement is strong in regards to Christology and the doctrine of the Trinity, but when it comes to application to the atonement, rests content with offering a rebuttal of 'divine violence' critiques of the atonement by means of the doctrine of the Trinity.[13]

In response to this deficiency, I will explore the Trinitarian resources for the doctrine of the atonement within Barth's theology. While to a limited extent I will exposit and defend Barth's doctrine of the Trinity *per se*, my primary purpose is to consider the resources therein for a robust construal of the doctrine of the atonement. I thus hope to offer a partial vindication of Sanders' claim (cited earlier) that Barth's doctrine of the Trinity energizes his account of all other theological loci by outlining some of the most prominent features of Barth's Trinitarian theology of the atonement.[14] Specifically, I will note the implications for the doctrine of the atonement found in Barth's account of the doctrine of the Trinity in *CD* I/1 §§8–9, namely: (1) The Root of the Trinity, (2) Unity in Trinity, (3) Trinity in Unity,

---

inspiration for their development in these areas, and he offers, I think, a more fertile soil for inquiry even if the ground is less broken and tilled than in some of these other theologians.

Concerning Moltmann I must add that I have significant reservations, particularly for his denial of monotheism and the ensuing difficulties in his revised appropriation of Patripassianism. Cf. Daniel Castelo, *The Apathetic God: Exploring the Contemporary Relevance of Divine Impassibility* (Colorado Springs, CO: Paternoster, 2009).

[11] Colin E. Gunton, 'Salvation,' in *The Cambridge Companion to Karl Barth*, ed. J. B. Webster (New York: Cambridge University Press, 2000), 143, 52–3.

[12] Pfleiderer, 'The Atonement'.

[13] McCormack, 'Ontological Presuppositions'. The context of this essay is such that this 'rebuttal' is much needed. My point is simply to express some disappointment concerning the absence of a more constructive point in addition to the defensive maneuver, surely explained by the space constraints of the edited volume. Cf. Thomas' dissatisfaction with McCormack's efforts on this front: Günter Thomas, "Der für uns 'gerichtete Richter". Kritische Erwägungen zu Karl Barths Versöhnungslehre', *Zeitschrift für dialektiscshe Theologie* 18, no. 2 (2002), 213–14.

[14] 'Trinitarian theology is not a restatement, but a revision of systematic theology in view of the Trinity' (Paul Louis Metzger, *Trinitarian Soundings in Systematic Theology* (New York: T & T Clark, 2005), 7).

and (4) the Triunity of God.[15] In each of these sections, I will summarize key aspects of Barth's doctrine of the Trinity analyzing the bearing thereof on the doctrine of the atonement by exploring and developing the implicit and explicit connections Barth makes.[16]

The Root of the Trinity

Barth introduces the doctrine of the Trinity (CD I/1, §8) by considering its root – its basis or foundation within the Christian faith. Recognizing that Scripture's witness to the activity of the Father, Son and Holy Spirit 'prefigures' the problems that manifested later in the doctrine of the Trinity (CD I/1, 314) without establishing its essential elements, Barth develops the doctrine of the Trinity out of the nature of specifically Christian revelation (as witnessed in Holy Scripture). He insists that in the event of revelation 'God Himself in unimpaired unity yet also in unimpaired distinction is Revealer, Revelation, and Revealedness' (CD I/1, 295), and more specifically still: 'The doctrine of the Trinity is simply a development of the knowledge that Jesus is the Christ or the Lord' (CD I/1, 334). Because the revelation is the self-revelation of God, Barth unconditionally denies the validity of any other norm or basis for the Church's knowledge of God and its dogmatic task. Consequently he denies the possibility of *vestigia trinitatis*: aspects or vestiges of the created order that bear an inherent similarity to the triunity of God, thereby serving as possible means for understanding and developing the doctrine of the Trinity (CD I/1, 333–47). I touch on these significant themes only briefly, for my intent is not to offer a full exposition of Barth's doctrine of the Trinity, and the 'root of the doctrine of the Trinity' is on the periphery of the scope of my project. However, Barth's point grants a strategic entry into our study, establishing the sphere and limitations of the present inquiry.

Essentially, Barth's Trinitarian account of revelation demands that we reject natural theology as a task of the church and more specifically as a means for developing or critiquing the doctrine of the atonement. In other words, according to Barth only the Scriptural witness to God's reconciling work provides the Church with the norm by which it is to pursue its

---

[15] My purpose is to offer an introductory survey of the Trinitarian resources for the doctrine of the atonement in Barth's thought. I will develop some elements in greater detail than others, while bypassing some entirely. I will also not address a second layer to this whole discussion, which has to do with the 'Trinitarian pattern' in Barth. On the nature of this pattern, see Hunsinger, *How to Read*, 85–6, 107–8.

[16] A work focusing on Barth's doctrine of the Trinity would need to defend Barth from various critiques. My purpose, however, is to explore Barth's Trinitarian theology for its resources in regards to the doctrine of reconciliation. I acknowledge that my treatment stands or falls with Barth's account.

theological vocation; any other considerations provide only a ministerial service to the Church (at best) and are subject to the definitive authority of the Scriptural witness.

For this reason, our experiences of reconciliation drawn from the world around us (e.g. political oppression and salvation, or the (dis)harmony between punishment and restoration in the judicial system) are not normative for the proclamation of the Church and its dogmatic task. In a later volume Barth draws this connection, writing that this rejection is necessary 'simply and solely because God Himself has revealed Himself as the Reconciler. And in doing so He has radically compromised all other reconciliations … He has shown Himself to be the end and the beginning of real reconciliations' (*CD* II/1, 78). Because God is the triune God known in Jesus Christ – and above all in his suffering on the cross[17] – we can know the meaning of reconciliation only in the person and work of Jesus Christ as witnessed by Scripture. On the flip side, however, knowing the true meaning of reconciliation puts us in a position to recognize and critique unchristian understandings of the atonement. Barth writes, for instance:

> This enterprise [of Hitler's Germany] was met by toleration and yet more toleration, in a desire to atone (in a very unchristian way!) for past mistakes. It was perhaps through blindness to the true nature and power of this enterprise, perhaps in the weakness which came from a bad conscience about the past, perhaps because they realized they had neglected their duty to arm themselves for war in order to save peace, that the victors of 1918 negotiated with Hitler.[18]

The conclusions drawn from our experiences of the various realms of the created order do, however, have a significant (though ultimately secondary) role to play. Barth famously writes that 'God may speak to us through Russian communism or a flute concerto, a blossoming shrub or a dead dog. We shall do well to listen to Him if He really does so' (*CD* I/1, 60). The Church should be 'grateful to receive [the one Word] also from without, in very different human words, in a secular parable, even though it is grounded in and ruled by the biblical, prophetic-apostolic witness to this one Word … Which in material agreement with it, illumine, accentuate or explain the biblical witness in a particular time and situation' (*CD* IV/3.1, 115).[19] While these parables are not a source of revelation, we must nonetheless respect them within their proper limits, and be grateful when they facilitate our task of understanding the biblical witness.

---

[17] Klappert, *Die Auferweckung*, 157, 80–1.

[18] Karl Barth, *This Christian Cause* (New York: Macmillan, 1941), 29–30.

[19] For an exposition of Barth's understanding of 'parables of the kingdom', cf. Hunsinger, *How to Read*, 234–80.

Accordingly, critiques or proposals concerning the doctrine of the atonement by Girardians, feminists and liberation-theologians serve the Church if and as they remind it of, or awaken it to the truth of Scripture through the various instances of reconciliation they champion from their respective spheres of experience. But the Church must listen, according to Barth! One could go so far as to say, for instance, that one simply cannot be a diligent student of the atonement today without giving sustained attention to Girardian approaches to the atonement – one of the most innovative theories in today's soteriological market – for we must never discount the possibility that this provocative theory might be a secular parable of the truth, reminding us of some aspect of Christ's reconciling work long forgotten or insufficiently appreciated.[20] Similarly, the argument offered below, chiefly consisting of an interpretation of Barth's theology, serves the Church best by reminding it of its proper task, for Barth's own thoughts are no more of a norm for the Church than those of René Girard (Barth, after all, had little interest in 'Barthians'). As I do not seek to defend the Scriptural basis of Barth's theology, my thesis is, quite simply, a reminder to the Church that will hopefully awaken it more fully to its exegetical task.

With this delimiting point in place, we have only begun to explore the vital role of the doctrine of the Trinity within that of the atonement, specifying the scope of the present work. In the following sections we begin to explore far more constructive aspects of this relationship, beginning with the role of the oneness of God.

Unity in Trinity

Barth begins his conceptual clarification of the subject of revelation, the triune God, with the 'final and decisive confirmation of the insight that God is One' (*CD* I/1, 348).[21] Drawing on the relationship between the doctrines of revelation and the Trinity, Barth affirms that the 'revealed name of Yahweh-Kyrios ... is the name of a single being, of the one and only Willer and Doer whom the Bible calls God' (*CD* I/1, 348). The persons in God are not three gods with three names, but One God with One name.

> According to Barth, the Christian faith depends on the belief that God is one. Everything depends on the fact that the content of the three

---

[20] This is true of Girard's earlier literary work. Later in his career Girard writes from a more explicitly Christian standpoint, such that his work should be heeded not as a 'secular parable' but as an exegesis of Scripture informed by the unique perspective of his earlier work.

[21] Richard Roberts questions whether it might be an over-emphasis. Roberts, *A Theology On its Way*, 87.

articles [of the Apostles' Creed] cannot be separated from each other, that in all that is said in these three articles ... it is not a matter of three divine departments, with a 'Director' for each. What is involved is the *one* work of the *One* God ... (*DO*, 42)

Scripture tells us of the Father in heaven, the incarnate Son, the work of the Spirit, but in such a way that this is the history of the one God with us. The only way to account for this diversity in Scripture (and the only way to overcome the Kantian denial of the possibility of revelation), according to Barth, is to take with full seriousness the claim that Jesus Christ is Lord, that he is Yahweh: not *a* lord, but *the Lord*. He is not another God, but the one God – there is one God throughout Scripture's witness. God reveals himself in such a way that as Revealer, Revelation and Revealedness, as Father, Son and Holy Spirit, God is one God. Apart from this foundation of the oneness of God, Barth worries that the Church's understanding of the Father, Son and Holy Spirit will collapse into a tri-theistic and conflict ridden account of God and his perfections – and consequently a collapse of the reconciliation of God with the world.[22]

Barth anchors his view of God's oneness by locating the 'personality' of God in his essence and therefore and on that basis in the three 'persons' (*CD* I/1, 350).[23] He equates the personal lordship of God with 'what the vocabulary of the early Church calls the essence of God ... the divine οὐσια, *essentia*, *natura* or *substantia*' (*CD* I/1, 349). The essence of God, or that by which God is what he is, is the personal lordship of God, which in God's free self-revelation concretely 'speaks as an I and addresses by a Thou' (*CD* I/1, 307). In Barth's thought, therefore, the essence of God, that which traditionally establishes the unity or the oneness of God, is fully personal. As a result, God is one personal being, who has one will and is one active agent – as robust a monotheism as one could ask for. Barth's is a decidedly Trinitarian monotheism, however, as 'God is the one God in three-fold repetition' (*CD* I/1, 350). This repetition is grounded in God's being (that is to say, it has no basis outside of God), such that he is the one God only in this repetition and moreover is the one God in each repetition. Thus the

---

[22] Klappert, *Die Auferweckung*, 176. Barth affirms that there is no conflict in God (between the Father and Son), meanwhile noting that the threeness of God, combined with the incarnation of the Son, provides the basis for atonement being a matter of Jesus 'earning' our grace, without resulting in competition within the Godhead. Karl Barth, *Unterricht in der christlichen Religion*, ed. Heinrich Stoevesandt (Zürich: Theologischer Verlag, 1925–26), 92.

[23] According to Gunton, 'Barth's view is that the concept of "person" is irredeemable' (Gunton, *The Barth Lectures*), 87. Against this, aside from the passages cited above, note the following claim: 'The *Lord, your* God is a God with a name, a face, a personality' (Barth, *Deliverance to the Captives*, 111).

one God who addresses us in a three-fold repetition does so personally in each case because God's essence is itself personal.

A fuller development of the theme of repetition awaits us in the next section, where Barth provides his account of the triune 'modes of being'.[24] For the time being, this brief account of God's self-repetition functions largely as a place-holder, while Barth focuses his attention on the oneness of God. His basic thrust is to locate the personality of God, the seat of God's willing and doing, in the very essence of God, and therefore and on that basis in the three 'persons' (or, to anticipate the next section, the three modes of being). The word 'person', Barth suggests, 'as used in the Church doctrine of the Trinity [one God in three persons] bears no direct relation to personality' (CD I/1, 351). But, while it is a relatively poor option for the necessary common term in the doctrine of the Trinity, it is in fact a rich and vital option for the essence of God. 'This one God is to be understood not just as impersonal lordship ... but as person, i.e. as an I existing in and for itself with its own thought and will. This is how He meets us in His revelation' (CD I/1, 358–9). Barth is emphatic that we speak not of 'three divine I's, but thrice of the one divine I' (CD I/1, 351), thereby establishing a Christian monotheism (CD I/1, 354) with a finality and decisiveness which leaves its mark on all ensuing developments. In God there is a single essence, and this essence, according to Barth, is fully personal.

Turning from exposition to the development of our thesis, God's unity plays an essential role in the doctrine of reconciliation via the gravitational force it exerts on what otherwise have a tendency to become disparate and unrelated themes – namely the unity we see in the various divine perfections prominent in treatments of the doctrine of reconciliation (the subject of the next chapter), and in the Trinitarian relations between Father, Son and Holy Spirit in the life of Jesus Christ.[25] We turn now to consider how the unity

---

[24] We cannot help mentioning God's threeness while exploring his oneness, however. Just as the one God never exists in any other way than as Father, Son and Holy Spirit, a theological consideration of God's oneness must not abstract from his threeness.

My sense is that Ovey over-emphasizes Barth's use of the concept 'repetition', which really only serves as a place holder until he develops his account of God's 'modes of being', although it is nevertheless the case that his interaction between Barth and patristic sources is quite helpful and a significant step in the right direction. Cf. Michael J. Ovey, 'A Private Love? Karl Barth and the Triune God', in Engaging with Barth: Contemporary Evangelical Critiques, eds David Gibson and Daniel Strange (Nottingham: InterVarsity Press, 2008), 227.

[25] A second implication concerning God's act which we will not consider at length is how God's oneness influences Barth's understanding of the history of Jesus Christ, where the death and resurrection 'are not two acts of God, but one. The two have to be considered not merely in their relationship but in their unity.' The reason for this, Barth writes, is that 'it is the one God who is at work on the basis of His one election and decision by and to the one Jesus Christ with the one goal of the reconciliation of the world with Himself, the conversion of men to Him' (CD IV/1, 342). God's

of the triune God not only safeguards[26] – for Barth notes, 'the *sense* and *sound* of our word must be fundamentally *positive*'[27] – but constitutes the antecedent basis in God for the reconciliation accomplished in Jesus Christ.

By affirming the oneness of the triune God, by asserting that God is one 'Willer and Doer' (*CD* I/1, 348), Barth cuts off at the root any break in unity, any division or antithesis between the Father, Jesus Christ and the

---

oneness compels Barth to unite the death of Christ and his resurrection, resulting in a highly developed soteriological account of the resurrection. See R. Dale Dawson, *The Resurrection in Karl Barth* (Burlington, VT: Ashgate, 2007); Thomas F. Torrance, *Space, Time, and Resurrection* (Grand Rapids, MI: Eerdmans, 1976). An account of reconciliation lacking a robust account of the soteriological significance of the resurrection is not only incomplete, for Barth: it denies the unity of God by denying the unity of his acts. Far too many works on the atonement omit a treatment of the resurrection, the most prominent being Anselm's *Cur Deus Homo*, which mentions the doctrine only tangentially.

[26] Unfortunately, though it is somewhat understandable given contemporary critiques of the atonement, many accounts of the doctrine of the Trinity in relationship to the atonement stop precisely at this point. Even more unfortunate is the frequency with which critiques of substitutionary atonement offer little more than caricatures of that doctrine. One of the most prevalent criticisms of the doctrine of the atonement today focuses on the unity or oneness of God, particularly on the relationship of the Father and the crucified Jesus Christ. This line of reasoning suggests that any substitutionary account of the doctrine of reconciliation, in which something happens to Jesus Christ in order that it might not happen to those whom he thereby reconciles to the Father, posits an intolerable distance or conflict between the Son and the Father. Often the criticism runs that the Son is of a different will than the Father, in his mercy taking upon himself the wrath of the Father so as to save us, such that the relationship in question ultimately serves as a paradigm for abusive human relationships. This reasoning suggests that substitutionary views of the atonement necessarily presuppose an intolerable (and horrific) break in the oneness of the Father and the Son. Nowhere is this critique more powerfully expressed than in Rita Nakashima Brock and Rebecca Ann Parker, *Proverbs of Ashes: Violence, Redemptive Suffering, and the Search for What Saves Us* (Boston, MA: Beacon Press, 2001). Barth himself is not immune from such critique. Cf. L. A. R. Bakker, 'Jesus als Stellvertreter für unsere Sünden und sein Verhältnis zu Israel bei Karl Barth', *Zeitschrift für dialektische Theoloigie* 2 (1986), 39–59.

Please note that in my critique I in no way intend to disparage the intense pain and anguish often motivating contemporary critiques of the atonement from feminist perspectives. My comment is directed against the doctrine of the Trinity presupposed by the theological critique, and not at all toward the abuse and suffering underlying and motivating that critique. As Eberhard Jüngel notes of 'the frightening possibilities of misuse to which the word "God" is submitted', 'forgetting about God does not help to prevent such God-pollution [misuse of the word "God"]; rather, the only thing that helps here is proper, responsible talk of God' (Eberhard Jüngel, 'What Does it Mean to Say, "God is Love"?', in *Christ in Our Place: The Humanity of God in Christ for the Reconciliation of the World*, eds Trevor A. Hart and Daniel P. Thimell (Allison Park, PA: Pickwick, 1989), 300–1.

[27] Barth, *The Humanity of God*, 59.

Holy Spirit, such that the life of Jesus Christ is an event in the life of the one God, deriving therein its power and efficacy. Neither in the willing of substitutionary reconciliation nor in its accomplishment do we deal with three gods, three wills or three acts which could possibly suggest a break, conflict or division within the triune God.[28] Because God is one in essence, and therefore one in both will and act, according to Barth there is and can be no division within God in the work of reconciliation. The one God, Father, Son and Holy Spirit, reconciles us to himself in such a way that every aspect of his act and will manifests the oneness proper to his being as God.[29] But in establishing this unity, that God is one 'Willer and Doer', Barth establishes how the events in the life of Jesus Christ can be both reconciliatory and revelatory – reconciliatory because the event derives its efficacy from the whole being of the one God acting for us; revelatory because the efficacy is the result of the act in which the being of God is fully present to be known.

Because God is one, because he is 'a single being … one and only Willer and Doer' (CD I/1, 348), the person and work of Jesus Christ confronts us with the one God in the fullness of his being, such that Jesus Christ is the final and complete revelation and reconciliation of God.[30] The work of Jesus is not the work of a god, or a part of God, but of the one God in his fullness, such that there is no possibility of the work of a second or third God or another part of God that would undermine or qualify this work by reacting to or superseding it. In the incarnate, crucified, abandoned and exalted Son we do not know a God different from the Father whom he reveals, and in the work of the Spirit in the Church this revelation is not altered or augmented but verified and applied, for 'in this event God allows the world and humanity to take part in the history of the inner life of His Godhead, in the movement in which from and to all eternity He is Father, Son and Holy Spirit, and therefore the one true God' (CD IV/1, 215). In the

---

[28] As McCormack notes, Barth's theology contains no resources whatsoever for understanding the relationship between the Father and the Son in the act of reconciliation as an abusive relationship. The closest thing that we could come to along these lines, he concedes with tongue-in-cheek, is a form of masochism in God. McCormack, 'Ontological Presuppositions', 364.

[29] Even the cry of dereliction (Mt. 27.46; Mk 15.34), a significant locus for this discussion, is not the cry of a person distinct from the Father suffering the wrath of the latter against his will, but rather a complex event in the life of the one God, wherein God abandons himself. In fact, not only does the cry of dereliction *not* posit an ontological rift between the Father and the Son, it is a key event in God's self-revelation. In the next section, we will explore in more depth some of the tensions that the present section is building which we shed some light on the cry of dereliction and other similar passages which might seem to indicate precisely the kind of division within the triune being of God I am here denying.

[30] 'If God is not truly and altogether in Christ, what sense can there be in talking about the reconciliation of the world with God in Him?' (CD IV/1, 183).

event of Jesus Christ, in his life and death for us, we know the one God, and are brought by him to share in the inner life of his Godhead.

This is true because the incarnation is an event in the life of the one God and therefore a 'work of the whole Holy Trinity' (*CD* IV/2, 44). It is not a distinct act of the Son in which the Father and Spirit participate or to which they react in some way. Rather, the life of Jesus Christ is the incarnation, death and resurrection of 'the one personal God' through the differentiated act of God's triune being (*CD* IV/2, 44). This is particularly evident in Barth's doctrine of election, wherein 'Jesus Christ was the choice or election of [the triune] God in respect of [the reality which is distinct from Himself]' (*CD* II/2, 102). Jesus, that is, was the choice of the Father, Son and Holy Spirit with respect to us, his creatures:

> In the beginning it was the choice of the Father Himself to establish this covenant with man by giving up His Son for him ... In the beginning it was the choice of the Son to be obedient to grace, and therefore to offer Himself and become man in order that this covenant might be made a reality. In the beginning it was the resolve of the Holy Spirit that the unity of God, the Father and Son should not be disturbed or rent by this covenant with man. (*CD* II/2, 101)

Why is the death and resurrection of Jesus the complete self-revelation of God? Do not we also need the revelation of the Father and the Spirit – and might not these revelations conflict? Barth's answer is that the death and resurrection of Jesus Christ is an event in the life of the triune God – an event willed and accomplished by the one God, Father, Son and Holy Spirit. We do not look elsewhere for the revelation of the Father and the Spirit because Jesus Christ is the way the triune God chose from eternity to fulfil his covenant and reveal himself as Father, Son and Holy Spirit. The life of Jesus, in other words, is a Trinitarian and not simply Christological event, such that Barth can affirm that the death of Jesus Christ was a matter of the 'suffering and dying of God Himself in His Son' (*CD* IV/1, 250). While it is true that this event happens 'in His Son' (as we will see in the next section), it is no less the case for Barth that this is the 'suffering and dying' of the one God according to the diverse modes of his being.[31]

Basically, then, the unity or oneness of God allows for the events in the life

---

[31] 'Of each divine work we need to say: (a) that it is *absolutely* the work of the undivided godhead; (b) that each person of the godhead performs that work in a *distinct* way, following the manner and order of that person's hypostatic existence; and (c) that particular works may be assigned *eminently* to one person, without rescinding absolute attribution to the undivided Trinity and without denying that the other two persons also participate in that work in the distinct modes proper to them' (John Webster, 'Trinity and Creation', *Intrnational Journal of Systemataic Theology* 12, no. 1 (2010), 16).

and death of the incarnate Son of God to be events in the life of the one God himself and therefore efficacious towards our salvation. These events derive their power from the being of God, without creating a division within the oneness or unity of God such as would render reconciliation impossible. Because the passion of Jesus Christ is the passion of the one God, the one Willer and Doer, it is absolutely effective, for 'the mystery of this passion … is to be found in the person and mission of the One who suffered … It is the eternal God Himself who has given Himself in His Son' (CD IV/1, 246), doing so 'without any alteration or diminution of His divine nature' (CD IV/1, 184), putting 'into effect the freedom of His divine love' and therefore his wisdom, righteousness, mercy and holiness (CD IV/1, 187–8).

The work of the incarnate Son reconciles us to God because Jesus Christ is himself God and not another or different god from the Father with whom we are reconciled. Rather, it guarantees our reconciliation with the Father with whom he is one (CD IV/1, 8). Because God is one we need not question the efficacy of the work of Christ with regard to the Father, for this work has behind and within it the full being and act of God from which to draw to accomplish its purposes (CD IV/1, 12–13, 553). Because God is one the life and death of Jesus Christ can be genuinely revelatory of the being of God,[32] for it is not the work of a god or part of God, but of the one God in his (triune) fullness: in Jesus Christ we know God himself. Because God is one the divine perfections are fully present and active in the incarnate Son, without breaking them apart among the Father, Son and Holy Spirit. The compassion or mercy of the Son does not counter and overcome the wrath and righteousness of the Father; rather, the love shown us in the work of Christ is the love of the Father for us. Likewise, the suffering of the incarnate Son is not his alone, but shared by the Father (and Spirit) as the suffering of the one God (CD IV/1, 245).

God's oneness profoundly shapes Barth's understanding of God's work of reconciliation. The being of God and therefore God's election and actions *ad extra* are properly understood, Barth holds, only when we begin from the standpoint that God is one, and that the work of Jesus Christ is the

---

[32] We saw in the previous chapter that, according to Barth, God's work of self-revelation and reconciliation are identical, for the two are the sides of a single coin: the event of God sharing his active and therefore effective being with us. 'The work of the Son or Word', Barth writes, 'is the presence and declaration of God which … we can only describe as revelation. The term reconciliation is another word for the same thing' (CD I/1, 409). This being the case, however, we can adapt Barth's statement concerning revelation to make the following claim: 'all antitrinitarianism is forced into the dilemma of denying either the reconciliation of God or the unity of God. To the degree that it maintains the unity of God it has to call [reconciliation] in question as the act of the real presence of the real God … To the degree that it is ready to maintain [reconciliation] but without acknowledging the substantial equality of the Son and the Spirit with the Father in heaven, the unity of God is called in question' (CD I/1, 352).

work of this one God, deriving from thence its meaning, significance and power. Only God's oneness secures the meaning and efficacy of Jesus' work of reconciliation through his death and resurrection by bringing it within the sphere of God's being and act, and only God's oneness establishes the basis for knowing God in Jesus Christ so as to fully appreciate who God is and what he has done for us. Any other standpoint quickly collapses into a denial of God's unity (polytheism) and the reconciliation he accomplishes in Jesus Christ. God's oneness, however, never exists in abstraction from, but always and exclusively in his threeness as Father, Son and Holy Spirit. Accordingly, we turn to consider more fully the role of God's threeness within the doctrine of the atonement.

Trinity in Unity

God's triunity does not allow for exposition of unity apart from trinity and vice versa. In the previous section Barth drew on the concept of God's self-repetition (or differentiation) as he emphasized God's unity. In the next section he offers the necessary elaboration of this concept in terms of God's *Seinsweisen*: modes (or ways) of being (*CD* I/1, 355).[33] In a detailed

---

[33] As noted by the editors in the preface to *CD* I/1, the expression *Seinsweise*, or 'mode of being' has no relationship to modalism, or *modalismus* in German (cf. *KD* IV/1, 215). Barth's intention was 'to refer back to the Cappadocian τρόπος ὑπάρξεως and the *modus entis* of Protestant Orthodoxy' (*CD* I/1, viii). Barth understands modes of being along the lines of eternal ways of existing, such that God never exists in a way other than this, and there is no fourth God who can be accessed behind these eternal ways of his being the one God (cf. Hunsinger, *Disruptive Grace*, 191n7).

While my primary purpose is not to defend Barth, this point merits attention. For many, Barth's understanding of God's *Seinweisen* undermines the relationality, love and fellowship between the Father, Son and Holy Spirit. Cornelius Plantinga Jr aptly expresses this sentiment, arguing that Barth's theory reduces 'three divine persons to modes or roles of one person, thus robbing the doctrine of God of its rich communitarian overtones'. He notes, however, that he does this 'while trying simultaneously to harvest from trinity doctrine all the best fruits of a more social view'. He concludes with the following verdict: 'To tell the truth, his theory cannot consistently yield these fruits. For modes do not love at all. Hence they cannot love each other.' Cornelius Plantinga Jr, 'The Threeness/Oneness Problem of the Trinity', *Calvin Theological Journal* 23, no. 1 (April 1998), 49–50. Others who argue in this vein include: Trevor A. Hart, *Regarding Karl Barth: Essays Toward a Reading of His Theology* (Carlisle: Paternoster Press, 1999), 107; Torrance, *Persons in Communion*, 115, 220. Later Alan Torrance softens his claim, suggesting the possibility of development in Barth's thought: Alan J. Torrance, 'The Trinity', in The *Cambridge Companion to Karl Barth*, ed. J. B. Webster (New York: Cambridge University Press, 2000), 82.

Paul Molnar convincingly defends Barth, drawing on multiple aspects of his thought, including the relationship between knowledge and communion, Barth's qualified affirmation of the term 'person', and the concreteness of Barth's understanding of modes

historical argument (*CD* I/1, 355–60), Barth contends that 'mode of being' is a relatively preferable concept to 'person' so as to express the 'common term' by which we understand the Father, Son and Holy Spirit (*CD* I/1, 355). Partly, this relative advantage has to do with the etymological shift in the meaning of the term person: in the nineteenth century the term 'person' incorporated the aspect of self-consciousness, such that it connotes tritheism when used in the doctrine of the Trinity (*CD* I/1, 357; *CD* IV/1, 204–5). Additionally, Barth draws on Reformed Orthodox and ultimately Eastern Orthodox understanding of ὑπόστασις, which means *subsistentia*, 'i.e., mode of existence or mode of being of an existent' (*CD* I/1, 360), which he considers to be an under-developed source in the Church's analysis of the concept of person (*CD* I/1, 359). As we have seen, however, this also has a great deal to do with Barth locating God's personhood in the one essence of God and therefore and on that basis in the 'persons' of the Trinity.

What then does it mean to affirm that the one God eternally exists, lives, and is who He is in these three distinct modes of being?[34] While it may

---

of being as the modes of being of the one personal God. Molnar, *Divine Freedom*, 242–5. While Barth does not dwell on the communal or relational elements of the Trinity in this passage (*CD* I/1, §9.2), I contend with Molnar that when viewed concretely as modes of being *of the one personal God*, Barth in fact gives us all the necessary resources by which to explore the relationality of the Father, Son and Holy Spirit in a way consistent with precisely those passages throughout the *CD* which speak of such the triune relationality (cf. *CD* I/1, 484; II/1, 532; III/3, §54.1). By the time we reach *CD* III/3, the relational emphasis of Barth's Trinitarian theology is fully evident. Katherine Sonderegger, 'Barth and Feminism', in *The Cambridge Companion to Karl Barth*, ed. J. B. Webster (New York: Cambridge University Press, 2000), 269. This account of the triune relationality, I believe, goes a long way toward addressing the difficulties perceived in Rowan Williams' incisive essay, eschewing the supposedly Moltmann-esque leanings Williams sees in CD IV/1: R. D. Williams, 'Barth on the Triune God', in *Karl Barth, Studies of His Theological Method*, ed. Stephen Sykes (New York: Oxford University Press, 1979), 175–6. Cf. 181–4.

Furthermore, Barth's emphasis on the modes of being *of the one personal God* provides solid grounds for the thesis that Barth does in fact honor Jowers' claim that 'He would do better to clarify than to reject the term "person"' (Dennis W. Jowers, 'The Reproach of Modalism: A Difficulty for Karl Barth's Doctrine of the Trinity,' *SJT* 56, no. 2 (2003): 246; cf. 244. While this may not be particularly evident in *CD* I/1, it is more apparent in later volumes, where Barth demonstrates the freedom to refer to the Son as a person. For example, Barth writes: '[He concludes] the peace the price of which He Himself willed to pay and did pay in the person of this man, and therefore in the person of His own Son' (*CD* IV/3.1, 414). Barth's intent is to locate God's personhood within the very essence of God and in this way to offer the proper safeguards for referring to the Father, Son and Holy Spirit as persons, though this intent may not be quite as clear as it could be. The same point goes a long way towards correcting Ovey's over-emphasis on the 'reflexivity' of Barth's God-talk, as opposed to its relationality (Ovey, 'A Private Love', 220–9).

[34] How it is that 'an essence can produce itself and then be in a twofold way its own

not be readily apparent at this point of the argument, in this section Barth develops the foundation of distinctness and otherness within the being of God which is at the root not only of the intra-triune relationality, but also, as we will see, of God's work *ad extra* (cf. *CD* II/1, 463). In a summary statement towards the end of §9, Barth writes: 'By the doctrine of the Trinity we understand ... the unity of God in the three modes of being ... or of the threefold otherness [*dreimaligen Anderssein*] of the one God in the three modes of being' (*CD* I/1, 375; *KD*, 396). It is precisely this 'otherness' that Barth aims to secure here. The one God exists and lives from all eternity as other to himself.[35] This other is not foreign to or separate from God, but is God himself in distinction from himself: God the Father, God the Son and God the Holy Spirit. The term *Seinsweise* is the conceptual vehicle by means of which Barth speaks of this distinctness while safeguarding himself from a lapse into tritheistic separation.

When Barth affirms the distinctness of God's modes of being as affirmed in this section in conjunction with the radical commitment to locating the personality of the one God precisely in God's essence, he provides us with all the necessary resources for the full intra-relationality of the Trinity so many commentators find missing. For Barth the one personal God lives out his life in eternity in these three simultaneous modes or ways of being, each of which is fully personal precisely because they are the modes of being *of the one personal God*. Accordingly, Barth writes of the love of the Son for the Father and of the 'indestructible fellowship between the two' (*CD* I/1, 432), and later in the *CD* brings the full weight of the intra-triune relationality to bear on the doctrine of reconciliation. Therein he writes that God is God in the concrete relationships of his modes of being, 'in the history which takes places between them ... The true and living God is the One whose Godhead consists in this history, who is in these three modes of being the One God ...' (*CD* IV/1, 203). God in himself, apart from his relationship with creation, has a history, lives in concrete relationships and loves in freedom (*CD* II/1, 275). While Barth does not develop the intra-triune relationality extensively in *CD* I/1, he presupposes and builds its foundation by locating the personality of God in God's essence and therefore and from eternity in the three modes or ways of the one God's personal being.

For a better understanding of this point, we turn to the possibilities within

product', how it is that 'an essence's relation of origin ... can subsist simultaneously and with equal truth and reality in the two different corresponding modes of being' and in this simultaneous subsistence relate to itself, we cannot say (*CD* I/1, 367). It is not the business of theology and any specific concept such as 'modes of being' to overcome God's mystery, but continually to wrestle with the mystery rationally.

[35] Webster explains: 'The triune God is one simple indivisible essence in an irreducible threefold personal modification. That is, God's unity is characterized by modes of being in each of which the entire divine essence subsists in a particular way' (Webster, 'Trinity and Creation', 8).

this account for our elaboration of the doctrine of the atonement, a move that Barth himself is eager to make. In his continued exposition of the doctrine of the Trinity, Barth anticipates our interest in the atonement:

> It is hard to see how the distinction of the mode of being of the Son of God from that of the Father – and the same distinction must also be made from that of the Holy Spirit – can be denied without speculatively changing and weakening the seriousness of God's wrath against sin ... into a mere tension within a totality which is known to us and can be surveyed by us. (*CD* I/1, 410)

Why does Barth claim that a denial of the distinction of God's modes of being entails a weakening or changing of the seriousness of God's wrath against sin?[36] In answering our present question we continue to delve into the antecedent possibility in God for the reconciliation accomplished in Jesus Christ: his triune being as Father, Son and Holy Spirit.

God can be our God and reveal himself as such precisely and solely because he is triune (*CD* I/1, 383), which is to say that the otherness proper to God's being, the relationality between Father, Son and Holy Spirit from eternity, is the principle of his revealing and reconciling activity, the principle of the concrete and unadulterated manifestation of the seriousness of his wrath. Only inasmuch as there is in God a self-distinction, a mode of God's being which is 'different from though not subordinate to [*nicht untergeordneten*] His first and hidden mode of being as God', can He exist for us (*CD* I/1, 316; *KD*, 334).[37] That is to say, God's being in three modes is

---

[36] I opt to discuss wrath here not because it ought to play a singularly decisive role in the doctrine of the atonement (though it is essential), but because of Barth's own use of the concept in relating it to the topic we are currently exploring.

[37] Elsewhere, Barth writes: 'In God's own freedom there is encounter and communion [*Begegnung und Gemeinschaft*]; there is order [*Ordnung*] and, consequently, dominion and subordination [*Überordnung und Unterordnung*]; there is majesty and humility [*Hoheit und Demut*], absolute authority and absolute obedience [*vollkommene Autorität und vollkommener Gehorsam*]; there is offer and response [*Gabe und Aufgabe*]. God's freedom is the freedom of the Father and the Son in the unity of the Spirit [*eben weil und indem sie die Freiheit des Vaters und des Sohnes in der Einheit des Heiligen Geistes ist*]' (Karl Barth, *Das Geschenk der Freiheit: Grundlegung evangelischer Ethik* (Zollikon-Zurich: Evangelischer verlag, 1953), 4; cf. Barth, *The Humanity of God*, 71).

It is important to note that Barth distinguishes between two forms of subordination within the Trinity. 'Subordination [*Unterordnungsverhältnis*] regarding their deity' (*CD* I/1, 393; *KD*, 414) denies the divine essence by positing variations in regards to the essence itself, while 'the relation of subordination [*Unterordnungsverhältnis*]' (*CD* I/1, 413; *KD*, 434) Barth favours is a matter of the distinction and relationality between the various modes of being of the one essence. In one of the clearest presentations of this distinction, Barth writes: 'this subordination [*Unterordnung*] and sequence cannot imply any distinction of being; it can only signify a distinction in the

the premise of a robust soteriology, such that God can take up sinful human nature into his own divine life in the person of the Son and in this way pour out 'his wrath out upon himself' in an intra-Trinitarian act.[38]

According to Barth, God can manifest his wrath against humankind in the fullness of its reality *while at the same time* reconciling us to himself because God exists alongside himself in the person of the Son. He can bring this event into his own proper life, dealing with our sin and death in the history of his triune being as Father, incarnate Son, and Holy Spirit, pouring out his wrath not upon us but upon himself in his mode of being as the incarnate Son who took upon himself the sins of the world.[39] In this way we are saved, for we bear the wrath of God not directly upon ourselves, but in the person of the incarnate Son; in the same way God justifies himself in face of his forbearance of human sin by doing away with it decisively in the death and resurrection of the incarnate Son. Only by God remaining God in the mode of being of the Father can he pour out his wrath upon the incarnate Son; only by his being God in the mode of the Spirit, who is the love between the Father and the Son, can God maintain his unity in this event; and only by becoming incarnate in the mode of the Son can God bring the sinful human nature into his own life so as to do away with it once and for all.[40] In short, only by being the Triune God

---

mode of being' (*CD* I/1, 413; *KD*, 434). Barth reaffirms and more fully explores the nature of this Trinitarian subordination in *CD* IV/1, 200–10.

[38] For an excellent treatment of the relationship between the doctrines of the Trinity, Christology and atonement, see McCormack, 'Ontological Presuppositions', 363–4. On atonement as an inter-Trinitarian act, cf. Barth, *Unterricht in der christlichen Religion*, 131.

[39] Critiques of the doctrine of the atonement in its more traditional forms often make two related mistakes. First, they do not operate with an adequate account of the doctrine of the Trinity, but presuppose a tritheistic account of God. Second, critiques often fail to take into account the premise that the Father does not relate to the Son simply, and is not moved by 'the suffering of an innocent man' (Bruce L. McCormack, *For Us and Our Salvation: Incarnation and Atonement in the Reformed Tradition* (Princeton, NJ: Princeton Theological Seminary, 1993), 30). Rather, the key is the incarnate Son *who bears our sin*. Cf. Maurer, '"Für uns" An unserer Stelle hingerichtet' 192. When Jesus 'stands under the wrath and judgment of God, *He* is broken and destroyed on God. It cannot be otherwise ... For God is in the right against Him. He concedes that the Father is right in the will and action which leads Him to the cross' (*CD* IV/1, 175). Why is the Father right in doing this? To put it simply, because the Son took upon himself our flesh – sinful human flesh. Drawing on such passages as 2 Cor. 5.21 and Gal. 3.13, Barth affirms that he became a 'man standing under the divine verdict and judgment, man who is a sinner and whose existence therefore must perish before God' (*CD* IV/1, 165ff.).The precise way in which Barth holds Jesus Christ to bear our sin is too difficult a topic to explore here, given the scope of my argument.

[40] Failing to note the Trinitarian context of such claims results in a radical misunderstanding of God's point, and the eventual need to jettison an account of God's anger or

can God bear his own wrath 'creatively'.[41] A god who does not exist in threefold otherness cannot take upon himself human nature without losing himself or drink the cup of his own wrath without destroying himself. He cannot do away with that which he opposes without doing away with those with whom he seeks fellowship and is consequently unable to reconcile humankind to himself in faithfulness to himself. He is unable to manifest his wrath against our sin without denying himself or destroying precisely that which he seeks to save.[42]

Barth's account of God's 'otherness' does not appear to be without difficulties, however. He seems to undermine his insistence on God's unity in his account of the suffering and dying of Jesus Christ as an act of God which took place for us (*CD* IV/1, 252).[43] He writes:

> The very heart of the atonement is the overcoming of sin ... He fulfils it – as man in our place – by completing our work in the omnipotence of the divine Son, by treading the way of sinners to its bitter end in death, in destruction, in the limitless anguish of separation from God [*in der grenzenlosen Qual der Gottesferne*]. (*CD* IV/1, 253; *KD* 278)

This 'separation' is central to Barth's understanding of the doctrine of reconciliation, and lies at the root of one of the primary developments of the doctrine of the atonement in the twentieth century: a soteriological emphasis on the passibility of the triune God.[44] At first glance, however, Barth's claim seems to contradict God's triunity, which denies separation in God: 'God's essence is indeed one, and even the different relations of origin

---

wrath entirely from an account of Christ's work. Cf. Bakker, 'Jesus als Stellvertreter', 50–1, 56.

[41] Maurer, '"Für uns" An unserer Stelle hingerichtet' 194.

[42] 'This is what it costs God to be righteous without annihilating us' (*CD* II/1, 399).

[43] Cf. Jowers, who suggests that 'Barth's idea of an eternal obedience rendered to the Father by the Son ... undermines Barth's case against subordinationism' (Jowers, 'The Reproach of Modalism', 246).

[44] Among those theologians who draw upon Barth in this line of thought, the most prominent include Jürgen Moltmann, Hans Urs von Balthasar and Eberhard Jüngel. Cf. Moltmann's comment that 'more recent studies on the doctrine of the Trinity [beyond those just mentioned, Moltmann also cites Kitamori, Mühlen and Hall] start from the passion of Christ and reject, along with the picture of the unmovable Sovereign Lord, the axiom of God's impassibility: the deepest ground for the passion of Christ is the *pathos* of God' (Jürgen Moltmann, 'The Motherly Father: Is Trinitarian Patripassianism Replacing Theological Patriarchalism?', in *God as Father*, eds Johannes-Baptist Metz, Edward Schillebeeckx and Marcus Lefébvre (New York: Seabury, 1981), 53–4). In this essay Moltmann does not mention Barth's influence or the fact that many of the theologians he mentions would not agree with him that monotheism and the doctrine of the Trinity contradict each other.

do not entail separations [*keine Trennungen*]' (*CD* I/1, 370; *KD*, 390).[45] Barth reaffirms his rejection of separateness within the Trinity just prior to the problematic passage we noted (*CD* IV/1, 253), writing that 'God is God in these two modes of being which cannot be separated [*nicht zu trennenden*]' (*CD* IV/1, 203; *KD*, 222). How then do we account for this ambiguity if not downright contradiction?

Unfortunately the ambiguity is largely on account of the English translation, for Barth consistently distinguishes between two different terms, affirming *Gottesferne* or *Sonderung* while denying *trennungen* within the Trinity. *Ferne*, or separation in the sense of 'distance', is not only acceptable but necessary, while *Trennung*, or separation in the sense of 'division from' is inconsiderable.[46] In the doctrine of reconciliation Barth utilizes the full Trinitarian resources of God's 'otherness', relying on it to provide the basis for the *Gottesferne* of the incarnate Son, while at the same time preventing a fatal collapse into *Trennung*. Precisely because God exists in three-fold otherness, the Son of God can go into the far country, *die Fremde*,[47] taking upon himself sinful human nature, and suffering as a result the anguish of separation (*Gottesferne*) from the Father (*CD* IV/1, 253; *KD*, 278). It is the separation or distance within the 'otherness' of the triune being which forms the antecedent basis in the one God for the reconciling *Gottesferne* experienced by Jesus.[48] Barth's theology

---

[45] Shortly after that Barth complicates this claim by adding that the distinction of the Father and Son 'affirms fellowship in separateness and separateness in fellowship [*in der Gemeinschaft die Sonderung und in der Sonderung die Gemeinschaft*]' (*CD* I/1, 484). In a later volume Barth denies separation within the divine perfections, 'which since they are His are not capable of any dissolution or separation [*Trennung*] or non-identity' (*CD* II/1, 332; *KD*, 374).

[46] Barth does not appear to be entirely consistent on this point, for later he writes: 'Eternity is God in the sense in which in Himself and in all things God is simultaneous [*einmal und zugleich*], i.e. beginning and middle as well as end, without separation, distance or contradiction [*ohne Trennung, Ferne und Widerspruch*]' (*CD* II/1, 608; *KD*, 685). Barth's use of *Ferne* in *CD* I/1 and IV/1 would seem to require that he accept it here in *CD* II/1 as well.

[47] Elsewhere Barth refers to God's 'self-alienation [*Selbstentfremdung*]' (*CD* II/1, 58; *KD*, 62).

[48] While David Lauber offers a helpful account of the relationship between Barth and von Balthasar's thought on the descent into hell, he overlooks an important dimension of Barth's thought when he uses Barth to question von Balthasar's 'use of "primal kenosis", "separation" and "distance"' – a point that obviously bears on our present concern. He writes that for Barth the separation Jesus undergoes in the abandonment of the Father and the descent into hell is 'a human experience, a human suffering of God'. While this is certainly the case, and indeed no 'ontological rupture' in the relationship between Father and Son occurs, Barth anticipates von Balthasar more closely than Lauber acknowledges (Lauber, *Barth on the Descent*, 60–1).
  It may also be the case that Barth anticipates to some extent von Balthasar's notion of primal kenosis, in that both root the suffering of the incarnate Son in a prior form of separation proper to the divine being and life. Along these lines, von Balthasar writes:

demands separation (*Ferne*; not *Trennung*) within the triune being of God rooted in God's otherness, for God 'does not change in giving Himself. He simply activates and reveals Himself *ad extra*, in the world' (*CD* IV/1, 204).[49] The separation or distance between the Father and the incarnate Son is thus an actualization of the distance within the immanent Trinity under the condition of the incarnation of the Son.

It is vital to note, however, that this actualization is under new circumstances (namely, the inclusion of a sinful human nature in the being of the Son), such that the distance now becomes one that includes suffering (whereas in the life of the immanent Trinity it did not). God 'really turns to us as the One He is and not under a mask ... because in the first instance distance and confrontation [*Distanz und Gegenüber*], encounter and partnership [*Begegnung und Partnerschaft*], are to be found in Himself' (*CD* IV/2, 343; *KD*, 383), but turns to us in these new circumstances and therefore in a way that now includes suffering. Barth's account of God's 'Trinity in Unity' thus provides him with the resources to account for the otherness within the being of God, an otherness capable of undergoing the separation (*Distanz* or *Ferne*) of the incarnate Son from the Father without

'We shall never know how to express the abyss-like depths of the Father's self-giving, that Father who, in an eternal "super-Kenosis", makes himself "destitute" of all that he is and can be so as to bring forth a consubstantial divinity, the Son ... God as the "gulf" ... of absolute Love contains in advance, eternally, all the modalities of love, of compassion, and even of a "separation" motivated by love and founded on the infinite distinction between the hypostases – modalities which may manifest themselves in the course of a history of salvation involving sinful humankind' (*Balthasar*, *Mysterium Paschale*, viii–ix).

[49] A possible rejoinder could draw from this very passage, in which Barth writes that God 'becomes what He had not previously been ... He empties Himself, He Humbles Himself', and in this way the separation in question is not within the being of God but between the incarnate Son and the Father (*CD* IV/1, 203). Continuing to read, however, we find that 'He does not do [this] apart from its basis in His own being, in His own inner life. He does not do it without any correspondence to, but as the strangely logical final continuation of, the history in which He is God.' In a fuller treatment, Lauber would need to account for the correspondence and continuation Barth so keenly emphasizes.

As an aside, I take Barth's point that this is a 'strangely logical final continuation', or what I might translate as 'the wonderfully consistent final continuation [*wunderbar konsequenter letzter Fortsetzung eben der Geschichte*]', to refer to the freedom with which God elected to be who he is in this new way, to do something new, which 'He had previously not been' (*CD* IV/1, 203). The strangeness refers to God's freedom in the act of election, while the consistency refers to the antecedent basis within God for this repetition or overflow, safeguarding God's constancy. Cf. Paul D. Molnar, 'The Function of the Immanent Trinity in the Theology of Karl Barth: Implications for Today', *SJT* 42, no. 3 (1990): 371n24. Thanks to Paul Molnar drawing my attention to this point.

resulting in a rupture or division (*Trennung*) within the being of the one God (as one might find in Moltmann, for instance).

In honour of Barth's emphasis on the unity of God, we must consider one further implication of God's threeness in regards to reconciliation, although at this point we can be much more brief. Barth's doctrine of the Trinity also provides him with the resources for the positive aspect of Christ's saving work (that which he saves us *for*). While the otherness within God is the principle for the negative aspect of Christ's work (focused on that which he saves us from by taking our condition upon himself and dealing with it within the triune life), it is also the basis of that for which God saves us: 'Himself, fellowship and intercourse with Himself' (*CD* I/1, 444), and 'eternal life as the continuance of man in fellowship with God Himself' (*CD* IV/1, 72). God does not need a second or third so as to have a counterpart, to be in relation. Within God's oneness is a 'distinction which affirms fellowship in separateness and separateness in fellowship [*in der Gemeinschaft die Sonderung und in der Sonderung die Gemeinschaft*]', a fellowship that he shares with us through the work of Christ and the impartation of the Spirit (*CD* I/1, 484). Later in the *CD* Barth re-affirms this point, writing: 'The triune life of God ... is the basis of His whole will and action even *ad extra*, as the living act which He directs to us ... of the relationships which He has determined and established with a reality which is distinct from Himself' (*CD* IV/2, 245). Barth's constant emphasis on the relationship and fellowship between God and his people flows from the eternal fellowship within God's triune being. God reconciles us to himself that we might have that which he has in himself and from eternity: fellowship with the triune God (*CD* II/1, 275; *CD* IV/1, 9; *CD* IV/2, 757).[50]

Triunity

Barth's third section on the doctrine of the Trinity dwells on the necessary dialectical interplay of the above two points. He adopts the term 'triunity' (*Dreieinigkeit*) to indicate this dialectical movement, a term suggesting threeness while emphasizing unity (*CD* I/1, 369) and thus itself indicative of the necessary movement required of our understanding. Barth then turns his attention (in the remainder of this section) to the two forms 'of the dialectic needed to work out the concept of "triunity"' (*CD* I/1, 371): (1) the doctrine of perichoresis and (2) the doctrine of appropriations combined with the rule *opera trinitatis ad extra sunt indivisa* (the external operations of the Trinity are undivided).

---

[50] The positive centre of the doctrine of the atonement is thus that God does not want to be God without us, but rather seeks to share his life with us (Ruddies, 'Christologie und Versöhnungslehre', 176).

The doctrine of perichoresis 'states that the divine modes of being mutually condition and permeate one another so completely that one is always in the other two and the other two in the one' (*CD* I/1, 370). The unity of the Father, Son and Holy Spirit, the one essence of God in these three modes of being, involves a fellowship, 'a complete participation of each mode of being in the other modes of being' (*CD* I/1, 370). This participation confirms the distinction of the three modes of being in that the participation and fellowship is genuine and necessary for the uniqueness of each, while also putting limits on the distinction, as no one mode exists or acts in distinction or separation from the others. In this way perichoresis does justice to the dialectic involved in working out the concept of triunity (*CD* I/1, 371).[51]

The second form of the dialectic involves the inter-related doctrine of appropriations and the rule *opera trinitatis ad extra sunt indivisa*. The differentiations or distinctions in God's self-revelation attested in Scripture, the distinctions in God's acts and his attributes such as those of 'Creator, Reconciler and Redeemer' are the subject matter of the doctrine of appropriations. According to Barth this doctrine assigns a 'word or deed to this or that person of the Godhead', bringing to our awareness in a provisional or temporary way the 'truly incomprehensible eternal distinctions in God' (*CD* I/1, 372), although, to be sure, this is a true knowledge despite its incompleteness, rooted in the distinctions within the one God and the order appropriate to the modes of God's being (*CD* I/1, 396). The doctrine of appropriations thus enables us to speak of and distinguish the Father, Son and Holy Spirit in terms of acts or attributes, although it does so according to specific rules: (1) the appropriation may not be arbitrary, but requires a 'manifest kinship' between the appropriations and the three persons (a kinship grounded in the distinctions between the modes of God's being); (2) the appropriation must affirm God's unity and thus be temporary or provisional and not ultimately exclusive; and (3) must be drawn 'literally or materially or both from Holy Scripture' if it is to be authentic (*CD* I/1, 374). On this basis we may distinguish the Father, Son and Holy Spirit (although never without danger) along such lines as creation, redemption and sanctification, meaningfully speaking of the persons of the Trinity in this way.

The second and necessary part of this dialectical outworking of the concept of triunity is the rule *opera trinitatis ad extra sunt indivisa*: the external or outward works of the Trinity are undivided. Despite a temporary hiddenness of the oneness of God in the designation by Scripture of a specific act or attribute to the Father, Son or Holy Spirit, this rule affirms that 'all God's work, as we are to grasp it on the basis of His revelation, is one act which occurs simultaneously and in concert in all His three modes of being' (*CD*

---

[51] In Barth, perichoresis is a function of God's oneness, rather than vice versa, as in so much contemporary theology. Cf. Hunsinger, *Disruptive Grace*, 190.

I/1, 375). That is to say, while Scripture may attribute creation to the Father, it is nevertheless an act that God accomplishes as Father, Son and Holy Spirit, the same going for the designation of other attributes or actions. God is the 'one Lord, the one Creator, the one Reconciler, the one Perfecter and Redeemer. He is all this as he is Father, Son and Holy Spirit' (CD IV/1, 205).

To be sure, the indivisibility in question affirms the distinction of God's modes of being, such that the indivisibility is a full and diverse one, rather than flat and homogenous. While the one Lord is the one Reconciler, this is not at all to say that the Father, Son and Holy Spirit are the reconciler in the same way, for 'one cannot say of God the Father that He was conceived and born, that He suffered, died and rose again' (CD I/1, 397). To reiterate an earlier point, the triune God becomes flesh according to the differentiated act of God's triune being, such that only the Son takes up a human nature.

Turning to our thesis, we find the doctrine of God's triunity energizing Barth's account of the doctrine of reconciliation. For instance, the doctrine of appropriations enables Barth to attribute acts or qualities to specific persons of the Trinity, such as the wrath of the Father that is poured out upon the Son. Scripture permits, even forces, Barth to make such differentiations, speaking 'in terms of [them] … with great seriousness, i.e., in such a way that we are in no position to remove them without exegetical wresting' (CD I/1, 372). Along these lines, Barth writes that Jesus was obedient in choosing 'to suffer the wrath of God in His own body and the fire of His love in His own soul' (CD IV/1, 95), and affirms with the *Heidelberg Catechism* that 'during the whole time of His life on earth Jesus … bore the wrath of God against the sin of the whole human race' (CD IV/1, 165). Even more boldly, he specifies that 'God' in such cases refers to the Father: the Son of God made flesh 'stands under the wrath and judgment of God … He concedes that the Father is right in the will and action which leads Him to the cross' and 'the suffering of children chastised by their Father' he there experienced (CD IV/1, 175).

The doctrine of appropriations never stands on its own, though: we must dialectically relate any conclusions made on these grounds to the rule *opera ad extra sunt indivisa*, such that we do not conclude that the Father's wrath of itself distinguishes the Father from the Son. Such a conclusion collapses into tritheism (and a non-Trinitarian understanding of the divine perfections), ultimately undermining the possibility of both revelation and atonement. To the contrary, Barth affirms the oneness of God's acts and perfections. Just after the passage last quoted, Barth writes:

In Him God has entered in, breaking into that *circulus vitiosus* of the human plight, making His own not only the guilt of man but also his rejection and condemnation, giving Himself to bear the divinely righteous consequences of human sin, not merely affirming the divine sentence on man, but allowing it to be fulfilled on Himself. (*CD* IV/1, 175)

He thus demonstrates the necessary dialectical tension between the doctrine and rule we have been examining, affirming the work of Christ simply as a work of the one God. And nowhere is Barth's commitment to the outworking of this dialectic more evident than in his account of Christ's passion in the life of God,[52] his modified affirmation of Patripassianism,[53] the consideration of which brings us to our governing interest in the relationship between the doctrines of the Trinity and atonement.[54]

This event of God's giving of Himself in which the 'divine sentence on man' is 'fulfilled on Himself' is a Trinitarian event in which the sentence and judgement of the Father is fulfilled on the incarnate Son: in Jesus' suffering and death. The imminent danger is that we too rigidly distinguish the Father and Son in this event, breaking apart the unity of God's being. Eschewing this danger, Barth writes:

> It is not at all the case that God has no part in the suffering of Jesus Christ even in His mode of being as the Father. No, there is a *particular veri* in the teaching of the early Patripassians. This is that primarily it is God the Father who suffers in the offering and sending of His Son, in His abasement ... [He suffers] in the humiliation of His Son with a depth with which it never was or will be suffered by any man—apart from the One who is His Son ... The fatherly fellow-suffering [*väterliche Mitleiden*] of God is the mystery, the basis, of the humiliation of His Son. (*CD* IV/2, 357; *KD*, 399)[55]

---

[52] Klappert, *Die Auferweckung*, 102.

[53] Patripassianism is the ancient heresy according to which the Father, like the Son, suffered on the cross.

[54] Cf. Jüngel, *God's Being is in Becoming*, 98–103. For one critical of Barth's position on this subject, see G. C. Berkouwer, *The Triumph of Grace in the Theology of Karl Barth*, trans. Harry R. Boer (Grand Rapids, MI: Eerdmans, 1956), 298–313.

[55] We must take Barth's endorsement of the *particula veri* seriously, as he elsewhere denies Patripassianism as a whole (*CD* I/1, 397–8), as pointed out by Molnar, *Divine Freedom*, 224.

As an indication of just how far Barth departs from the tradition on this point, note the following passage from Tertullian: 'For what is the meaning of 'fellow-suffering,' but the endurance of suffering along with another [*Quid est enim compati quam cum alio pati*]? Now if the Father is incapable of suffering [*impassibilis*], He is incapable of suffering [*incompassibilis*] in company with another; otherwise, if He can suffer with another [*compassibilis*], He is of course capable of suffering [*passibilis*] ... Well, but how could the Son suffer, if the Father did not suffer with Him? My answer is, The Father is separate from the Son, though not from Him as God [*Separatur a Filio, non a Deo*]' (Tertullian, 'Against Praxeas', in The Ante-Nicene Fathers, ed. Alexander Roberts and James Donaldson (Peabody, MA: Hendrickson, 2004), 626;

Elsewhere, he adds:

> With the eternal Son the eternal Father has also to bear what falls on the Son ... In Jesus Christ God Himself, the God who is the one true God, the Father with the Son in the unity of the Spirit, has suffered [*miterlitten*] what it befell this man to suffer to the bitter end ... It is of this fellow-suffering of God Himself [*Mittleiden Gottes selbst*] borne on earth and also in heaven to the greater glory of God and the supreme salvation of man; it is of the God who has not evaded, and on the very grounds of His deity could not evade, this suffering with and for the world [*Mitleiden mit der Welt*], that the crucified man Jesus Christ speaks ... He speaks ... [of] the peace the price of which He Himself willed to pay and did pay in the person of this man, and therefore in the person of His own Son, and therefore in His fatherly heart [*väterlichen Herzen*]. (*CD* IV/3.1, 414–15; *KD*, 478)[56]

While Barth does not mention the 'rule' or 'doctrine' with which we are here concerned, they lie just below the surface, manifest in the dialectic of God Himself on the one hand and the incarnate Son and the Father on the other.[57] The doctrine of appropriations affirms that we can and must distinguish between the Father and the incarnate Son, such that only the Son is incarnate and suffers death and abandonment of the Father. On the other hand, the rule *opera ad extra sunt indivisa* demands that we step back, dwelling on the fact that Christ's passion is the work of the one God, such that 'the death of Jesus Christ in God-abandonment, precisely as a human experience, is understood by him to be an event in God's own life', the life of the one God.[58] This explains why, as Berthold Klappert notes, Barth is more inclined to speak of the suffering of God (*theopaschitisch*) than the New Testament emphasis on the suffering of Christ (*hyiopaschitisch*), interpreting the prevailing New Testament witness in light of the *theopaschite* statement in 2 Cor. 5.19.[59] For this reason Barth refers

---

Chap. XXIX). Latin text drawn from: Tertullian, *Tertvlliani Opera: Pars II, Opera Montanistica* (Turnholti, Belgium: Typographi Brepols Editores Pontificii, 1954), 1203; Chap. XXX.

[56] Cf. *CD* IV/1, 485; *CD* IV/3.1 297; Barth, *Deliverance to the Captives*, 80; Barth, *Table Talk*, 52.

[57] As Jowers points out, though, the 'rule' is in fact present in Barth's condemnation of Patripassianism earlier in the *CD* (*CD* I/1, 397), supporting my inference that it is a premise in this discussion as well (Jowers, 'The Reproach of Modalism', 239).

[58] McCormack, *Orthodox and Modern*, 189.

[59] Klappert, *Die Auferweckung*, 182–3n58. For one quite concerned about Barth's *theopaschitism*, cf. Berkouwer, *Triumph*, 297ff. Klappert's point is not so much that 2 Cor. 5.19 is a proof text for theopaschitism as that the general thrust of the passage, emphasizing that it was God who was active in Jesus Christ, seems to encourage such

to the 'fellow-suffering of God Himself' and subsequently distinguishes that suffering according to the various 'ways of God's being', such that the Father, in fact, suffers with the Son in his 'fatherly heart' precisely by giving him up to this suffering.[60]

According to Barth, as long as the Church properly balances the doctrine of appropriations and the rule *opera ad extra*, it has the right and responsibility to use provisional and temporary distinctions and appropriations (such as 'the wrath of the Father') in its theological discourse. This conclusion has a double edge in relation to current discussions. First, it forces critiques of the doctrine of the atonement based on a putatively fatal distinction between the Father and Son (typically referred to as a form of divine child abuse) to a greater depth of analysis, such that they must examine the arguments not only for appropriations (which, as we have seen, are one-sided even when warranted), but also for the balancing presence of the rule *opera ad extra sunt indivisa*. Likewise, this conclusion demands that proponents of traditional forms of the atonement be wary of concluding or giving unnecessary grounds for others to conclude that such appropriations finally and absolutely distinguish the Father, Son and Holy Spirit.

Summary

The doctrine of the Trinity offers the Church far more than a preventative measure to ward off criticisms of traditional interpretations of Christ's saving work – it is the essential foundation and vital force within the doctrine of reconciliation, the appreciation and development of which is a necessary part of that for which the Church must unfailingly strive: gratitude rooted in understanding the being and act of God in the atoning

---

an interpretation, particularly when read in light of certain entailments of the doctrine of the Trinity.

[60] Paul Molnar notes that 'in this analysis there remains a clear distinction between the Father and the Son and between the Father's suffering as a mystery grounded in the immanent Trinity and the creature's suffering which, while not part of God's nature, is experienced by God for the salvation of creatures' (Molnar, *Divine Freedom*, 225). The distinction is a crucial one. The uniqueness of Christ's suffering is rooted in Scripture's witness and as a reflection of the doctrine of appropriations. On the other hand, the term 'suffering', which is predicated of both the Father and the incarnate Son, is equally vital, in that it honours the rule *opera ad extra sunt indivisa*.

Eberhard Jüngel emphasizes this point, claiming that 'one must not exclude from this suffering the Father who gave his Son over to suffer death ... Thus the Father, too, participates with the Son in the passion, and the divine unity of God's modes of being proves itself in the suffering of Jesus Christ' (*Jüngel, God's Being is in Becoming*, 102). Barth thereby provides precisely the 'Trinitarian differentiation over the event on the cross', which Moltmann somehow finds lacking in Barth's theology. Cf. Moltmann, *The Crucified God*, 203; Jüngel, *God's Being is in Becoming*, 102n15).

work of Jesus Christ. Barth offers the church a great service in this regard, for he sought the key to dogmatics in the doctrine of the Trinity and, once he found it, proceeded to put it to great use. Unfortunately, the specific use Barth made of the Trinity in his development of the doctrine of reconciliation has received relatively little attention to date, and I have sought to remedy this condition, examining some the most essential aspects of Barth's doctrine of the Trinity and the role these play in his account of the atonement.

Barth helps us to see how the doctrine of the Trinity forces us to work on Scriptural grounds, eschewing the use of shared experience as a normative basis; how the unity of God is the precondition of the work of the incarnate Son reconciling us to God; how God's threeness is the condition for God's ability to take up into his own life the sinful human condition through the incarnation of the Son so as to save us by doing away with our sin and guilt in faithfulness to himself and sharing with us the fellowship proper to his triune being; how we can speak of the unified and differentiated work of the Father, Son and Holy Spirit in the work of Christ, without lapsing into tritheism. More radically, Barth drew on the doctrine of the Trinity to initiate the twentieth century's development of the doctrine of the atonement with his construal of a reformulated Patripassianism – a thesis that Moltmann, Balthasar and others were to develop greatly in subsequent years.[61]

Barth's use of the doctrine of the Trinity also impacts of our understanding of the Christ's saving work at a more general and highly significant way. 'The point in all Trinitarian theology', writes Barth, is 'distinction in unity and unity in distinction' (CD I/1, 440), although of course he is careful to specify this relation concretely with regard to God's being in act so that it does not achieve the dangerous independence of an abstract concept. With such specification in place, however, the general point concerning Trinitarian unity in distinction attains considerable significance, cultivating our theological sensitivity for an awareness of instantiations or applications of the triune God's unity in distinction. In other words, Barth greatly heightens our sensitivity to the complex and vital role of unity and diversity within theological thought generally and in the doctrine of the atonement in particular. In the next chapter, we will delve into this line of thought, examining an especially significant manifestation of Barth's sensitivity to unity in diversity within the doctrine of the atonement, rooted in his Trinitarian understanding of the divine perfections.

---

[61] Remarkably, Barth does not tend to feature in works on contemporary passibilists. While Moltmann, von Balthasar, Jenson and Jüngel all feature regularly on such lists, Barth remains conspicuously absent, despite his considerable influence on so many of these theologians.

Test Case: The Trinity and Exemplarist Understandings of the Atonement

As Barth would decry a study of the atonement operating exclusively at a general or conceptual level, I conclude this and the next two chapters by applying the argument to a specific standpoint of the atonement. The natural candidate for this chapter would be to consider the role of the Trinity in the theory of penal substitution, as the thesis of this chapter offers significant grounds for defending this theory from contemporary critiques.[62] Despite the fact that I find penal substitution (properly construed) to be a vital aspect of a full understanding of the work of Christ, however, I opt otherwise for two reasons. First, penal substitution has been ably and charitably defended in recent years, and I am of the conviction that yet another defence here would add little to the discussion, beyond the implications readily apparent from the argument above.[63] Second, my own project is not merely to rehabilitate the main trajectories of the atonement throughout the history of the doctrine,[64] but to go beyond that, helping the church to embrace new and relatively undeveloped aspects of Christ's saving work. That said, in this particular case I will focus on one of those supposedly 'main trajectories', although one that is frequently minimized by those with a more traditional approach to Christian doctrine: exemplarism.[65]

---

[62] A second likely candidate would be to explore the relationship between Barth's Trinitarian account of the atonement and the resurgence in divinization theologies. Cf. Michael J. Christensen and Jeffery A. Wittung, *Partakers of the Divine Nature: The History and Development of Deification in the Christian Traditions* (Grand Rapids, MI: Baker Academic, 2007); Stephen Finlan and Vladimir Kharlamov, *Theōsis: Deification in Christian Theology* (Eugene, OR: Pickwick, 2006). For a Barthian response to this resurgence, cf. McCormack, 'Participation in God'; Neder, *Participation in Christ*.

[63] Among those defences of penal substitution that I find to be most helpfully, ably and charitably written, see Boersma, *Violence*; James I. Packer, 'What Did the Cross Achieve?: The Logic of Penal Substitution', *Tyndale Bulletin* 25 (1974), 3–45; Garry Williams, 'Penal Substitution: A Response to Recent Criticisms', in *The Atonement Debate: Papers from the London Symposium on the Theology of Atonement*, eds Derek Tidball, David Hilborn and Justin Thacker (Grand Rapids, MI: Zondervan, 2008).

[64] A number of books have pursued this line of thought, including: Aulén, *Christus Victor*; Fiddes, *Past Event and Present Salvation*; Gunton, *The Actuality of Atonement*; John Seldon Whale, *Victor and Victim* (Cambridge: Cambridge University Press, 1960).

[65] Exemplarism as a theory of the atonement has a rather convoluted history. Some trace its heritage back to the twelfth-century theologian Peter Abelard, although it appears that this may have more to do with the polemics of Bernard of Clairvaux and Abelard's propensity to stir up trouble for himself than with the actual content of his thought. Cf. Richard E. Weingart, *The Logic of Divine Love: A Critical Analysis of*

The difficulty with exclusively exemplarist accounts of the atonement, of course, is that they fail to grasp the full significance of Christ's saving work (and with it the significance of our sinful condition), often with the result that Christ's death on the cross becomes comparable to other martyrdoms in the history of the church (or other religions).[66] Consequently:

> It cannot be ignored that many men have suffered grievously, most grievously, in the course of world history ... Many who have suffered at the hands of men have been treated no less and perhaps more unjustly than this man [Jesus]. Many have been as willing as He was to suffer in this way. Many in so doing have done something which, according to their intention and it may be in fact, was significant for others, perhaps many others, making a redemptive change in their life. (CD IV/1, 245–6)

In fact, some have been more willing to suffer in this way – one thinks of

the Soteriology of Peter Abailard (London: Clarendon, 1970); Thomas Williams, 'Sin, Grace, and Redemption', in The Cambridge Companion to Abelard, eds Jeffrey E. Brower and Kevin Guilfoy (New York: Cambridge University Press, 2004). Regardless of whether Abelard was in fact an exemplarist, it is clear that what came to be known as exemplarism had a definite role to play in medieval theology, although not as a distinct 'theory', as Thomas included it as one of those aspects of the atonement brought together in Christ's 'fitting' work. Cf. Adam Johnson, 'A Fuller Account: The Role of 'Fittingness' in Thomas Aquinas' Development of the Doctrine of the Atonement,' IJST 12, no. 3 (2010), 302–18. It is worth noting that Barth himself has a positive word for Abelard's account of the atonement, noting that it must merit our approval. Barth, Unterricht in der christlichen Religion 81.

To find a theologian holding to exemplarism as a discreet and sufficient theory of the atonement, one must move much closer to the present day. Cf. Alister E. McGrath, 'The Moral Theory of the Atonement: An Historical and Theological Critique,' SJT 38, no. 2 (1985), 205–20. Consequently, the current presupposition of 'three main views of the atonement throughout the history of the church' is historically questionable. Various forms of exemplarism are common today, however, especially when combined with some demythologized rehabilitation of the Christus Victor or ransom theory. Cf. Girard, I See Satan; Darby Kathleen Ray, Deceiving the Devil: Atonement, Abuse, and Ransom (Cleveland, OH: Pilgrim Press, 1998); Weaver, The Nonviolent Atonement. The Christus Victor theme seems to be particularly favoured today, much for the same reason that Dorothee Sölle opted for the term 'reconciliation' several decades ago: 'Its linguistic advantage is that it is more abstract ... it is not already appropriated and filled out with images' (Dorothee Sölle, Christ the Representative: An Essay in Theology After the 'Death of God' (London: SCM Press, 1967), 13. I doubt whether such flexibility is beneficial when unmoored from the biblical foundation of the term.

[66] Or what is to keep Jesus from being yet another 'irrelevant example', not worth imitating because 'no one believe[s] it possible'? (Thomas Keneally, Schindler's List (New York: Touchstone, 1982), 325).

Plato's account of the death of Socrates, or the martyrdom of Polycarp, in comparison to the agony of Christ in the garden of Gethsemane. To this list of usual suspects, Barth rather pugnaciously adds: 'Why is [Jesus'] attitude so different ... from that displayed by ... many Communists ... even by the German general Jodl, executed as a war-criminal in Nuremberg?' (*CD* IV/1, 265). Inasmuch as an exemplarist approach looks to Christ simply as a martyr, simply as an example which changes us through inspiration and is thus distinct from us only as a matter of degree rather than of kind, it falls radically short of a full understanding of the person and work of Jesus Christ and his reconciling and revealing work.

With that said, however, Barth's inter-working of the doctrines of reconciliation and revelation via the doctrine of the Trinity constitutes the basis for a thoroughly reoriented version of exemplarism, putting this theory of the atonement on a firm foundation. In fact, Barth affirms the noetic aspect of Christ's work so emphatically that some go so far as to conclude that his is merely an exemplarist theory of the atonement![67] Alister McGrath, for example, writes:

> for Barth ... Christ is supremely the revealer of the knowledge of the true situation of humankind, by which humans are liberated from false understandings of their situation. For Barth, the death of Christ does not in any sense change the soteriological situation ... Rather, he discloses the christologically determined situation to humans.[68]

---

[67] A number of commentators misinterpret Barth's conjoining of revelation and reconciliation, the most notable instance being Alister McGrath. In a light revision of some of his earlier work, and with little or no apparent effort at engaging contemporary Barth scholarship, McGrath interprets Barth as standing with the *Aufklärer* (Enlightenment thinkers) who understand Christ as a revealer of knowledge rather than one who changes the soteriological situation (Alister E. McGrath, 'Karl Barth's Doctrine of Justification from an Evangelical Perspective', in *Karl Barth and Evangelical Theology* (Grand Rapids: Baker Academic, 2006), 188. As Trevor Hart notes in his critique of McGrath's position, 'while it is possible to set up a polarity between the epistemic and the soteriological in some theologies, such a polarity is alien to the basic substance of Barth's understanding' (Trevor A. Hart, 'Revelation,' in *The Cambridge Companion to Karl Barth*, ed. J. B. Webster (New York: Cambridge University Press, 2000), 54). John Webster critiques McGrath's position as well, but from the vantage point of the '*moral* character of the relation of God to humanity' (John Webster, *Barth's Ethics of Reconciliation* (New York: Cambridge University Press, 1995), 5–8). Ironically, while McGrath's critique misses the mark, it goes a long way towards establishing the validity of my thesis: that within Barth's doctrine of the atonement is a fully developed 'revelation' theory of the atonement, which takes up and transforms many of the exemplarist approaches to that doctrine so common in the Enlightenment and beyond.

[68] McGrath, 'Karl Barth's Doctrine of Justification', 188.

While it is safe to say that the above statement is radically mistaken,[69] Barth does emphatically affirm that Christ came in order to reveal, to make known and to teach – and that this aspect of Christ's work is in no sense secondary to or derivative from his reconciling work.

In answer to the question *Cur Deus Homo*, Barth writes:

> We shall not be answering incorrectly, but indicating the background against which we have to understand everything else, if we begin by simply repeating that He wills this and does this in an outward activation and revelation of the whole inward riches of His deity in all its height and depth, that He wills it and does it especially that the world created by him might have and see within it, in the Son as the image of the Father, its own original, that He wills it and does it for the sake of His own glory in the world, to confirm and proclaim His will not to be without the world, not to be God in isolation. (*CD* IV/1, 212)

This passage contains several notable features. First, Barth understands this to be the 'background against which we have to understand everything else'. We are not dealing with an implication or extension of the heart of the matter – this is the context for understanding all else that follows. Second, according to Barth, God intends this act to result in his creatures in some sense 'having' and 'seeing'. While Barth elsewhere establishes the proper safeguards concerning 'possession' of God or revelation, here the emphasis runs in the other direction – God became man in order that we might have and see him. Finally, this act of incarnation is 'an outward activation and revelation of the whole inward riches of His deity'.[70] It is this conjunction of 'activation and revelation' which we will consider for the remainder of this section.

The key to this conjunction between 'activation and revelation' and the resulting reorientation of exemplarism is Barth's doctrine of the Trinity, particularly as it relates to Christology and revelation.[71] God is in himself

---

[69] At the heart of this interpretative blunder is a significant misunderstanding of the nature and implications of Barth's doctrine of revelation, as it is integrated with the doctrines of the Trinity and Christology, and clarified in Barth's treatment of God's being in act.

[70] Elsewhere, with a nod to Irenaeus, Barth states that 'all His activity consists simply in a recapitulation [*Wiederholung*] of His own being. It means that He is also *Himself* outwards in relation to another' (*CD* II/1, 532; *KD*, 598).

[71] Hart likewise contends that the crucial manoeuvre in terms of Barth's unification of revelation and reconciliation has to do with his doctrine of the Trinity: polarity 'between the epistemic and the soteriological ... is alien to the basic substance of Barth's understanding. This is not because he reduces salvation to the dispelling of ignorance through the bestowal of 'knowledge', but because he links these two

living, and relates to his creation by sharing his own proper life with his creation. As Trevor Hart says:

> The 'knowledge' which Barth insists can and does take place … is not an objectifying 'knowledge about'; … it is above all self-involving and self-transforming communion with God as personal Other. For Barth, therefore, revelation and reconciliation/atonement are two aspects of the same reality: they are both ways of referring to what happens and what must happen in order for humans to be drawn into a personal knowing of God.[72]

The key is the sharing or the self-involving act of God which is simultaneously self-revealing and reconciling: the former because it is the very being of God present with us in this event so as to be known, and the latter because it is the very being of God active and therefore effective among and for us. One can equally affirm, therefore, that God saves us by means of his self-revelation, or reveals himself by reconciling us to himself: God's self-revelation is God's act of reconciliation and vice-versa.[73] The centre of the Christian faith is 'the Word of the act or the act of the Word … The

themes together systematically in a way which broadens his model of salvation from a typically Western preoccupation with forensic and moral categories and integrates it more adequately with the doctrine of God as Trinity' (Hart, 'Revelation', 54). Cf. Ruddies, 'Christologie und Versöhnungslehre', 175–7.

[72] Hart, 'Revelation', 42, 54–5.

[73] 'Revelation is reconciliation, as certainly as it is God Himself: God with us; God beside us, and chiefly and decisively, God for us' (Karl Barth, 'Revelation', in *God in Action* (Manhasset, NY: Round Table Press, 1963), 17).

It is not strictly necessary, of course, that revelation and reconciliation be identical. Revelation could just as well mean destruction, and some form of reconciliation could occur in which the rebellious parties are simply put in their places. It is a matter of God's free decision to be in fellowship with human kind that calls for the integration of revelation and reconciliation via God's sharing of himself with his creatures. Such integration is hinted at throughout the Old Testament. On the most remarkable passages in this vein is that of Isa. 6, where Isaiah 'saw the Lord sitting on a throne' (6.1), to which he responds: 'Woe is me! I am lost, for I am a man of unclean lips, and I live among a people of unclean lips; yet my eyes have seen the King, the LORD of hosts!' (6.5). Isaiah knows how closely God's self-revelation and the destruction of the impure go hand in hand. Nevertheless, a remarkable event happens: 'Then one of the seraphs flew to me, holding a live coal that had been taken from the altar with a pair of tongs. The seraph touched my mouth with it and said: "Now that this has touched your lips, your guilt has departed and your sin is blotted out"' (6.6–7). Revelation without atonement, without the removal of guilt and blotting out of sin, means death to the unclean. But the Lord's concern is to commission his witness, sending him to his people – his purpose is to be in fellowship with his people as their Lord. And for this reason, reconciliation and revelation are inseparable – above all in Jesus Christ, but also to a significant measure in the Old Testament.

Word, the Logos, is actually the work, the *ergon*, as well; the *verbum* is also the *opus*' (*DO*, 67).

It is for this reason that Barth writes that 'without the knowledge of God there is no salvation. God's design in His whole action with us ... is in fact that we may know God' (*CD* II/1, 180). Again, 'this seeking and creating [in the work of Creation] is heightened in the work of revelation itself, which is identical [*identisch*] with the reconciliation of sinful man in the incarnation, death and resurrection of the Son of God.... What God does in all this, He is: and He is no other than He who does all this' (*CD* II/1, 274; *KD*, 307). For Barth there is absolutely no distinction between God's self-revelation and the reconciliation accomplished by the death and resurrection of Jesus Christ – they are, strictly speaking, identical.[74] But if that is the case, Barth has validated one of the chief commitments of exemplarism (for the work of Jesus Christ was to reveal, to make known, to teach and to be an example) without in any sense undermining an objective account of the atonement – precisely because God reveals himself in this objective act of reconciliation. Revelation and reconciliation are identical because God reconciles us to himself by bringing his own proper Triune being to bear upon our sinful condition, by seeking and creating fellowship with us by being Himself with and for us.[75]

At the same time as the reconciliation effected by Jesus Christ is the revelation of God, it is the revelation of both sinful and reconciled humankind. 'Jesus Christ is the fellow-man who goes before us as an example and shows us the way ... He is the fellow-man who goes before us as an example and shows us the way because and in the power of the fact that He is "for us ..."' (*CD* IV/1, 229). As this example, as the one who reveals our true nature and vocation, he likewise exposes and reveals our sin: 'only when we know Jesus Christ do we really know that man is the man of sin, and what sin is, and what it means for man' (*CD* IV/1, 389).[76] To integrate these two claims, Jesus Christ is an example inasmuch

---

[74] Although not all these passages make this point quite so strongly, see *CD* I/1, 119, 409; *CD* II/1, 547; *CD* IV/1, 72, 117.

[75] In this, Barth is not so different from the Gospel of John, where the Son is given authority over all flesh that he might give them eternal life (Jn. 17.1–2). This authority has everything to do with the conflict with Satan and the theme of propitiation present throughout the book, wherein we see the active development of Christ's atoning work. However, in the next verse, Jesus explains what he means by 'eternal life', saying: 'This is eternal life, that they may know You, the only true God, and Jesus Christ whom You have sent' (Jn. 17.3). For neither John nor Barth is there a dichotomy between Christ's saving work and the knowledge of God. The two are identical.

[76] This is only confirmed by Barth's claim that: 'Whether they recognise it or not, He is their Head from all eternity. He can be more to them than an example. He can do that which He does actually do in the atonement, representing God to them and them to God. His history can be their own history of salvation' (*CD* IV/2, 36). He is more

as he calls us to follow him. 'The lifting up of themselves for which He gives them freedom is not a movement which is formless, or to which they themselves have to give the necessary form. It takes place in a definite form and direction' (CD IV/2, 533) – a form and direction derived from Christ himself as he 'discloses and reveals Himself to a man in order to claim and sanctify him as His own and as His witness in the world' (CD IV/2, 534).

Why did God become man? What was God's purpose in the death and resurrection of Jesus Christ? According to Barth we can and must affirm that God's purpose was to reveal himself – to seek and create fellowship by making himself known to us, and in so doing to make us known to ourselves.

While there are numerous other standpoints from which we can and must view this event, these other standpoints do not minimize, qualify or undermine the full validity of this statement. We can properly understand the death and resurrection of Jesus Christ from any biblically warranted standpoint only inasmuch as we recognize that this is the event of God's self-revealing activity and that his purpose in this event was to make himself decisively and finally known here and in this way and in these circumstances.

than an example inasmuch as he represents humankind to God and thereby decisively reveals to us our human nature.

4

ATONEMENT AND ATTRIBUTES

Drawing on the previous chapter we now turn to the role of the doctrine of the divine perfections within an account of Christ's saving work. This investigation is integrally related to the doctrine of the Trinity because the perfections in question are those of the essence of the triune God, and receive their fundamental shape and pattern from the doctrine of the Trinity. In other words, the present chapter is a continuation and elaboration of some of the key points raised in the previous chapter, offering the decisive confirmation of the way in which the doctrine of the Trinity plays the critical role of ensuring the correct proportions of the Christian doctrine of atonement.[1] The structure of this chapter will differ from its antecedent, however. Whereas the chapter on the Trinity developed several distinct aspects of the doctrine of the Trinity and their implications for the atonement, this chapter engages in a more sustained and focused analysis of Barth's doctrine of the divine perfections, building toward the development of a single thesis which has a significant bearing upon our understanding of the atonement.

Of all the different forces combining to constitute the terrain of the doctrine of the atonement, the selection and application of the divine attributes is one of the greatest,[2] carving out winding gullies and leaving the soaring columns which characterize the theological landscape. What attribute(s) most clearly define(s) the being of God manifest in the cross? What is the relationship between God's love and his wrath? Is God necessarily just while he freely chooses whether to be merciful? Answers to

---

[1] This is a modification of Webster's broader point concerning the doctrine of salvation (Webster, '*Rector et iudex*', 40).

[2] A typical treatment of this topic affirms something along the following lines: 'It is only when we see the atoning work of Christ against the background of a carefully thought through doctrine of God that the unity of mercy and righteousness can be seen and allowed to come into expression in our formulation of the doctrine of the atonement' (McCormack, *For Us*, 28). My purpose is to expand the scope of this discussion beyond questions pertaining to a handful of attributes.

questions such as these largely account for the unique topography one finds in each distinct theory of the atonement. The purpose of this chapter is to familiarize ourselves with the shaping influence of this doctrine, allowing Karl Barth to guide us to a broader vista of Christ's saving work by exploring his understanding of the divine attributes (henceforth perfections) and applying the fruit of that study to the doctrine of reconciliation. Barth's treatment of these two theological loci and their inter-relationship is highly suggestive, but as we will see his theology of the divine perfections offers a basis for critiquing and extending his treatment of the doctrine of reconciliation.

Our specific concern in this chapter is with the basic dogmatic moves underlying Barth's exposition of the divine perfections in CD II/1[3] in order to assess the harmony of this treatment with that of the doctrine of reconciliation in CD IV, inasmuch as the latter depends upon and interacts with the material developed in the former.[4] First, I take a preliminary glance at the divine perfection Barth apparently emphasizes within his treatments of the doctrine of reconciliation. I then develop some of the central aspects of Barth's theology of the divine perfections. On that basis I conclude with a constructive criticism of Barth's doctrine of reconciliation, proposing a modified approach which more fittingly complies with his theology of the divine perfections.

A First Glance: Barth's Forensic Treatment of Reconciliation

Scholars vary widely in their assessment of Barth's relationship to penal substitution, as evidenced in Garry Williams' recent survey of the discussion. He notes that, according to Cornelius Van Til, Barth denies penal substitution, H. Cunliffe-Jones holds that Barth affirms it, R. G. Crawford

---

[3] Robert B. Price, 'Letters of the Divine Word: The Perfections of God in Karl Barth's *Church Dogmatics*' (PhD diss., University of Aberdeen, 2007), 188.

[4] That is not to suggest that I will explore the question of Barth's theological development. Along those lines, see Bruce McCormack's thesis that Barth errs in CD II/1 (pp. 396, 402) by making the 'death of Christ a satisfaction offered to the divine righteousness', and in doing so 'abstract[ing] righteousness from love as mercy' (McCormack, *For Us*, 30). Given the argument below, I am inclined to think that McCormack overstates his case for the ordering of holiness and righteousness 'under the heading of perfections of the divine loving' (McCormack, *For Us*, 28). Ultimately, love is not and cannot be any more central to the being of God than his righteousness. As long as it is the righteousness *of God* to which satisfaction is made, then we are in no danger. If anything, the problem with Barth's account of the atonement in CD II/1 is that he largely omits the positive aspect of Christ's work of acting righteously for us and establishing us in righteousness as God's new creation.

suggests he has moved beyond it, while Bruce McCormack claims he rescues it; Williams himself thinks finds Barth 'alters penal substitution beyond recognition'.[5] For our purposes, regardless of Barth's specific relationship to the traditional understanding(s) of penal substitution, this debate highlights the fact that Barth develops his substitutionary account of reconciliation within a forensic/judicial framework rooted in a 'central [judicial] metaphor',[6] thus making the debate plausible in the first place.[7]

[5] Williams, 'Karl Barth and the Doctrine of the Atonement', 256–7.
[6] Gunton, *The Actuality of Atonement*, 112. Correctly, I think, Gunton places Barth within the trajectory of Anselm, Luther and Forsyth (why omit Calvin?), all of whom create variations on the judicial conceptual theme. Barth's appreciation for Anselm extends well beyond his famous engagement with the latter's *Proslogion* in Karl Barth, *Anselm: Fides Quaerens Intellectum*, trans. Ian W. Robertson (New York: Meridian Books, 1960). While it is certainly true that Barth is critical of Anselm's *Cur Deus Homo*, he is far more appreciative of this work than Watson seems to recognize (Gordon Watson, 'A Study in St Anselm's Soteriology and Karl Barth's Theological Method', *SJT* 42, no. 4 (1989), 493–592. As Eberhard Busch notes, Barth's 'first intensive encounter [in the summer of 1926] gave him a great deal to think about – "somehow" he is certainly right' (Eberhard Busch, *Karl Barth: His Life from Letters and Autobiographical Texts*, trans. John Bowden (Philadelphia, PA: Fortress, 1976), 169, 205. Turning to the *CD*, we see Barth's comment that 'we must not make this [that he has suffered this punishment of ours] a main concept, as in some of the older presentations of the doctrine of the atonement (especially those which follow [*Nachfolgen*] Anselm of Canterbury) ... or that ... He 'satisfied' or offered satisfaction to the wrath of God' (*CD* IV/1, 253; *KD*, 279). This is likely not directed towards Anselm himself (as the latter saw a dichotomy between punishment and satisfaction), but rather against those who came after him ('follow' [*Nachfolgen*] is here meant chronologically, as opposed to materially in the sense of adhering to his teaching). While Barth critiques Anselm for minimizing God's forgiveness in favour of his righteousness (*CD* IV/1, 486–7), effectively siding with Thomas in doing so, this should in no way minimize Barth's debt to and appreciation for Anselm's contribution to the doctrine of the atonement, manifest, among other ways, in Barth's appropriation of Anselm's questions (*CD* IV/1, 212, 407) and in his reformulation of a satisfaction theory (focused on God's loving wrath) of the atonement. Cf. *CD* IV/1, 254–5, 276, 281. Elsewhere, Barth refers to Christ's work as that of 'making satisfaction and interceding', among other things (Barth, *The Humanity of God*, 47). For more on Barth and Anselm, cf. Bakker, 'Jesus als Stellvertreter', 43–4; Klappert, *Die Auferweckung*, 221–2. Of further interest may be Günter Thomas' article, although there is some question as to whether he accurately interprets Anselm's doctrine of satisfaction (Thomas, 'Der für uns "gerichtete Richter"', 212–14).
[7] Klappert and McCormack note this forensic framework in Klappert, *Die Auferweckung*, 198, 277; McCormack, *For Us*, 32. This emphasis is no less true for the fact that 'although the traditional themes of punishment and penalty are not eliminated from Barth's account of Christ's death, they are displaced from being central or predominant' (Hunsinger, 'Karl Barth's Christology', 136). Barth develops his understanding of the relationship between grace and judgement within a primarily forensic or judicial standpoint of the atonement. It is interesting to note that it has received some attention among 'non-violent' studies of the atonement, largely due to the emphasis highlighted

Barth's emphasis on a judicial framework, it appears, was consistent. He offers one of his first sustained reflections on Christ's saving work in the *Church Dogmatics* in his treatment of the divine perfections (published in 1940), in the context of the divine grace and holiness and the divine mercy and righteousness (*CD* II/1, 351-406).[8] In a representative passage, he writes: 'The fact that it was God's Son... who took our place on Golgotha and thereby freed us from the divine anger and judgment, reveals first the full implication of the wrath of God, of His condemning and punishing justice [*verurteilende und strafende Gerechtigkeit Gottes*]' (*CD* II/1, 398; *KD*, 450). Six years later, in the *Dogmatics in Outline*, he writes: 'In the death of Jesus Christ God has accomplished His law [*Recht*]... He has acted as Judge [*als Richter*] towards man' (*DO*, 116; *DG*, 137). Barth continues his emphasis on God's justice in *CD* IV/1 (published 1953) in the section 'The Judge Judged in Our Place' (pp. 211–83). Summarizing his argument, he writes:

We are now at the end of the important section dealing with ... what Jesus Christ was and did *pro nobis* ... To this question we have given four related answers. He took our place as Judge [*als der Richter*]. He took our place as the judged [*als Gerichteter*]. He was judged

by Hunsinger. Cf. Michael Hardin, 'Out of the Fog: New Horizons for Atonement Theory', in *Stricken by God? Nonviolent Identification and the Victory of Christ*, eds Brad Jersak and Michael Hardin (Grand Rapids, MI: Eerdmans, 2007), 56n7.

So far as I am aware, there is little question that Barth's account is substitutionary. He writes: 'we have had to develop [our theology] in this first part of the doctrine of reconciliation as the doctrine of substitution [*Stellvertretung*]' (*CD* IV/1, 273; *KD*, 300). Colin Gunton notes that 'Barth is definitely therefore putting forward a substitutionary Cross', proceeding to note how Barth's account differs from a strictly penal view (Gunton, *The Barth Lectures*, 183). Elsewhere Barth writes that 'the picture before us is that of an inconceivable exchange [*unbegreiflichen Tausches*], of a *katalage*, that is, a substitution [*Vertauschung*]. Man's reconciliation with God takes place through God's putting Himself in man's place [*Stelle*] and man's being put in God's place [*Stelle*], as a sheer act of grace. It is this inconceivable miracle which is our reconciliation [*Versöhnung*]' (*DO*, 115; *DG*, 135). Cf. Barth, *Table Talk*, 52.

My own view is that Barth's doctrine of reconciliation includes within it all that penal substitution affirms, while offering larger and more encompassing account of Christ's substitutionary work.

[8] McCormack, *For Us*, 28. Barth offers a treatment of the atonement earlier in *CD* II/1 (pp. 148-62) where he writes along the same forensic/juridical lines: 'He has taken to Himself the very accusation which was directed against us, the very judgment which was passed upon us. He has borne the punishment which was rightly ours' (p. 152). Earlier (1934), Barth wrote: 'Yes, exactly in the depths of our misery He intercedes for us, and substitutes Himself for us, warding off the wages justly due us and suffering and making restitution what we could not suffer and where we could not make restitution.' Barth, 'Revelation', 16–17.

[*gerichtet*] in our place. And He acted justly [*Rechte getan*] in our place. (*CD* IV/1, 273; *KD*, 300)[9]

Judge, judged, judgement and justice: judicial/forensic terminology seems to be at the heart of Barth's treatment of Christ's person and work. Although he certainly brings other aspects of God's being into his account, justice is the primary attribute in his account (but to be sure this is done in such a way that it is properly and consistently related to God's mercy and grace).[10]

But does Barth warrant his emphasis of the judicial aspect of Christ's work *pro nobis*, considered from the vantage-point of the doctrine of the divine perfections? How does he understand God's perfections, and does his account exonerate this emphasis on one aspect of God's being? To answer these questions we will explore three of the foundational aspects of Barth's theology of the divine perfections, each of which is thoroughly rooted in the doctrine of the Trinity. First, we consider in some depth the Trinitarian nature of Barth's account, both in terms of its dogmatic location and the basic pattern of his treatment. Second, we briefly note the dialectic of love and freedom shaping the structure of Barth's account. Finally we explore Barth's resistance to systematization through his focus on the triune and

---

[9] Although I am not able to address this here, note Thomas' interesting critique of Barth's judicial understanding of Christ's work, based on the fact that in the Old Testament judicial matters take place in a three-fold relation (between the judge, plaintiff and defendant) rather than two-fold relation (between the judge and the one judged) (Thomas, 'Der für uns "gerichtete Richter"', 219–22.

[10] Barth does not limit himself to the forensic framework. For instance, he preaches to the prisoners in Basel: 'He took human nature upon himself ... in order to put an end to the world's fight against him and also itself, and to replace man's disorder by God's design ... he not only bandaged, but healed the wounds of the world ... he delivered us from evil and took us to his heart as his children ... It happened through this man on the cross that God cancelled out and swept away all our human wickedness, our pride, our anxiety, our greed and our false pretences.' Summing up, he says: 'This is reconciliation: his damnation our liberation, his defeat our victory, his mortal pain the beginning of our joy, his death the birth of our life' (Karl Barth, 'The Criminals with Him', in *Deliverance to the Captives* (New York: Harper & Row, 1961), 79–80). Barth's forensic emphasis occurs within a broad and varied affirmation of different aspects of Christ's work, as suggested by Bloesch's comment that 'all the mainline views of the atonement are to be found in Barth in some degree or other, but he brings into the pictures something new. He does not abandon traditional concepts such as substitution, satisfaction, and penal redemption (despite what Arnold Come alleges), but he sees them in a new context. He deepens and radicalizes their meaning' (Donald G. Bloesch, *Jesus is Victor! Karl Barth's Doctrine of Salvation* (Nashville, TN: Abingdon, 1976), 43). To add to Bloesch's point, one can find much more than the 'mainline views' – hints of Irenaeus (*CD* II/1, 532), Anselm (*CD* II/1, 400), Hugo Grotius (*CD* II/1, 401), John McCleod Campbell (*CD* IV/1, 172, 259) and others permeate Barth's work (not to suggest that these 'hints' indicate intentional references to these theologians or their views).

living God. The result of this inquiry will be a firm platform from which to assess Barth's doctrine of reconciliation in its relationship with that of the divine perfections, which in turn provides the material for my constructive criticism.

The Trinity and the Divine Perfections

The single most significant factor for understanding Barth's doctrine of the divine perfections is its relationship to the doctrine of the Trinity. Daniel Migliore, acclaiming Barth as 'the most influential Trinitarian theologian of the modern era', contends that the latter 'finds the key to a Christian doctrine of the divine attributes … in a Trinitarian understanding of God centered in the person and work of Jesus Christ'.[11] Price notes this connection throughout his dissertation, arguing that:

> For Barth, the Trinitarian relations both ground and limit what he is willing to say … In other words, God's triunity can clearly be seen here as more basic to Barth's understanding of God than the divine perfections. From the very first descriptive paragraph of his exposition … Barth is not merely presupposing a doctrine of the Trinity, but actively employing it as a primary dogma in shaping secondary dogmatic concepts.[12]

Barth explicitly develops his account of the divine perfections upon the foundation of the doctrine of the Trinity, and furthermore allows the pattern established by the latter to characterize his understanding of the perfections individually and in relation to each other. To better understand Barth's interweaving of these two dogmatic loci, I distinguish between the Trinitarian (1) *basis* and (2) *pattern* of Barth's doctrine of the divine perfections.

Trinitarian Basis

The first and most obvious point to consider is Barth's location of the doctrine of the divine perfections within that of the Trinity. According

---

[11] Daniel L. Migliore, *Faith Seeking Understanding: An Introduction to Christian Theology* (Grand Rapids, MI: Eerdmans, 2004), 84. Not all of Barth's expositors are optimistic about the Trinitarian nature of Barth's treatment of the perfections. Gunton argues that, despite Barth's intent, his view is essentially binitarian (Colin E. Gunton, *Act and Being: Towards a Theology of the Divine Attributes* (Grand Rapids, MI: Eerdmans, 2003), 103). Von Balthasar, in a more general comment, suggests that Barth, like Thomas, does not allow the Trinity to play a central role in shaping his theology. Hans Urs von Balthasar, *The Theology of Karl Barth: Exposition and Interpretation*, trans. Edward T. Oakes (San Francisco, CA: Ignatius, 1992), 260.

[12] Price, 'Letters', 131.

to Barth, God is one personal essence or being (*Wesen* or *Sein*) eternally existing in three modes of being (*Seinsweisen*). The three-fold repetition of the one divine essence accounts for the unity of God, who is one person and bears one name, as well as God's threeness, as he exists only in the repetition of his own being and therefore in eternal and personal relationship to himself. Barth integrates his doctrine of the divine perfections with that of the Trinity by specifying them as the perfections of the one divine essence: 'to speak of God's attributes as we must and may do, since we are speaking of Him on the ground of His revelation, means therefore to speak ... of His being [*Wesen*]' (*CD* II/1, 323; *KD*, 364).

Each of God's 'many individual and distinct perfections ... is nothing else but God Himself, His one, simple, distinctive being [*sein eines, einfaches, ihm eigenes Wesen ist*]' (*CD* II/1, 322; *KD*, 362). Each perfection is identical with the one being (*Wesen*) of God, for 'if we are dealing with God ... every quality predicated of God, as the description of a specific self-exposition of the predicated Subject, can only denote God Himself ... in the perfection of His being [*seines Seins*]: in scholastic parlance, not a mere *accidens*, but the *substantia* or *essentia* of God; this substance or essence in a specific self-exposition, but in its totality' (*CD* IV/2, 756; *KD*, 858).[13] Barth thus clearly locates the divine perfections in the divine essence (and therefore in the threefold repetition of that essence as the Father, Son and Holy Spirit), carefully coordinating the doctrines of the Trinity and divine perfections. Accordingly, 'no attribute, no act of God is not in the same way the attribute or act of the Father, the Son and the Spirit' (*CD* I/1, 362; cf. 375).[14] As God exists and lives eternally only in his three modes of being, so the perfections of God exist only in the Father, Son and Holy Spirit as the perfections of this one being in its three modes. The perfections thus characterize God's own eternal life of fellowship with himself and serve as the antecedent basis in God for the kind of fellowship and life he shares with us.

In confirmation, Barth writes: 'since God is Father, Son and Holy Ghost, i.e., loves in freedom, every perfection exists essentially in Him [*Indem Gott der Vater, der Sohn und der Heilige Geist ist und das heißt: liebt in der Freiheit, ist ihm jede Vollkommenheit wesentlich zu eigen*]' (*CD* II/1, 323, *KD*, 363). This sentence, isolated between two passages of fine print and seemingly out of context in the beginning of Barth's summary treatment of 'The Perfections of God' (*CD* 2.1, §29), is highly informative. That God is

---

[13] Earlier in the *CD*, Barth wrote: 'it may be said of this essence [*Wesen*] of God that its unity ... consists in the threeness of the "persons"' (*CD* I/1, 349–50; *KD* 369).

[14] 'All the attributes of God are identical with God's essence; but his essence is his being and act as Father, Son and Holy Spirit' (John Webster, *Holiness* (London: SCM, 2003), 32). Later, Webster adds that the 'different divine attributes do not, therefore, denote separate parts of God ... Rather the enumeration of divine attributes is simply a designation of God's simple essence' (Webster, *Holiness*, 37).

triune and that He loves in freedom is an analytic truth for Barth. That God 'loves in freedom' is simply a restatement of the doctrine of God in terms of the perfections of God's being (*Wesen*) rather than the personality of his being (doctrine of the Trinity). But because this is so, because the perfections of the divine being are expressions and translations of the loving freedom of God, it follows that they are likewise expressions of the divine being, and exist essentially in God. Since God is Triune, since God is the One who by very nature loves in freedom, every perfection exists essentially in him.

To sum up: it is impossible to know the triune God without knowing the divine perfections and vice versa, because they are two aspects of the one divine essence that confronts us in the act of self-revelation. While the doctrine of the Trinity speaks of the subject of the act of revelation, the doctrine of the divine perfections speaks of perfections of this subject, and in this way the two doctrines are inseparable. It is thus

> impossible to have knowledge of God Himself without having knowledge of a divine perfection [and vice versa] ... For as the triune God, both in regard to His revelation and to His being in itself, He exists in these perfections, and these perfections again exist in Him and only in Him as the One who, both in His revelation and in eternity, is the same. (*CD* II/1, 323–4)

The Trinitarian Pattern

With this first step, however, we have only just begun to consider the integration of these two doctrines. While locating the doctrine of the divine perfections within that of the Trinity is Barth's first and decisive step, of itself this does not seem particularly impressive. The significance of his vision becomes far more evident as he draws upon the resources within this move, marshalling the doctrine of the Trinity to shape his exposition of the divine perfections.[15] The most decisive influence along these lines is that

---

[15] Barth is careful to distinguish these two doctrines (Trinity and divine perfection). A translation error refers to God's grace as a 'distinctive mode of God's being' (*CD* II/1, 353). In fact, Barth does not use 'mode' language here, which he reserves to distinguish the doctrine of the Trinity. As Price notes, '"Sein und Sichverhalten Gottes" is twice rendered "God's mode of being" (rather than, e.g., "God's being and conduct"), suggesting a fourth hypostasis in the Godhead to readers familiar with the parallel rendering of Barth's well-known *Seinsweise*' (Price, 'Letters', 58n11). What then is the difference between a mode of God's being and a perfection of his being? Recall from Chapter 2 that Barth distinguishes between the spirit and nature of God. The two are inseparable of course, but God is both in their inseparability. To speak of a mode of God's being emphasizes the eternal self-repetition of the personal God, while to describe the perfections of the divine being refer to the diversity in which the divine nature exists. The one personal God in the fullness of the divine perfections exists from eternity and in no other form than in the three modes of his being as Father, Son and

the doctrine of the Trinity provides the internal basis within the doctrine of God for the same pattern of the one and the many to be played out within the divine perfections. As the one living God is simultaneously many, existing from eternity in self-repetition as Father, Son and Holy Spirit, so his perfections likewise are both one and many, receiving this utterly unique and decisive characteristic from the doctrine of the Trinity.

Barth speaks of the 'unity of identity and non-identity, movement and peace, simplicity and multiplicity' of the divine being that 'is inevitable if God is triune', affirming that 'it certainly follows from God's triunity that the one whole divine being ... must be at the same time identical with itself and non-identical, simple and multiple, a life both in movement and at peace' (CD II/1, 660).[16] Decisively for our interests, he notes a correspondence in which the particular triunity of God (one personal essence in three eternal modes of being) demands certain implications for the consideration of the perfections of God's being. Because God is the triune God, who exists only as Father, Son and Holy Spirit, it follows that the perfections of God's one being bear the impression of that triunity. Barth carefully specifies this correspondence, however, opting for a formal (unity in diversity) rather than a material (unity in trinity) pattern that governs his treatment of the divine perfections. 'It does not follow from His triunity that his being is three-fold in the sense that His perfection consists of three parts ... His being is whole and undivided, and therefore all His perfections are equally the being of all three modes of the divine being' (CD II/1, 660).[17] While the number of divine perfections could, supposedly, have been three just as there are three divine modes of being, the more important claim is that the doctrine of the Trinity involves a specific kind of unity in diversity within and proper to the divine being which in turn serves as the foundation for understanding the unity in diversity of the perfections of that being (which, according to Scripture, turn out to be far more than three). As the

Holy Spirit, wherein both the spirit and nature of the Godhead is fully and eternally repeated. Modes of being is therefore a more foundational dogmatic concept, which includes and gives shape to the idea of the divine perfections.

[16] Following Barth, I do not make extensive use of the doctrine of divine simplicity in this book. While Barth affirmed the doctrine (CD II/1, 445–61), he was concerned that it not take on a life of its own in abstract form where it can become a controlling principle (CD II/1, 329). Rather, in affirming that God is simple, Barth sought to ensure that 'the relation between subject and predicate' remained irreversible (CD II/1, 448), such that 'He is One [or simple] even in the distinctions of the divine persons of the Father, the Son and the Holy Spirit' (CD II/1, 445). In short, Barth is deeply committed to divine simplicity, as long as we allow the triune God in his history with us to shape our understanding of what his unique simplicity means.

[17] This is the basis for Holmes' point that 'Just as God's oneness includes his threeness, the one God includes within himself a multitude of perfections' (Holmes, Revisiting, 76). The 'just as' in question pertains to the formal pattern of the doctrine of the Trinity permeating Barth's doctrine of the divine perfections.

doctrines of the Trinity and the divine perfections explore the one divine essence, the pattern derived from the former provides the basis for properly understanding the latter.

In other words, the specific unity in multiplicity of the Trinity justifies and necessitates the distinct but related form of the unity and multiplicity of the divine perfections, as the two are the repetitions of the self-same being. 'Because we are thinking of God Himself, we are thinking of the One who at the same time, in confirmation and glorification of His oneness, is also many' (CD II/1, 323). This pattern of the one and the many, rooted specifically in the triune being of God, profoundly shapes Barth's treatment of the perfections both structurally and in specific detail, demanding an exacting unity to the whole, while likewise calling for great diversity and breadth in his treatment.

That the one God is many thus opens the door to the doctrine of the divine perfections 'in an exact parallel [genauen Parallele] to the concern of the doctrine of the Holy Trinity', without necessitating a form of modalism in which God's perfections are a function of his relationship to that which is outside of himself (CD II/1, 326–7; KD, 367).[18] That is to say, Barth affirms that the 'multiplicity, individuality and diversity of God's perfections are rooted in His own being and not in His participation in the character of other beings' (CD II/1, 333; cf. 612). The one God brings the multiplicity of his perfections that are proper to his eternal triune life to bear upon his creation for the purpose of seeking and creating fellowship with it. This multiplicity, however, is the multiplicity of God's oneness. Returning to our Trinitarian parallel, 'as it is of decisive importance not to dissolve the unity of the Godhead tritheistically ... so it is of equal importance to interpret God's glory and perfections, not in and for themselves, but as the glory of the Lord who alone is able to establish, disclose and confirm them as real glory' (CD II/1, 327). There exists 'another' within the Trinity and within the divine perfections only inasmuch 'as it is still one and the same thing' (CD II/1, 368). As we move from a first to a second, we do so solely because the second is 'utterly identical' with the first [dieses Zweite ganz und gar das Eine ist] (CD II/1, 375; KD, 422). Accordingly, in each perfection we encounter the 'one complete essence' of God (CD II/1, 491). The unity of God thus prevents a tritheistic understanding of the perfections in which God's perfections can be more or less essential, or so distinct as to be in conflict.

Naturally enough, Barth brings the Trinitarian doctrine of perichoresis developed in CD I/1 to bear upon his discussion of the divine perfections,

---

[18] According to Christopher Holmes, 'Barth's chief worry is that a doctrine of the divine attributes funded by nominalism understands God's simplicity to exclude multiplicity' (ibid., 55). Whether or not this is Barth's 'chief worry', it is certainly a view that he is eager to ward off.

so as to facilitate this inter-working of their unity and diversity and further integrate the doctrines of the Trinity and divine perfections. Noting the *perichoresis* of God's three *Seinsweisen*, Barth concludes that 'the divine being draws from [the doctrine of perichoresis] ... the outer perfection of its form, its thorough-going distinctiveness, as the unity of identity and non-identity, movement and peace, simplicity and multiplicity' (*CD* II/1, 660) of its account of the divine perfections. Christopher Holmes explains that 'as the three modes of being of God only live in and through one another, so the perfections of God live through and in one another'.[19] While Barth delves into each distinct perfection in full cognizance that this one perfection is the whole essence of God, he does so inclusively, such that the material development of any one perfection always seeks to assume and anticipate 'in the true sense the content' of that which is to follow (cf. *CD* II/1, 440). Because each perfection is the perfection of the one essence of God and fully expresses the nature of that one essence, it necessarily includes within it the multiplicity of the other divine perfections in which the one divine essence consists.[20]

To anticipate, we can begin to sense the momentous implications that such a Trinitarian view of the divine perfections has for the doctrine of the atonement. Every concrete account of Christ's work depends on one or more divine perfections as that which gives traction to its account of the dilemma of sin and the intervention of God in Christ. The unity and diversity of God's perfections demands that our account of God's work in Christ reflect this unity and diversity, exploring the relationship of each of the divine perfections to Christ's work, pushing us well beyond the well-known territory of thinking through Christ's passion in light of God's mercy and wrath or his love and righteousness.

The Love/Freedom Dialectic

The Trinitarian pattern of the divine perfections does not mean, however, that the order of their treatment is haphazard or inconsequential. Just as we know the Father through the incarnate Son as revealed to us by the Holy Spirit, just as we know the hidden God through his self-revelation, so we know the divine perfections in a dialectic of revealedness and hiddenness,

---

[19] *Ibid.*, 59.

[20] In line with the perichoretic relationship between the divine perfections, Barth draws on his distinction between *Ferne* and *Trennung* pertaining the notion of separation within the doctrine of the Trinity so as to allow for a distinction [*unterscheiden*] without separation [*trennen*] in the divine perfections (e.g. *CD* II/1, 360; *KD*, 405). On this basis, for example, Barth writes that 'God's knowledge, will and action cannot be divided [*abspalten*]', although we can distinguish them and speak of them individually (*CD* II/1, 578; *KD*, 651).

in which we take as our 'fundamental point of departure the truth that God is for us fully revealed and fully concealed in His self-disclosure' (*CD* II/1, 341). In the act of self-revelation, God reveals himself as the hidden God, which is to say that he is the one who creates fellowship with us and makes himself known to us only 'in the miracle of His good pleasure' and therefore not by any actualization of our own inherent capacities and abilities (*CD* II/1, 182).[21] The doctrine of the divine perfections seeks to reflect this relationship between revelation and hiddenness in the structure of its account.

Barth's thesis concerning the simultaneity of God's hiddenness and self-revelation is essential for properly understanding the structure of his account of the divine perfections, especially given a particularly infelicitous comment by Barth in this context. He writes: 'this unity and this distinction [of God's self-disclosure and also his concealment] corresponds to the unity and distinction in God's own being between His love and His freedom [*Diese Einheit und dieser Unterschied trifft nun aber zusammen mit der Einheit und dem Unterschied in Gottes Wesen: zwischen seiner Liebe und seiner Freiheit*]' (*CD* II/1, 343; *KD*, 385–6). As Price notes, 'these lines are easily misread as implying that it is *strictly* in God's love that he is knowable and *strictly* in his freedom that he is unknowable'.[22] Were this to be the case, Barth would deny precisely the unity which he seeks to affirm, such that God's hiddenness and revelation are not simultaneous but rather are two different events, rooted in two different aspects of God's being – freedom and love respectively. But love does not correspond to God's self-revelation any more than his freedom corresponds to his hiddenness, for 'we do not know what love is and we do not know what freedom is; but *God* is love and *God* is freedom' (*DO*, 39). In Christ, God's love is just as much hidden as his freedom is revealed, which is to say that both God's love and God's freedom are simultaneously revealed and hidden – a claim equally valid for each of the divine perfections.[23]

---

[21] That 'God is fully revealed and fully concealed in his self-disclosure' (*CD* II/1, 341–4), and that 'the hiddenness of God is the inconceivability of the Father, Son and Holy Spirit' (*CD* II/1, 197) undermines Colin Gunton's thesis concerning an imbalance in Barth's account of the divine perfections inasmuch as it focuses on the Father and Son while ignoring or minimizing the Holy Spirit (Gunton, *Act and Being*, 102–3). The basis of Gunton's argument is the assumption that the perfections of love relate to the Son and those of freedom to the Father. In fact, love and freedom are equally manifest in the Son, and therefore Gunton's Trinitarian critique fails to hit the mark. As Barth notes, 'no attribute, no act of God is not in the same way the attribute or act of the Father, Son and Spirit' (*CD* I/1, 362). Cf. Price, 'Letters', 58.

[22] Price, 'Letters', 48.

[23] *Ibid.*, 49. A significant implication of Barth's approach is that it eschews a distinction between the divine perfections as those of 'God for us' and 'God in Himself' (*CD* II/1, 345). God in his freedom is for us, and in his love is unknowable to us apart from

What then are we to make of this correspondence? According to Price, 'the correspondence between the dialectic of God's revelation (unveiling and veiling) and the dialectic of his being (love and freedom) which Barth intends to capture is as follows: each perfection is unveiled when considered on its own and veiled when considered in light of its unity with its counterpart and with the other perfections'.[24] Because we cannot 'confess simultaneously both our knowing and our not knowing' as is demanded of us by the doctrine of the divine attributes (CD II/1, 342), we must emphasize both factors, 'alongside each other and therefore successively – God's self-disclosure and also His concealment' (CD II/1, 343). Returning to Price's point, we call attention to God's self revelation by considering one of the divine perfections on its own (in light of the event of God's self-revelation in Jesus Christ), but then acknowledge the hiddenness of that divine perfection by proceeding to consider it in light of the other divine perfections. While Barth here emphasizes the movement from love to freedom, 'the logic works the other way round when it comes to the perfections of the divine freedom'.[25] The key to the correspondence thus lies in the relationship of unity and simultaneity governing the two dialectics, rather than a strict correspondence of love to revealedness and freedom to hiddenness.[26]

And what of the structure of Barth's treatment of the divine perfections, characterized as it is by the relationship between love and freedom? According to Price, 'it is crucial to realize ... that there remains a distinction between the two dialectics, and that it is the dialectic of God's being, the dialectic of his loving and his freedom, and not the dialectic of his revelation (veiling and unveiling), which orders Barth's exposition'.[27] Barth does not move from the known to the unknown (dialectic of revelation), but rather within that which is both known and unknown (dialectic of God's being), in such a way that 'the dialectic between love and freedom of God can be a means to this end'.[28] This dialectic is only a means because ultimately the Trinitarian foundation of the divine perfections eschews any ultimate pairing of the divine perfections. Any 'counterparts' within the divine perfections ultimately take place within and are subsumed by a far broader

his self-revelation. Barth thus entirely excludes the distinction between immanent and economic attributes as having no basis in the event of revelation and therefore in the theological task of the Church.

[24] Ibid., 50.
[25] Ibid. Cf. CD II/1, 440–1.
[26] The same holds true for Barth's claim concerning 'the movement of life in which God is God ... corresponding exactly to His revelation of Himself as God' (CD II/1, 350). The point, once again, is to affirm the exact correspondence of the 'full reciprocity' and to deny a 'difference of value' (CD II/1, 350).
[27] Price, 'Letters', 49.
[28] Ibid.

and richer relationship with the other divine perfections. Nonetheless, the dialectic of revelation (veiling and unveiling) throughout Barth's treatment plays a significant if chastened role. Although this dialectic is not identical to that of the divine being, it nonetheless emphasizes the order of divine revelation, facilitating the theological task in its attempt to root itself first and foremost in what God has in fact done for us, facilitating the eschewing of natural theology. The order of love and freedom, therefore, is not essential but rather pragmatic.[29] As Holmes notes, 'the duality ... is

[29] To be sure, Barth writes that 'the order in which these two series of divine attributes are formulated is not a matter of indifference'. Although it may seem that 'we can begin and end at either point ... without incurring any particular danger', in fact 'the logical rigour of the dialectic which occupies us must not conceal from us the fact that we are not concerned with any sort of dialectic but with the very special dialectic of the revelation and being of God' (CD II/1, 348). Barth's point is polemical, however. His concern is with the tendency of theologians to first treat of God's being in general and only then of his triune nature. In principle, there is no impediment to beginning with the freedom of God, as long as the freedom in question is that made known to us in Christ. While Barth goes so far as to claim that there is an 'intrinsic order of the divine life', in which 'He is first of all the One who loves and then and as such the One who is free', and that this 'sequence can be reversed only arbitrarily and at the cost of great artificiality and misapprehension' (CD II/1, 351–2), this is, in fact, a blurring of the distinction between the dialectics of revelation and the being of God which is ultimately inconsistent with Barth's thought, motivated largely by polemical concerns.

   To balance the passages just quoted, it might be helpful to note a passage in which Barth argues for the reversibility of the treatment of the divine love and freedom. Towards the end of his treatment of the perfections of the divine loving, Barth offers a provisional conclusion, noting that he has just explored the idea of God's love as that of the 'grace, mercy and patience of God' in relationship to a 'second set of ideas – holiness, righteousness and wisdom' (CD II/1, 422). The first set expresses or translates the love of God, while the second does so by expressing 'with greater distinctness than the first ... the fact that it is His free and therefore distinctively divine love'. What is so important for my thesis is that Barth then claims that 'our experience would have been the same if we had begun with the second set of ideas [i.e. those relating to the divine freedom]. In our next section [CD II/1, §31] we shall in fact begin with the ideas which more definitely characterize and describe the freedom of God as His love. And we shall then find the same thing' (CD II/1, 422). In other words, Barth here concedes the possibility of beginning with the perfections of the divine freedom.

   It is altogether too easy to see why G. Williams questions the nature of this sequence, writing: 'It is one thing to say that divine mercy and righteousness must always agree in their outworking ... It is quite another thing to claim, as Barth does, that "divine mercy necessarily precedes" righteousness ... Barth eschews the picture of the divine attributes as points on the surface of a sphere, all equidistant from the centre, thereby rejecting the classical doctrine of divine simplicity (CD II/1, 376). Such a privileging of mercy is incompatible with the equal ultimacy of the divine attributes entailed by the classical and Reformed doctrine of God' (Williams, 'Karl Barth and the Doctrine of the Atonement', 259). A comparison of this passage with CD II/1, 406 shows that Barth's position is not as opposed to the classical Reformed tradition on this point as might appear. Barth's emphasis has to do with an order within equality based on the

also *relative*; the perfections appropriate to love and those appropriate to freedom are the perfections of the same indissoluble Subject who is both love and freedom; the same speaking and acting subject who posits himself as Father, Son and Holy Spirit. And yet, the duality, though not absolute, must, nonetheless, be preserved.'[30]

Barth's acknowledgement of this duality characterizes the structure of his exposition of the perfections, as he begins with the perfections of the divine love (*CD* II/1, §30) and follows with those of the divine freedom (*CD* II/1, §31). Within these two movements Barth further utilizes this thesis, pairing perfections of the divine love with those of the divine freedom that 'express with greater distinctness than the first ... the fact that it is His free and therefore distinctively divine love' (*CD* II/1, 422), and vice versa with the perfections of the divine freedom. At every point of Barth's treatment, however, the material development threatens to burst its banks and overwhelm the framework of the dialectic between God's love and his freedom, for ultimately the foundational Trinitarian framework will not allow such a dialectic to suffice.

Resisting Systematization

Through his focus on the living God via the person and work of Jesus Christ, Barth's treatment of the divine perfections consistently resists systematization, noting 'that what appears to be an unavoidable systema-tization [*unvermeidlicher Systematik*] is only a means to an end' (*CD* II/1, 352; *KD*, 396).[31] Appreciating this theme guides us into the heart of Barth's exposition of the divine perfections, inoculates us against prevalent misinterpretations of his thought, and prepares us for our query concerning the relationship between the doctrine of the atonement and that of the divine perfections.

For Barth, as we saw in Chapter 2, the act of God in Jesus Christ as witnessed by Scripture is the centre of and concrete basis for his theology. Naturally, therefore, Jesus Christ is the centre of and concrete basis for his account of the divine perfections. Barth writes:

> Any denial of the fullness of God's presence in [Jesus Christ] will precipitate us into darkness and confusion ... Without the key to the whole ... we will not find ... [or] be able to recognize and praise Him as God, for we will meet Him only in the diversity, in the curious

logic of revelation, which is itself rooted in the very logic of the Trinity in the eternal generation and submission of the Son.

[30] Holmes, *Revisiting*, 61.
[31] Cf. *CD* II/1, 442.

details and puzzling contradictions of His presence. We will then have to fall back, according to the best of our knowledge and belief and our judgment from some other point of view, upon another basis of unity for His presence. (*CD* II/1, 319)

The fullness of God's presence in the person and work of Jesus Christ is the key to the unity of the divine perfections – in Jesus Christ God is present in such a way that everything he is, all the perfections that are proper to his being as God, are fully enacted in this event. This is the 'key to the whole', as Barth calls it. Consequently, unifying concepts or systematizing patterns play a strictly subservient role in Barth's treatment, depending on their relationship to this 'key' to prevent their becoming merely attempts 'according to the best of our knowledge', or 'judgment[s] from some other point of view'.

That is to say, the relation of subject and predicate is irreversible (*CD* II/1, 448, 493): the subject Jesus Christ is the ultimate basis and warrant for the predicates we attribute to God. 'We do not know what love is and we do not know what freedom is; but *God* is love and *God* is freedom. What [these are] we have to learn from Him. As predicate to this subject it may be said that He is the God of free love' (*DO*, 39). We do not take that which is known and attribute it to God. Rather, through our knowledge of God in the person and work of Jesus Christ we come to know what he is like, we come to recognize his perfections through their outworking in the life of God. Likewise, the subject Jesus Christ is the ultimate basis and warrant for the concepts and systematization we use in speaking of the divine perfections – just as we allow the subject to inform us of his perfec-tions (an irreversible order for Barth), so we allow the subject to inform us of the concepts or ordering principles we use (e.g. the traditional conception of communicable and incommunicable attributes [cf. *CD* II/1, 345]).

All that to say, Barth gives precedence to the subject of revelation, striving to bring his treatment and ordering of the multitude of divine perfections into alignment with this one subject. As Price notes:

> The welcome sharpness of Barth's initial description of a given perfection fades as exposition continues, and one suddenly finds oneself staring yet again at some aspect of how God has reconciled the world to himself in Christ. But this is precisely Barth's point. He has not lost the plot, but brought it to its climax. God's perfections are those of his enacted identity and must remain transparent to it.[32]

God's perfections are those of the living God – the priority is incontestable. The very term for which Barth opts, 'perfection', is intended to point 'at

---

[32] Price, 'Letters', 181.

once to the thing itself instead of merely to its formal aspect' (*CD* II/1, 322); the 'thing itself' is the one perfect essence of the triune God enacted in the person and work of Jesus Christ. The task of the doctrine of the divine perfections is thus to name and describe again and again the ever rich God in the abundance of the perfections in which his unity consists.

Barth, then, derives the concepts he employs, and the predicates he ascribes to the divine being, from the one perfect being of God fully manifest to us in the person and work of Jesus Christ. As a result, 'there is no divine predicate with a special content of what God is – there is only the divine subject in the fullness of the divine predicates' (*CD* II/1, 300). Likewise, no proposition (i.e. divine predicate) is the 'final word or guiding principle [*lezten Wort … Leitsatz oder Prinzip*]' (*CD* II/1, 407; *KD*, 458). Thus, for instance, despite the fact that in the *CD* we move from God's grace to his holiness, in doing so we do not cling 'stubbornly to our idea of grace as the focal point [*Mittelpunkt*]' (*CD* II/1, 359; *KD*, 403), for it is God himself 'whose simplicity is abundance itself' (*CD* II/1, 406) that is the focal point. To speak properly of God's perfections, we must constantly keep on the move, therefore, 'by realizing that that one focal point may bear other names and thus by allowing the one focus to express other ideas and in that way to control what we think and say' (*CD* II/1, 359).[33]

While in principle this seems straightforward, Barth gives ample reason for us to think that we have misunderstood him or that he contradicts himself. Christopher Holmes, for example, suggests that glory 'performs such important theological work in Barth's account of the perfections because glory, *as the chief perfection*, attests that God "is not only the Lord (*Herr*), but the Lord of glory (*Herrlichkeit*): and conversely, that all

---

[33] Our need to keep moving from perfection to perfection has to do with the fact that 'Barth is playing once again on the distinction between a given perfection as itself the divine essence and as a concept by which we indicate the divine essence' (*ibid.*, 71). Given that any perfection is itself the divine essence, and God's essence exists only in a diversity and multiplicity proper to God's own being, we must follow and acknowledge this diversity in practice (rather than merely noting it in theory while actually dwelling on a small list of favourite perfections). If we are to know God, we must seek to honour the fullness of his perfections by constantly progressing in our consideration of further perfections of the one God. Any given perfection, at the same time, however, is a 'concept by which we indicate the divine essence' and therefore inadequate, necessitating once again our appropriation and re-appropriation of new perfections. Barth writes: 'In our heart and on our lips, in our mode of knowledge, this thing grace is in no sense so fully and unambiguously clear, or above all so rich and deep, as it is in the truth of God which by this concept we apprehend – yet apprehend as we men apprehend God by faith, i.e., in such a way that our knowledge must needs expand and grow and increase. For this reason the idea of grace, not in itself, not in God, but in our mode of knowledge, requires qualification and expansion' (*CD* II/1, 358).

glory is the glory of God the Lord (*die Herrlichkeit Gottes des Herrn*)".'[34] More often interpreters bestow the honour of 'chief perfection' to love, or a combination of love and freedom. Along these lines Stephen Holmes writes that 'Barth offers good reasons for his decision, but the language appears in danger of suggesting that "love" and "freedom" are the *controlling perfections* of God, under which all else must be arranged'.[35] To be sure, Barth offers substantial support for this interpretation:

> Whatever else we may have to understand … in relation to the divine being, it will always have to be a definition of this being of His as the One who loves. All our further insights about who and what God is must revolve around this mystery – the mystery of His loving. In a certain sense they can only be repetitions and amplifications of the one statement that 'God loves.' (*CD* II/1, 283–4)[36]

---

[34] Holmes, *Revisiting*, 54–5 (emphasis added). Holmes sees 'glory as the chief sum of the divine perfections … because… [it] describes, it a manner unique to all the perfections of God's love and freedom, the self-movement in which God exists and in which he calls the creature to participate. Put very simply, to know God's glory is to know God in his act of self-declaration' (Holmes, *Revisiting*, 89).

[35] Stephen R. Holmes, 'The Attributes of God', in *The Oxford Handbook of Systematic Theology*, ed. J. B. Webster, Kathryn Tanner and Iain R. Torrance (Oxford: Oxford University Press, 2007), 60 (emphasis added). Kevin Vanhoozer, for example, writes that: 'In Barth's *Church Dogmatics*, love operates as a kind of "control attribute" that regulates the other divine perfections' (Kevin J. Vanhoozer, 'Introduction: The Love of God – Its Place, Meaning, and Function in Systematic Theology', in *Nothing Greater, Nothing Better: Theological Essays on the Love of God*, ed. Kevin J. Vanhoozer (Grand Rapids, MI: Eerdmans, 2001), 15). Cole makes much the same claim (Cole, *God the Peacemaker*, 37). Gunton refers to God's love and freedom as the 'two main attributes of God (Gunton, *The Barth Lectures*, 85). Lauber notes that 'these couplets [grace and holiness, mercy and righteousness, patience and wisdom] fall under divine love and are not to be considered on a par with divine love. God is not love and holiness, for example; rather, God is love and this love is holy love' (Lauber, *Barth on the Descent*, 14).

[36] To note just one more of many such statements, Barth writes: 'We must not cling to any of our ideas. For this reason we must constantly be prepared to allow our ideas to be qualified and expanded. We have already recognized this in presupposing the great reciprocal qualification and expansion of the two leading ideas [*Hauptbegriffe*] of the love and freedom of God' (*CD* II/1, 358; *KD*, 403).

To further complicate the matter, the perfections of the divine love repeat and amplify (*CD* II/1, 283–4), distinguish (*CD* II/1, 353, 359), enrich, clarify and intensify (*CD* II/1, 411), express or translate (*CD* II/1, 422) and determine (*CD* II/1, 464) the divine love. These concepts (and others like them) would seem to lend support to the idea that God's loving freedom is set apart from the other divine perfections in some significant and ultimately problematic way, given the Trinitarian nature of Barth's theology of the divine perfections.

How are we to understand the prominence of the divine love (and freedom) within Barth's account of the divine perfections? Does he sidestep the Trinitarian groundwork he so carefully establishes for the perfections, opting instead for his own master-concept?

If Barth in fact elevates one of the divine perfections to a level of prominence over the others such that it is a 'master concept' or exerts a 'controlling' function, it is less than clear which perfection(s) actually play(s) this role. While God's loving freedom is a strong candidate, we have seen that Christopher Holmes favours the divine glory. God's unity is a strong candidate as well, however:

> All the perfections of God's freedom can be summed up by saying that God is One. And to this extent all the perfections of His love ... and all the perfections of the divine being taken together, can be summed up in this one conception. If we understand it rightly, we can express all that God is by saying that God is One. (*CD* II/1, 442)[37]

Elsewhere, Barth makes similar claims of other divine perfections, such as of the divine constancy and grace.[38] While in certain passages Barth emphasizes God's loving freedom, the details of his treatment complicate rather than corroborate this interpretation.

Further complicating the issue is the fact that Barth does not specify the manner in which God's loving freedom is the leading idea, controlling concept or *Hauptbegriffe*. Rather, he argues that alongside the interdependence of the perfections, we must speak of any given perfection independently (*Selbständig*), 'as if it were the one and only standpoint [*Gesichtspunkt*]' (*CD* II/1, 491; *KD*, 552). The supposed 'control' exerted by God's loving freedom is limited indeed if we can speak of each of the divine attributes independently as God's one, complete essence (*CD* II/1, 491). In fact, it throws such a concept almost entirely into question. This is all the more clear as Barth qualifies himself at certain key points, such as when he writes that '*in a certain sense* [further insights about God's perfections] can only be repetitions and amplifications of the one statement that "God loves"' (*CD* II/1, 283–4, emphasis added). This is true 'in a certain sense' inasmuch as the statement that 'God loves' is in fact a statement

---

[37] As Price notes, 'It is not the *concept* of the divine unity to which Barth refers in this instance, but the divine unity itself, and therefore the very essence of God' (Price, 'Letters', 67).

[38] Cf. *CD* II/1, 491. Berkouwer, for example, notes the prominence of the divine grace in: Berkouwer, *Triumph*. Cf. Bloesch: 'For Barth the heart of the atonement is not the punishment of sin (though this is not excluded) but the triumph of grace over sin' (Bloesch, *Jesus is Victor*, 28–9). Barth gives good reason for this emphasis in *CD* IV/1 §58, where he speaks quite dominantly of grace, such as in pp. 145–7. Cf. Barth, *DO*, 16.

about the one essence of God. Inasmuch as any perfection is the essence of the one God, statements about God's other perfections can only be repetitions and amplifications of that one perfection. What is true of the statement 'God loves' is thus equally true of the statement that 'God is patient' or 'God is eternal'.

As Price suggests, 'it is God's being, the revealed divine identity, which both determines the structure of exposition and controls its individual elements. Love and freedom are simply conceptual shorthand for aspects of God's identity; they possess no independent function'.[39] Barth's discussions of God's love and freedom (CD II/1, §28.2–3) constitute a vital concrete specification of God's 'being in act' (CD II/1, §28.1), a first step towards naming the one God again and again on the basis of his enacted identity in preparation for a further exploration of the unity in diversity of the being of God in his account of the divine perfections.[40] The *Hauptbegriffe* of the love and freedom of God are indeed 'leading ideas' in the sense that they constitute the first concrete step of speaking of the one essence of God in its multiplicity. The only control or force they exert on the other divine perfections, however, rests in their faithful witness to the enacted being of God – to which our exposition of the other attributes must likewise witness. The control, in other words, has to do with the divine being and not with love and freedom.

---

[39] Price, 'Letters', 51. Critiquing Kevin Vanhoozer and Cornelius Van Til, Price continues: 'It is therefore misleading to claim that, in Barth's account, "love operates as a kind of 'control attribute' that regulates the other divine perfections", or, far worse, that according to Barth "all the attributes of God are subordinate to the one attribute of love or grace."'

[40] Although I do not develop this thesis in the present work, I understand CD II/1, §§28–31 to be a progressive development and expansion of the same theme: the being of God. §28.1 introduces the theme of God's livingness, while §28.2–3 develops that theme concretely in light of the loving freedom in which God lives. §29 steps back from this progression to address certain questions about the relationship of Barth's understanding to the traditional views of the doctrine, while §§30–1 offer Barth's fullest expansion of the same single theme. The implication of this view of §§28–31 is that God's love and God's freedom are no more essential to God's being than the fact that he is the living God or any of the other perfections considered in §§30–1. Rather, they constitute the second movement in Barth's expansion of his theme. To understand this kind of approach to covering theological material it is quite helpful to keep in mind Barth's appreciation for the music of Mozart. Cf. Karl Barth, *Wolfgang Amadeus Mozart*, trans. Clarence K. Pott (Grand Rapids, MI: Eerdmans, 1986). As George Hunsinger notes, 'in the style of composition there is a certain music to the argument. What first appears as mere repetition turns out on closer inspection to function rather like repetition in sonata form. It is the author's method of alluding to themes previously developed while constantly enriching the score with new ideas' (Hunsinger, *How to Read*, 28).

Accordingly, I contend that while he does not say as much, Barth could have begun his account of the being of God with any of the perfections of the divine loving (such as grace or patience), emphasizing them dialectically with any of the perfections of the divine freedom. After all, Barth writes that the concrete perfections chosen as the *Hauptbegriffe* have 'the basic character only of a trial and proposal', with no authoritative direction from Holy Scripture (*CD* II/1, 352). It is God's being manifest, decisively in the person and work of Jesus Christ, which is the ultimate basis for our theology of the divine perfections in both their unity and multiplicity. In each of the perfections we see the whole divine essence, and yet we keep on the move, honouring the multiplicity of God's one essence as it confronts us in his act of self-revelation.

While it may seem that Barth privileges a specific attribute or pair of attributes within his account of the doctrine of God, an impression strongly confirmed in the secondary literature, in fact Barth is not interested in such a project. Underlying his rejection of such an elevation or hierarchicalization within the divine perfections is his consistent focus on the doctrine of the Trinity, the doctrine of the living God that brings with it an exceptionally strong focus on God's self-revelation and an equally strong eschewal of abstract systematizations which are ultimately foreign to the Gospel. The net effect is an account of the divine perfections in which the unity and diversity proper to the doctrine of the Trinity and focused on God's self-revelation in the person and work of Jesus Christ make for a highly dynamic exposition of God's being.

The Fullness of the Perfections in Christ's Reconciliation

Having surveyed some of the key aspects of Barth's theology of the divine perfections, we return to our original question: what is the relationship between the doctrines of reconciliation and the divine perfections in Barth's theology or, put differently, what influence does Barth's understanding of the divine perfections have upon his doctrine of reconciliation? Earlier we noted that Barth seems to operate with a fairly traditional emphasis on the judicial/forensic aspect of the atonement. But is this manoeuvre consistent with his view of the divine perfections, and does he in fact adhere to a strictly judicial/forensic framework?

As we have seen, Barth locates the divine perfections in the one divine essence lived out eternally in God's three modes of being. Given the unity of the perfections (rooted in the doctrine and pattern of the Trinity), Barth affirms that God's perfections consist and confirm themselves in all that God does. He writes: 'the divinity of the love of God consists and confirms itself in the fact that in Himself and in all His works God is gracious, merciful and patient, and at the same time holy, righteous and wise' (*CD* II/1, 351), and again: 'the divinity of the freedom of God consists and confirms itself in the fact that in Himself and in all His works God is One, constant and eternal, and therefore also omnipresent, omnipotent and glorious' (*CD* II/1, 440). In short, one of the fundamental insights of Barth's doctrine of the divine perfections is that God is all that he is in all that he does – the divinity of the love and freedom of God consist and confirm themselves by the fact the fullness of the divine perfections are present and active in all that God does.[41]

This is not to say, however, that the fullness of God's being is equally apparent in all that God does. Integrating this thesis with the doctrines of election and revelation (recall the specification of God's being in act via the doctrine of election in Chapter 2), Barth claims:

> What God is as God, the divine individuality and characteristics, the *essentia* or 'essence' of God, is something which we shall encounter either at the place where God deals with us as Lord and Saviour, or not at all… [for] He has given no less than Himself to men as the overcoming of their need, and light in their darkness. (*CD* II/1, 261)

Reaffirming this point within his doctrine of reconciliation, Barth writes:

> God for us men, God in His majesty, God the Father, Son and Holy Spirit, God in all the fullness of His divine being, God in His holiness, power, wisdom, eternity and glory, God, who is completely self-sufficient, who does not need a fellow in order to be love, or a companion to be complete: God for us men. If that is what He is, if that is what He is as the true and real and living and only God – as the One who Himself willed to become man, and in so doing proved and revealed that He cares for man, and that He does so originally and properly and intensely, if He is this God, the *Deus pro nobis*, the covenant-God, then He is so, not as limited and conditioned by our freedom, but in the exalted freedom of His grace. (*CD* IV/1, 39)

The first point resonating throughout this passage is that God is present in Christ in the fullness of the divine perfections. As he states shortly thereafter, God 'does not merely give [man] something … He gives Himself, and in so doing gives him all things' (*CD* IV/1, 40). Equally significant, however, is the point that it is in this event, this history of the person and work of Jesus Christ, that the fullness of God's perfections confronts us in such a way as to be known and understood by us – and only here! While God's perfections are equally and fully present in all of his acts, God has ordered

---

[41] Cf. *CD* II/1, 111, 228, 327, 351, 352, 422, 440, 495, 515, 608, 655.

his relationship with creation and humankind towards a centre, and it is only in this centre that the whole becomes clear.

The foundation for our knowledge of the divine perfections, therefore, is God's self-revelation in the incarnate Son of God, Jesus Christ.

> What does it meant that 'God was in Christ' (2 Cor. 5.19)? It obviously means that all that God is, without either needing or being subject to any change or diminution or increase, is characterized by the fact that He is everything divine, not for Himself only, but also, in His Son, for the sake of man and for him. (*CD* IV/2, 86)

But 'Jesus Christ was and is for us in that He suffered and was crucified and died' (*CD* IV/1, 244). [42] All that God is, God's essence in the oneness and multiplicity of its perfections, is characterized by the fact that He is everything divine in the life, suffering, crucifixion, death and resurrection of Jesus Christ. For Barth, the perfections of God witnessed throughout Scripture find their final and decisive affirmation and clarification in this one event: the death and resurrection of Jesus Christ. Dying 'in the full possession of all the divine perfections' (*CD* II/1, 514), the incarnate Son brought the full reality of the being of God to bear upon our sin, for 'it needed nothing less than God Himself to remedy the corruption of our being and ourselves' (*CD* IV/1, 251). That is to say: it needed nothing less than the fullness of the divine perfections to remedy our corruption and bring the covenant to fulfilment.

Without developing this connection explicitly, Barth lays the foundation for the following thesis: *in regards to the divine perfections, the doctrine of reconciliation must honuor the Trinitarian oneness and multiplicity of the being of God by witnessing to the role of the divine perfections in their distinct individuality and in their inter-relatedness, while eschewing the ultimate preeminence of any one perfection or group of perfections.* In the act of reconciliation, Jesus brings the fullness of the divine perfections to bear upon our sinful condition. The church is therefore bound by God's self-revealing and saving work to understand the doctrine of reconciliation in light of each of these perfections, both in their distinctness and inter-relatedness. [43]

---

[42] In this case Barth omits reference to the resurrection temporarily as matter of properly attending to Christ's suffering and death. He emphasizes the resurrection both in its unity with and distinction from Christ's death in *CD* IV/1, 283–357 (and elsewhere).

[43] One could easily put this thesis in terms of Hunsinger's notion of 'dialectical inclusion', wherein 'each part is thought to contain, from a certain vantage point, the entire structure. The part includes within itself the entire pattern and way of functioning of the whole. The part is not just a division of the whole but a reiteration of it (Hunsinger, *How to Read*, 58). Again, this time more fully: 'the patterns within which the mysterious unity of soteriological objectivism and personalism seemed

In fact, Barth comes close to affirming my thesis, bringing his theology of the divine perfections to explicit fulfilment within his doctrine of the atonement. Renouncing Melito of Sardis' view that 'for the redemption of the world ... [God] den[ied] the immutability of His being ... [and was] in discontinuity with himself' (*CD* IV/1, 184), Barth affirms that God becomes man 'without an alteration of His being' (*CD* IV/1, 185), and that 'who God is and what it is to be divine is something we have to learn where God has revealed Himself and His nature, the essence of the divine' in Jesus Christ (*CD* IV/1, 186). He proceeds to affirm that in Jesus Christ God 'enters our being in contradiction [*Sein im Widerspruch*]' (*CD* IV/1, 186; *KD* 203), establishing communion between himself and his creature by putting 'into effect the freedom of His divine love', which he specifies as his immutability, sovereignty, grace, faithfulness, omnipresence, omnipotence eternity, wisdom, righteousness, holiness, mercy and glory (*CD* IV/1, 187-8).[44] If indeed each of these perfections individually and in relation to one another are the one essence of God in its fullness, and the one essence of God is fully present in the person and work of Jesus Christ as Barth here suggests, then we have no other option than to conclude that we must speak of the doctrine of the person and work of Jesus Christ, of reconciliation, in terms of the fullness of the divine perfections, both in their individuality and inter-relatedness. Unfortunately, although Barth comes within a hair's breadth of it he does not, to my knowledge, develop this implication of his thought in this way.

Barth's Forensic Model of Reconciliation?

But does Barth develop his account of reconciliation in harmony with the above thesis that we found to emerge from his account of the divine

to Barth to fall were largely those of Actualism and dialectical inclusion. The motif of Actualism made it possible to speak of the unity of a single, once-for-all event which yet occurred uniquely and mysteriously in a variety of differentiated and self-transcending forms. At the same time, the formal "Trinitarian" pattern of dialectical inclusion made it possible to speak of each form of this occurrence in such a way that the whole was always somehow present in each one of the forms without making any of them (whether subsequent or prior) superfluous. Each distinctive form of this occurrence made its own contribution to the unified whole, and yet nothing less than the whole was present as such in each distinctive and irreplaceable form. This dialectical inclusion or reciprocal coinherence of each differentiated form in the unified whole, and of the unified whole in each differentiated form, was itself an internally ordered or structured occurrence. For the occurrence as such had a "center" and a "periphery," and never the one without the other. All the differentiated, living, and actualistic forms constituting the whole were unified by the unique and once-for-all form of the event alive at their center – Jesus Christ himself' (Hunsinger, *How to Read*, 107–8).

[44] Barth makes similar statements in several places. See *CD* IV/1, 79–80, 126, 129–30, 417, 487, *CD* IV/2, 588 and Barth, *The Humanity of God*, 48–9.

perfections? As we saw at the beginning of this chapter, Barth gives every indication of operating within a forensic/judicial framework in which God's justice and righteousness are preeminent. What are we to make of this apparent conflict? A careful examination of Barth's doctrine of reconciliation suggests that he holds to a more nuanced position which, though not without weaknesses, is thoroughly amenable to the thesis I am advancing.[45]

In the midst of his exposition of Christ's passion in the *Dogmatics in Outline*, Barth makes the following caveat:

> Let me add that no doctrine of this central mystery can exhaustively and precisely grasp and express [*erschöpfend und präzis erfassen und aussprechen*] the extent to which God has intervened for us here [*inwiefern hier Gott für uns eingetreten ist*]. Do not confuse my theory [*Theorie*] of the reconciliation with the thing itself [*der Sache selber*]. All theories of reconciliation can be but pointers [*Alle Versöhnungstheorien können nur Fingerzeige sein*]. (*DO*, 116; *DG*, 137)

This theological 'aside' is noteworthy for two reasons. First, Barth uses the term 'theory' infrequently – this is one of the comparatively few instances in which he uses it reflexively, referring to his own position as a theory. Equally interesting is the difficulty Barth notes: appreciating the extent to which God has intervened for us. Why is this a difficulty for Barth, as 'God renders up Himself', his whole being, to accomplish our reconciliation (*DO*, 116)?

While Barth does not say as much, my sense is that Barth carefully distinguishes his theory [*Theorie*] from the thing itself [*Sache*] because any human and therefore finite and limited account of reconciliation will emphasize certain aspects of God's intervention while omitting or minimizing others so as to offer a concrete testimony to Christ's saving work. Such omissions and emphases are a necessary feature of any *Theorie* of reconciliation, determining both its significance and limitations. In the same way that Barth's selection of the divine perfections for consideration in *CD* II/1 was 'arbitrary' because ultimately 'we are drawing upon the ocean … [and] are therefore faced by a task to which there is no end' (*CD* II/1, 406), our selection of the perfections to emphasize in a specific account of the atonement is likewise arbitrary.[46] Our limited accounts of reconciliation simply cannot say all that there is to be said: we explore the work of

---

[45] Thomas expresses his dissatisfaction with Barth's over-emphasis of the juridical framework, but so far as I can find does not explore the possibility of a broader line of inquiry within Barth's thought. Cf. Thomas, 'Der für uns "gerichtete Richter"', 219.

[46] Athanasius' comment, while focused on the achievements of Christ rather than on the role of the perfections within his work, is of a similar vein: 'Such and so many are the Saviour's achievements that follow from His Incarnation, that to try to number them is like gazing at the open sea and trying to count the waves' (Athanasius, *On the Incarnation*, 93).

Christ through concrete and limited theories which witness truly though incompletely to the thing itself.

In this distinction between *Theorie* and *Sache*, with its seemingly arbitrary emphasis of certain elements at the expense of a whole which is too great to speak of, we are once again operating on trinitarian grounds, and it will be helpful to recall and expand an insight from the previous chapter. According to the rule *opera ad extra sunt indivisa*, Father, Son and Holy Spirit necessarily work conjointly. The doctrine of appropriations, however, allows for the attribution of a 'word or deed to this or that person of the Godhead' so as to temporarily bring to our attention in a concrete way the 'truly incomprehensible eternal distinctions in God' (*CD* I/1, 372), provided we do this in cognizance of the aforementioned 'rule'. Relating this to the divine perfections and theories of the atonement, the 'rule' states that the divine perfections are fully and equally present and active in Christ's reconciling work. The 'doctrine', however, allows for us to temporarily and provisionally attribute specific divine perfections, as it were, to theories of the atonement, so as to bring to our attention the truly incomprehensible richness of Christ's saving work. In this view, theories of the atonement are equivalent to and justified by the applications of the doctrine of appropriations, and at the same time are properly delimited by an awareness of the underlying 'rule'.

Turning to the *CD*, we find a similar passage which explains Barth's forensic treatment of reconciliation in *CD* IV/1. Concluding his answer to Anselm's question (*Cur Deus homo?*), Barth writes that his 'first statement is complete in itself, that it comprehends all that follows, and that it can stand alone' (*CD* IV/1, 273). He then notes 'the different ways in which the New Testament speaks of this *pro nobis*', taking a retrospective survey of the ground already covered, offering the following explanation:

> When we spoke of Jesus Christ as Judge and judged, and of His judgment and justice, we were adopting a definite standpoint [*bestimmte Anschaulichkeit*] and terminology [*Begrifflichkeit*] as the framework [*Rahmen*] in which to present our view [*Aufweises*] of the *pro nobis*. In order to speak with dogmatic clarity and distinctness we had to decide on a framework [*Rahmen*] of this kind ... But exegesis reminds us that in the New Testament there are other standpoints [*Anschaulichkeiten*] and terminologies [*Begrifflichkeiten*] which might equally be considered as guiding principles [*Ordnungsprinzipien*] for dogmatics. (*CD* IV/1, 273; *KD*, 301)[47]

---

[47] There is thus a similarity between the exegetical *Ordnungsprinzipien* (*CD* IV/1, 273; *KD*, 301) mentioned in this passage and the dogmatic *Hauptbegriffe* alluded to earlier (cf. *CD* II/1, 358; *KD* 403), in that both admit of a definite flexibility. In fact, this

This passage corroborates my interpretation of the *Dogmatics in Outline*. Barth adopts a definite standpoint by which to make his exhibition of the *pro nobis*, fully conscious of other standpoints which could serve in that capacity. Here, however, the notion of *Aufweises gemachen* (making an exhibition or demonstration) replaces that of *Theorie*, and Barth specifies that the standpoints he refers to are the Biblical accounts of the efficacy of Christ's work, rather than the standpoint offered by the various divine perfections.[48] At no point does a *Theorie* or *Aufweisen* sufficiently capture the thing itself, the *Sache* of reconciliation, but serves as a concrete and in itself complete development of reconciliation from a definite perspective which must be held in proper relation to the other standpoints presented in Scripture (an approach to unity and diversity firmly rooted in Barth's Trinitarian theology).

Barth specifies these standpoints [*Anschaulichkeiten*] as the financial, military and cultic imagery used in the New Testament to speak of the work of Christ (*CD* IV/1, 274), offering a 10-page recapitulation of 'The Judge Judged in Our Place' from the vantage point of the cultic *Anschaulichkeit* (*CD* IV/1, 274–83). The implications of these few pages for Barth's doctrine of reconciliation are momentous, not least for the fact that he essentially confesses that his treatment of 'The Judge Judged in Our Place' is but a sketch of the doctrine of the atonement, although one that in and of itself is whole and complete (notice the Trinitarian pattern at work). He brackets the entire discussion of §59.2, arguing that it is a definite and complete statement, although one alongside other equally valid standpoints or guiding principles – a point rooted in the Trinitarian pattern of unity and multiplicity we have seen throughout his doctrine of the divine perfections. This 'bracketing' not only allows for but demands the development of other 'definite and complete' statements of the doctrine, all of which together constitute a whole.

In this passage Barth opens the door to a wider vista of the doctrine of reconciliation, but does he open it far enough? Does he demand with sufficient clarity that in addition to the forensic standpoint we move on to further standpoints? To adapt one of Barth's statements to the present context, does he urge us to move forward without 'leaving behind what we have already said' by offering 'further analysis and elucidation of this first affirmation' by 'plac[ing] alongside our first affirmation a second and a third: not with the idea of adding something new, but with the idea of continually saying the one thing', that God so loved the world that he

---

flexibility is essential to their role, and when this is forgotten both exegetical and dogmatic problems will shortly follow.

[48] The second of these differences is relatively inconsequential. The two can and should be integrated, as the biblical accounts rely on divine perfections in order to make their explanations.

reconciled it to himself in Jesus Christ, 'on the presupposition of what has already been said, in ever new forms' (CD II/1, 368)?

A Modest Correction

Despite the strengths of Barth's argument, a modest correction is in order for the limited concession to multiplicity Barth acknowledges concerning other standpoints for the doctrine of reconciliation. While noting the fundamental possibility of adopting other frameworks for the doctrine of reconciliation, his argument in this section is insufficient for two reasons. First, at times it tends towards being a rather grumpy acknowledgement rather than a resounding imperative. Second, the exegetical route Barth maps out to further developments of the doctrine is but one of several different approaches which together lead us to the full diversity of the biblical witness.

Regarding the nature of Barth's acknowledgement, his fundamental point is positive in nature: we are permitted to 'think out the whole event within the framework' of other standpoints (CD IV/1, 274) – something that, in fact, the Church will always do (CD IV/1, 273). Sprinkled throughout, however, are comments such as the following: 'it is surely enough if we are ready to use the particular force of these categories in an occasional and subsidiary manner', and 'a place should be found for this group of images' (CD IV/1, 274). To be sure, he notes that 'if we fail to notice these variations, there will be a formal if not a substantial lacuna in our presentation, and we shall also miss certain definite insights' (CD IV/1, 273), but at times one gets the sense that Barth thinks of this as a task that is possible although maybe not necessary, or one that should be done but may in fact not prove too helpful. A marked lack of energy and excitement overshadows the whole, where a sense of freshness and vigour ought to teem forth resulting from the awareness of these new frameworks for interpreting the work of Christ, the necessity with which we must engage them, and the promise of the definite insights we stand to gain. Adapting an earlier statement of Barth's, we must 'magnify the plenitude of the divine being [in reconciliation] by not lingering unduly over any one [standpoint of the atonement] or letting it become the final word or the guiding principle, but by proceeding from one to another, from the second to the third. As we do so, we realize that even if we make a provisional halt at the third, this does not mean that we have spoken the last word' (CD II/1, 407).

While the above (somewhat begrudging) tendencies are clearly not the only ones present, they are evident and unfortunately minimize the force of the passage. Thus, while Barth opens a door of possibility in this passage which significantly broadens the task of the doctrine of reconciliation, the light shining through this entry lacks the warmth and radiance we might expect. In fact, the light is so dim that Justyn Terry interprets Barth as believing 'that he had so captured the essence of the work of reconciliation in terms of the judgment of God that all else he would say about the doctrine could be seen as commentaries on [his account of the atonement in light of the judicial metaphor]'.[49] While such an explanation runs counter to Barth's Trinitarian understanding of the divine perfections and their bearing on the doctrine of reconciliation, Terry's point nevertheless confirms the tepidity of Barth's argument in this passage.

A partial explanation for this tone has to do with the question Barth addresses in this passage: why begin with the judicial framework? In other words, Barth is less focused on the obligation to move on to other standpoints (an imperative that is, in fact, present in this passage) than he is upon defending his particular standpoint. In what John Drury calls a 'rare moment of sensitivity to cultural relevance',[50] Barth admits that 'material which is already difficult would have been made even more difficult by trying to understand it in a form which is now rather remote from us', and that even had we tried to adopt a sacrificial standpoint, we could not have done so as well, distinctly and comprehensively, given the 'particularly good basis in the Bible' for the judicial standpoint (CD IV/1, 273, 275). In response, the first reason (cultural distance) seems fraught with peril and uncharacteristic timidity. The second reason (biblical basis), however, offers a plausible reason for beginning with this standpoint, but little or none for minimizing, ignoring, or subsuming the other standpoints within those better attested ones. In short, while Barth's selection of the judicial framework is defensible, and his opening of the door to other trajectories within Scripture for developing parallel treatments of the doctrine of the atonement with their own distinct contributions is exceptional, there is, in spite of all this, an unfortunate tone to the passage and a less than thunderous call to take up the theological task and proceed to develop these other biblical standpoints for the doctrine of the atonement.

A second avenue exists for critiquing Barth's point, however, for the door itself, the exegetical route he opens to further study, is unfortunately

---

[49] Terry, *Justifying Judgement*, 107. Terry goes on to point out that 'exactly how this use of judgment relates to other metaphors of atonement, however, Barth does not say' (Terry, *Justifying Judgement*, 108). The reason that Barth does not offer such an account is that he is simply not thinking along these lines. Barth has no interest in 'primary' and 'subordinate' metaphors of the atonement, with the exception of noting the biblical emphasis (as distinct from dogmatic priority). Only the doctrine of divine perfections can provide the proper hermeneutic for interpreting Barth here. It is clear that Barth's interest does not lie in prioritizing or ranking the 'metaphors' of the atonement, given his approach to exploring the atonement from the standpoint of the sacrificial imagery in the Bible in *CD* IV/1, 275–85, in which he seeks to 're-state and verify' his argument 'in another direction' (*CD* IV/1, 275).

[50] Drury, 'The Priest Sacrificed in Our Place', 8.

(although understandably) narrow.[51] Reconciliation is the work of the triune God in Jesus Christ to confront sin in all its aspects and fulfill God's creative/covenantal purposes, with a particular focus upon the efficacy of Christ's death and resurrection towards this end. Accordingly, the doctrine of reconciliation is a whole formed of the various doctrinal loci represented above, including at the very least the doctrines of God (Trinity and divine perfections), Christ and Sin, brought together by means of an explanation as to the efficacy of the incarnate Son of God's death and resurrection for overcoming our sin and fulfilling in us God's covenantal purposes. The frameworks Barth mentions (forensic, financial, military and cultic) pertain to those passages in Scripture that speak boldly and clearly of the efficacy of Christ's death and resurrection. However, the Bible contains a host of less direct but equally significant trajectories relevant to the doctrine of reconciliation within the doctrines of God (i.e. Trinity and perfections), Christology or sin, for example, which access less familiar frameworks for the doctrine of reconciliation, allowing us to appropriate and more fully comprehend passages speaking of the efficacy of Christ's death and resurrection that we might otherwise tend to overlook. For instance, to adapt Paul Jones' question: 'What rewards might accrue … were a Christian doctrine of [the atonement] to begin with a discussion of divine patience?'[52] Or what might we find if we explore more deeply God's relationship to his people as bridegroom, or the role of the Temple as God's saving presence in the Old and New Testaments? Barth does well to open the door to multiple frameworks for the doctrine of reconciliation, but unfortunately uses but one of several possible doctrinal avenues.

Barth would have been consistent, and more revolutionary for the doctrine of reconciliation, had he drawn from his account of the divine perfections, demonstrating that the biblical witness to the divine perfections grants us yet another entry-point to the spectrum of frameworks which further the Church's task of appreciating the fullness of the riches that we have in the work of Christ. Because he derives his elaboration of the divine perfections from the being in act of God in the person and work of Jesus Christ, these same perfections grant us a definite insight into the work of Christ which either fit within the frameworks already mentioned, or open our eyes to new and relatively undeveloped standpoints ripe for exploration.[53]

---

[51] Barth seems to be somewhat more aware of the danger of overly narrow accounts of the biblical diversity earlier in his career. Cf. Barth, *Unterricht in der christlichen Religion*, 80.

[52] Jones, *Humanity of Christ*, 6.

[53] Barth is deeply concerned that the 'concrete life of the Church and of the members of the Church is a life really dominated by the exegesis of the Bible' (CD I/2, 533). It is largely this concern which motivates him to develop his doctrine of reconciliation within a forensic framework: he finds it to be the most distinct and comprehensive framework developed in Scripture. Recognizing this, I am not suggesting that the

Why didn't he make this step? Two possibilities come to mind. First, he was seeking to adhere to the biblical witness by attending to those themes it most thoroughly develops. While more could have been done, this is in and of itself commendable. Second, it may simply be a unique characteristic of the present age that we are somewhat more sensitive to diversity than were previous eras.[54] Why does Robert Peterson's book find so much more diversity in Calvin's doctrine of the atonement than Paul Van Buren's?[55] Why are we suddenly so sensitive to the diversity within Abelard's view of the cross?[56] While it is not the case that in the past theologians were impervious to diversity, it may simply be that one of the strengths of the present age lies in its sensitivity in this area – a sensitivity that Barth did not share in quite the same degree with regard to Christ's saving work.

Substitutionary Framework: The Four-Fold 'For Us'

Fortunately, Barth does not leave us without direction for how we might proceed in exploring the doctrine of reconciliation from the vantage point offered us by the divine attributes. At the 'end of the important section dealing with ... the particular question [of] what Jesus Christ was and did *pro nobis*, for us and for the world' (*CD* IV/1, 273), Barth gives a retrospective look at the ground just covered. In so doing he lays out the substitutionary framework which emerges from his exposition of Jesus Christ as the 'Judged Judged in Our Place', and which he believes will hold equally true for other standpoints for exploring Christ's reconciling work.[57] 'Whatever we say further', he writes:

> depends upon the fact that in the sense we have noted He was the Judge judged in our place. All theology, both that which follows and indeed that which precedes the doctrine of reconciliation, depends upon this *theologia crucis* [theology of the cross]. And it depends upon it under the particular aspect under which we have had to

doctrine of reconciliation simply use the various divine perfections to freely develop new aspects of Christ's saving work independent of an exegetical basis. Rather, because Barth derives the divine perfections from the being-in-act of the Triune God centred in the person and work of Jesus Christ, the divine perfections are themselves necessarily rooted exegetically in such a way as to open our eyes to aspects of Christ's saving work which are themselves found in Scripture.

[54] Vanhoozer, 'Atonement in Postmodernity', 369.
[55] Robert A. Peterson, *Calvin and the Atonement* (Fearne, Scotland: Christian Focus Publications, 2008); Paul M. Van Buren, *Christ in Our Place: The Substitutionary Character of Calvin's Doctrine of Reconciliation* (Edinburgh: Oliver and Boyd, 1957).
[56] Weingart, *The Logic of Divine Love*; Williams, 'Sin, Grace, and Redemption'.
[57] For a summary of this four-fold framework, cf. Klappert, *Die Auferweckung*, 277–86.

develop it in this first part of the doctrine of reconciliation as the doctrine of substitution [*Lehre von der Stellvertretung*]. (*CD* IV/1, 273; *KD*, 300)[58]

This doctrine of substitution, concretely developed in the account of the judge judged in our place, involves a 'fourfold "for us"' filled out by means of the particular framework adopted from Scripture for referring to the work of Christ. In this particular case (i.e. forensic/judicial), Jesus 'took our place as Judge. He took our place as the judged. He was judged in our place. And He acted justly in our place' (*CD* IV/1, 273).

Having laid out the gist of his doctrine of substitution, Barth briefly tests his exposition by recapitulating his account of Christ's work from the cultic standpoint (*CD* IV/1, 275) – a process in which a fundamental structure becomes apparent and is vindicated precisely through this recapitulation.[59] Therein, Barth explores in brief the idea that just as 'Jesus Christ took our place as Judge ... He is the Priest who represented us' (*CD* IV/1, 275). Combining the second and third aspects of substitution, he notes that just as Jesus was judged in our place, so 'He gave Himself to be offered up as a sacrifice to take away our sins' (*CD* IV/1, 277). Concluding, he notes that just as Jesus acted justly, so 'in our place He has made a perfect sacrifice' (*CD* IV/1, 281).

This is a significant passage for several reasons. First, returning to a concern mentioned at the beginning of the present chapter, it offers a partial explanation of why Barth's thought transcends (while simultaneously incorporating) the doctrine of penal substitution.[60] Barth's focus is on the presence of God in Christ, accomplishing the fulfilment of the covenant by means of his substitutionary work. Specifically, in this case, he dwells on the being of God as judge. While this gives Barth the resources to incorporate the role of punishment and penalty (and therefore the concerns of penal substitution), Barth's concern is larger than simply describing the mere overcoming of our plight. That is to say, Barth is just as concerned with the fourth 'for us' of Jesus' work (in which he acts justly in our

---

[58] Cf. *DO*, 115.

[59] This process involves the three following elements: (1) representing us by filling an office (Judge or Priest), (2) representing us by submitting to the demands of that office (convict or sacrifice), and (3) representing us by fulfilling the demand of that office (acting justly in our place or offering a perfect sacrifice). This structure itself is not salvific, and is never present apart from a concrete manifestation within a particular sphere of biblical imagery. Cf. Drury, 'The Priest Sacrificed in Our Place', 1–2. While I somewhat alter Drury's point concerning the 'procedure' Barth chooses by integrating the first and third procedures, his paper is essentially correct, and was quite helpful in drawing my attention to this passage and exploring its meaning.

[60] For Barth's affirmation of penal substitution, cf. *CD* II/1, 152, *CD* III/2, 602–4, the carefully nuanced position in *CD* IV/1, 252–5, and Barth, *Table Talk*, 52.

place) as he is in the second and third (in which he bears our judgement or punishment). To put it quite simply, Barth thinks that an over-emphasis on punishment simply cannot do justice to the justice of God manifest in the substitutionary work of Christ. Moreover, Barth is so concerned with the being of God in Christ that he also cannot merely dwell on the justice or righteousness of God. As has been argued in this chapter, other standpoints within the Scriptural witness beyond and distinct from those of a forensic/judicial framework demand his attention.

The second point I wish to make from this passage is that the doctrine of substitution is a consequence of and not the basis for the unity of the work of Christ. Barth's argument, in other words, is not that the work of Christ is unified because it is substitutionary, but rather that it is unified because God is the one present in Christ making this substitutionary work effective. The weight of Barth's thought falls upon the presence of God in this particular act. The act, that is, derives its significance from the subject whose act this is. This explains why Barth begins his doctrine of reconciliation with an account of 'God with us' (*CD* IV/1, 3), and only explicitly formulates a doctrine of substitution as such in what nearly amounts to an appendix to his argument.[61] While we have ample warrant to refer to Barth's account of Christ's work as being a substitutionary theory of the atonement, we best honour this commitment of Barth's by placing our emphasis on the fact that God was, in Christ, reconciling the world to Himself. In this way we are less inclined to abstract or generalize our understanding of 'substitution', and more prone to interpret the relevant concepts or predicates in light of the inalienable subject: the triune God.

Once in place, the substitutionary framework Barth develops on the basis of Christ's work (as God's chosen means by which to bring his life to bear upon us for our salvation) serves as a framework for future explorations in the doctrine of the atonement, in which we incorporate different divine perfections into this framework to test whether and how it resonates with the biblical witness. At this point, significant care is needed lest the systematic task outpace the biblical witness upon which it rests, and stray from its proper task.[62] Scripture itself witnesses events

---

[61] While there is merit to Lauber's claim that this is a 'programmatic statement', there is also reason to hold it somewhat loosely. Lauber adds, however, that 'Barth's view cannot simply be described as a strain of "substitutionary" atonement or "penal substitution" without qualification. These catch-all phrases obscure Barth's concentration on the narrative of Jesus Christ' (Lauber, *Barth on the Descent*, 2). The fact that the four-fold doctrine of representation is 'at the center of Barth's theology' in no way abscures this fact (Bakker, 'Jesus als Stellvertreter', 40).

[62] The same danger attends other doctrines. Once the doctrine of the Trinity of one God in three persons or modes of being has been developed, for example, it can quickly outpace the explicit development of these themes in Scripture. See Karen Kilby's cautionary point in this regard (Karen Kilby, 'Is an Apophatic Trinitarianism

it does not recount (Jn 21.25); just as this does not trouble us, neither should the idea that it would witness to a reality which it does not fully explore or integrate. Our task, with regard to my thesis, is first and foremost to use it as a hermeneutic by which to become more sensitive to the Scriptural account. When this account is incomplete, however, when it partially develops aspects of Christ's work, our business is to move beyond Scripture scripturally, elaborating and completing these accounts by working analogically between the different aspects of Christ's substitutionary work, while noting the tentative and exploratory nature of our theories, exercising care not to build upon a foundation other than that provided in Scripture. In other words, this systematic thesis is necessarily ordered towards theological interpretation of Scripture, and must not to take on an independent life of its own, although it is bound to give a conceptually unified and pastorally relevant account which may and will often go beyond the explicit affirmations in Scripture in a manner called for, guided by and faithful to Scripture.

Conclusion

My thesis, drawn from Barth's theology, is that *the doctrine of reconciliation must honour the oneness and multiplicity of the being of God by witnessing to the role of the divine perfections in Christ's reconciling work (both in their distinct individuality and in their inter-relatedness), eschewing the ascription of ultimate preeminence to any one perfection or group of perfections.* While Barth did not himself make this claim, I have argued that it is the consequence of the trajectory established by his doctrine of the divine perfections, and is suggested in Barth's account of the doctrine of reconciliation without being fully developed as such. While Barth himself tends to favour a forensic treatment as the concrete standpoint from which to approach the doctrine of reconciliation, he clearly establishes that this is but one of multiple frameworks by which to accomplish this task. My goal was to appreciate and extend this element of Barth's thought, more firmly establishing the necessity of developing these other frameworks and expanding the exegetical avenues to open up doors to yet further possibilities through noting the implications of Barth's theology of the divine perfections.

Possible?', *IJST* 12, no. 1 (2010) (65–77). At the other end of this spectrum we find Webster's claim: 'the ruler and judge over all other Christian doctrine is the doctrine of the Holy Trinity' (Webster, '*Rector et iudex*', 35). By extension, as Webster holds theological interpretation of Scripture to be 'a way of reading which is informed by a theologically derived set of interpretative goals', the doctrine of the Trinity is likewise ruler and judge over the interpretation of Scripture (John Webster, 'Editorial', *IJST* 12, no. 2 (2010), 116).

The implication of this thesis is that the Church is bound by the biblical witness to God's self-revealing work of salvation to understand the doctrine of reconciliation in light of each of the divine perfections, both in their distinctness and inter-relatedness. Limiting ourselves to a consideration of certain of God's perfections in Christ's work is unwarranted and detrimental. The same holds for granting one perfection (or a group of them) a controlling position over the others within our understanding of Christ's work: the doctrine of the divine perfections, as Barth understands it, will not tolerate such a thought.

Why is such limitation so dangerous? After all, isn't it simply an application of the doctrine of appropriations with regard to the atonement? The danger lies in the fact that love, freedom, mercy, knowledge ... all the perfections in and of themselves are 'not merely neutral. Power [and the same can be said for the others[63]] in itself is evil' (CD II/1, 524). Our concern is with the power [and love, freedom, mercy ...] of God, and in this way and to this extent with omnipotence, with real power' (CD II/1, 524). By focusing over-much on a single divine perfection, we run the danger of minimizing or forgetting the fact that as a perfection of God it is identical with the essence of God only inasmuch as it is identical to and in relationship with a host of other perfections. If we abstract one perfection from the others, we run the risk of abstracting from the being and act of God altogether and our theology quickly suffers the consequences. While the doctrine of appropriations allows for temporary elevation of a given perfection for consideration within the doctrine of the atonement, the rule *opera ad extra sunt indivisa*, which is the constant companion of the doctrine of appropriations, demands that we return again and again to the one God whose perfections these are, and thus move on to the consideration of his other perfections, lest we risk ceasing to think of the Triune God and his reconciling work altogether.

Must we then integrate each and every divine perfection into our account of the atonement? Do we have to say everything at once to say anything? Just as Barth did not integrate all the divine perfections into his doctrine of God (CD II/1, 406), we do not need to integrate them all into our understanding of the death and resurrection of Jesus Christ in order to have an adequate understanding. There is no readily apparent end to this task, and for that reason it is an ongoing calling and responsibility. At the same time, we must strive to integrate each and every divine perfection into our account of Christ's reconciling work, for our incapacity does not alter the task at hand, but serves as a reminder of the necessary incompleteness of, and ongoing need for, the theological vocation of the Church in the present day.

This dialectic leaves us with the ongoing task of exploring the relationship between the divine perfections and our reconciliation in Christ, exerting

---

[63] Cf. CD II/1, 407 on 'love in general'.

care to fall into neither of two errors. First, we must not elevate any one or group of perfections to a position of superiority or control over the others, but recognize that in any concrete treatment of one or several of the divine perfections we are engaging in a theological exercise that speaks truly if incompletely of the work of Christ. Second, we ought not to fear delving into a concrete exposition of the doctrine of reconciliation rooted in a single perfection (such as justice or righteousness), knowing that each of the perfections of God is itself the fullness of the one essence of God.

Test Case: The Patient One Patient in Our Place

My purpose in this book is not simply to reproduce Barth's thought, but to extend his theology constructively. For that reason, and with the additional incentive of preventing my argument from becoming overly abstract, I offer a test-case at the conclusion of each of the main chapters. In the previous chapter, we saw that Barth's doctrine of the atonement can and should be seen as an exemplarist theory of the atonement par-excellence. Now, at the conclusion of the present exploration of the relationship between the doctrines of reconciliation and the divine perfections, I take an altogether different approach, sketching a standpoint of Christ's substitutionary work from the perspective of the divine patience. My thesis is that just as Jesus was 'the judge judged in our place', so, from the standpoint of the divine patience, he was the patient one patient in our place. While the perfection of divine patience does not lend itself so poetically as that of justice to Barth's four-fold "for us," it nevertheless opens the door to a complete aspect or theory of the atonement, making us privy to 'certain definite insights' (CD IV/1, 273).[64]

Barth introduces the concept of patience (CD II/1, 406–22) by tying it irrevocably to the being of God: 'God acts [patiently] ... That He does so lies in His very being. Indeed, it is His being. Everything that God is, is implied and included in the statement that He is patient' (CD II/1, 408). Barth then defines God's patience as 'His will ... to allow another ... space and time for the development of its own existence, thus conceding to this existence a reality side by side with His own, and fulfilling His will towards this other in such a way that He does not suspend or destroy it as this other but accompanies and sustains it and allows it to develop in freedom' (CD II/1, 409–10).[65] God comes to us in the person of Jesus Christ as the one who

---

[64] That is, it would open our eyes to the aspect, enabling us to develop a theory.

[65] Barth's use of patience (אֶרֶךְ רוּחַ אֶרֶךְ אַפַּיִם, μακροθυμία ὑπομονη and ἀνοχη) as a divine perfection rests on a firm biblical foundation. Cf. God's patience with Cain after the first murder, his patience with Israel manifest so clearly throughout the book of Joshua, and Jonah's complaint against God's patience with Nineveh (Jon. 4.2).

is patient in this way (the first of the four elements of Barth's substitutionary account).

But the biblical witness is not monolithic with regards to God's patience – God visits the iniquity of the fathers on the children! Barth asks: 'where is in fact the patience of God.... How often, to how many people, and how destructively His impatience also seems to take effect! How radically His wrath, too, seems to take its course!' (*CD* II/1, 415).[66] Barth's answer is that

Especially significant is the recurring theme of patience reverberating throughout the Old Testament drawing from Exod. 34.6–7: 'The LORD passed before [Moses] and proclaimed, "The LORD, the LORD, a God merciful and gracious, slow to anger [אֶרֶךְ אַפַּיִם], and abounding in steadfast love and faithfulness, keeping steadfast love for thousands, forgiving iniquity and transgression and sin, but who will by no means clear the guilty, visiting the iniquity of the fathers on the children and the children's children, to the third and the fourth generation".' (Cf. Num. 14.18; Pss., 86.15, 103.8, 145.8; Neh. 9.17; Joel 2:13; Nah. 1.3). Exodus 34 is particularly significant for, as Walter Brueggemann notes, it is 'a formulation so studied that it may be reckoned to be something of a classic, normative statement to which Israel regularly returned, meriting the label "credo"' (Walter Brueggemann, *Theology of the Old Testament: Testimony, Dispute, Advocacy* (Minneapolis: Fortress, 1997), 216). For Barth's exegesis of this biblical material, see *CD* II/1, 407, 412–15.

It is worth noting, however, that Barth's definition of patience is somewhat different from that of biblical scholars. As J. Horst puts it, 'the data in the OT and LXX show that in the struggle to understand God's μακροθυμία there is always an unresolved certainty whether it will finally serve to deliver the man who in prayer tries to seek refuge in it' (J. Horst, 'μακροθυμία', in Theological Dictionary of the New Testament, eds Gerhard Kittel, Geoffrey William Bromiley and Gerhard Friedrich (Grand Rapids, MI: Eerdmans, 1964), 4.378). Horst thus emphasizes the way in which patience (μακροθυμία ορ ἀνοχή) often has the sense of withholding imminent and deserved judgment: 'Have patience [μακροθύμησον] with me, and I will pay you everything' (Mt. 18.26), and 'What if God, desiring to show his wrath and to make known his power, has endured with much patience [μακροθυμίᾳ] the objects of wrath that are made for destruction?' (Rom. 9.22). There is also a positive sense of the word, however, in which the emphasis is on the awaited positive outcome: 'The LORD is gracious and merciful, slow to anger [אֶרֶךְ אַ פִּים] and abounding in steadfast love' (Ps. 145.8), and 'I received mercy for this reason, that in me, as the foremost, Jesus Christ might display his perfect patience [μακροθυμίᾳ] as an example to those who were to believe in him for eternal life' (1 Tim. 1.16). James E. West emphasizes this positive aspect of the divine patience: 'When used of God, it describes God's willingness to wait calmly for the people to return in repentance so they can claim God's offer of forgiveness' (James E. West, 'Patience', in *The New Interpreter's Dictionary of the Bible*, ed. Katherine Doob Sakenfeld, Samuel E. Balentine and Kah-Jin Jeffrey Kuan (Nashville, TN: Abingdon, 2006), 4.396. Barth's decision, it seems, is to split the difference between these two emphases, making a general point amenable to either use of the word, in which the gift of space and time for the development of a unique and distinct existence is granted to another, although clearly this gift takes place within the framework of God's covenantal purposes.

66 A fuller account of the divine patience would also need to take into account the divine impatience, and the forms of sin as both patience and impatience.

these are 'all temporary and as such symbolic judgments and punishments. They are not the outbreak of the genuine wrath and judgment of God. They are not the eternal death, the abandonment and precipitation into nothingness, which Israel and with Israel all humanity deserved ... That which we all deserved has been suffered in our place and in Israel's place by the only righteous One' (CD II/1, 420).[67] The tension throughout Scripture between God's patience and the outbreaking of these temporary and symbolic manifestations of his wrath (no matter how harsh they may seem to be to us) is ultimately a tension that takes place within a higher order of patience – the patience of God directed towards the work of Christ when he justifies himself passing 'over former sins' (Rom. 3.25–6).

But this raises a significant question for Barth's understanding of the divine patience within the economy. Barth is clear that God is patient in that he gives us 'space and time for the development of [our sinful] existence, thus conceding to this existence a reality side by side with His own' only inasmuch as this space and time is ordered towards and presupposed by the work of Christ. But when he explores the work of Christ in this context, he abandons the theme of divine patience in favour of an account of the divine wrath and righteousness. 'For the sake of manifesting His righteousness in Jesus Christ, God exercised ἀνοχή, in these times' (CD II/1, 418). But does the divine patience come to an end in the passion of Jesus Christ? Has the divine patience held back the wrath and righteousness of God all this time, only now to relinquish its duty in allowing the 'genuine wrath and judgment of God' (CD II/1, 420) to be poured forth? Unfortunately, this seems to be the path Barth takes. He offers us, however, a glimpse of the path we should take to rethink the role of the divine patience in the passion of Jesus Christ – a path that becomes all the more evident in the work of theologians in the past 50 years on the theology of Holy Saturday.[68]

---

[67] Lauber notes that Barth refers to our death as 'a *sign* of God's just judgment on us' in CD III/2, 596 (Lauber, *Barth on the Descent*, 22). It should be noted, however, that according to Horst, 'the wrath of God, though manifested aleady, R[om]. 2:5; cf. 1.18; 9.22f., will reach its climax only on the day of wrath, 2.5' (*TDNT* 4.382).

[68] 'Holy Saturday' refers to the day between Good Friday and Easter Sunday in which Jesus was dead. More specifically, it offers a theological account of Jesus Christ's experience of death, hell and God-abandonment, interpreting the substitutionary death of Christ as a Trinitarian event with a particular emphasis on some form or degree of divine passibility. Properly speaking, Barth's is not a theology of Holy Saturday. He uses 'the descent into hell ... as an interpretative key that unlocks the meaning of the crucifixion ...' but only in von Balthasar do we move beyond Barth 'by treating the descent into hell as an event in its own right' (*ibid.*, 40–1).

There are two trajectories for rooting this line of thought Scripturally. The first (and weakest) approach is to find in 1 Pet. 3.18–22, Rom. 10.6, Eph. 4.8–10 and Acts 2.12–28 more or less direct references to this event. The second possibility (these are not mutually exclusive) emphasizes the cry of dereliction (Mt. 27.46 and Mk. 15.37) in conjunction with Jesus' teaching concerning the nature of hell and the widespread

Recall that for Barth God's patience is 'His will ... to allow another ... space and time for the development of its own existence, thus conceding to this existence a reality side by side with His own, and fulfilling His will towards this other in such a way that He does not suspend or destroy it as this other but accompanies and sustains it and allows it to develop in freedom' (*CD* II/1, 409–10). It is natural to think of ourselves as the 'other' in this passage – God gives us space in time, without suspending or destroying us, in anticipation of the saving work of Christ. But Barth's theology demands that we always think first in terms of Jesus Christ, and only second in terms of humankind. What happens if we rethink the above definition in terms of the incarnate Son of God bearing our sins?

In this line of thought, God continues to manifest his patience – in fact, manifests it here as nowhere else – in his will to allow Jesus Christ space and time for the development of his own existence as 'the bearer and Representative of sin' (*CD* IV/1, 254), as one who is dead in our place, fulfilling His will towards him by giving him over to eternal death and abandonment and precipitation into nothingness (*CD* II/1, 409–10, 420, paraphrase).[69] The patience of God is thus fully enacted not in forbearance, not in the tension between forgiveness and wrath throughout the Old Testament, but in the death of Christ in God-forsakenness, in the silence of Holy Saturday.[70] Adapting Barth's thought, we can affirm that 'it was to His being in death [*Sein im Tode*] that he had gone as the end of His way into the far country, in fulfillment of His [patience] in our place' (*CD* IV/1, 305; *KD*, 336), in his taking 'the existential measure of everything that is sheerly contrary to God, of the entire object of the divine eschatological judgment, which here is grasped in that event in which it is "cast down".'[71] In the work of Christ God does not cease to be patient but manifests

---

biblical conviction that Jesus bore the sins of the world. In other words, the 'doctrine of the descent into hell' is largely 'not the product of the exegesis of isolated biblical passages; rather it is the logical consequence of a synthetic reading of Scripture, and rigorous reflection on the implications of the *pro nobis* character of Jesus Christ's life and passion' (Lauber, *Barth on the Descent*, 76–112, esp. 10–11).

[69] Note the similarity to von Balthasar's claim: 'The real object of a theology of Holy Saturday ... consists in something unique, expressed in the 'realization' of all Godlessness, of all the sins of the world, now experienced as agony and a sinking down into the "second death" or "second chaos," outside of the world ordained from the beginning by God' (Balthasar, *Mysterium Paschale*, 51–2).

'Jesus suffers *eternal* corruption in his death. In other words, Jesus Christ enters hell in his death' (Lauber, *Barth on the Descent*, 23).

[70] 'Only if God is as steadfast as Jesus in accepting the terrible pain of this moment of holding back can God carry human sin to the uttermost' (John Goldingay, *Psalms* (Grand Rapids, MI: Baker Academic, 2006), I.342).

[71] Balthasar, *Mysterium Paschale*, 174.

Strangely, Alan Lewis critiques Barth in this regard: 'We have found nothing in the logic of Barth's later thought to prevent him from anticipating some successors in specifying not just the *suffering* but also the *death* of Christ as a Trinitarian event ...

the depth, the full extent of his patience, for Holy Saturday 'is precisely a day of waiting, a hiatus and a barrier ... And it is across this motionless, unhurried interstice between yesterday and tomorrow, this deadly stasis of inertia which faith has been constrained to speak of as descent into hell, that God's own self is suspended on Holy Saturday.'[72] In the time between Good Friday and Easter Sunday, Jesus Christ suffers the patience of God in the outworking of his being as the one great sinner (CD IV/1, 254) as the one who dies in abandonment from the Father (the second and third 'for us' of Barth's doctrine of substitution).[73]

But Jesus Christ suffers under the patience of God as the one who is truly patient in our place (the fourth and final 'for us'). He bore the wrath and abandonment of the Father, and was raised on the third day as God's decisive verdict that he was in fact sinless, was in fact the patient one for us and in our place – the one who bore in himself our impatience and its fruits in all the fullness of its demonic power.[74] He who was perfectly patient took the place of all us impatient sinners, by offering Himself, by substituting a perfect patience for us. This is 'the closing of the time of the divine ἀνοχή, the time of the mere πάρεσις of human sins endlessly repeating themselves, the time of the alternation of divine grace [or patience] and divine judgment ...' (CD IV/1, 281). But in this closing of the divine patience a new time of divine patience opens, not in the form of forbearance but in the form of

As it was, Barth allowed the human weakness and humiliation of Calvary's knowledge of God's nature. But he was less willing to allow the godforsakenness and termination of Good Friday to obtrude mortality, separation and disruption into God's own triune life' (Alan E. Lewis, *Between Cross and Resurrection: A Theology of Holy Saturday* (Grand Rapids, MI: Eerdmans, 2001), 214). Partly this has to do with Lewis' appreciation of Moltmann's understanding of the doctrine of the Trinity, and partly it rests on a misunderstanding of Barth. For a further critique, see Lauber, Barth on the Descent, 145–9.

[72] Lewis, *Between Cross and Resurrection*, 412–13. The line of thought following this quote requires some careful specification if not reformulation. It is interesting that Lewis appropriates the work of divine patience to the Holy Spirit in the event of Holy Saturday.

[73] Barth writes that 'His vicarious bearing of the sin of all Israel and indeed the whole world, points beyond the comfortless but tolerable situation of the righteous man of the Old Testament as alienated from God in *Sheol* ... [For] here God is wholly and unreservedly and in full seriousness against man. Here God metes out to man the kind of treatment he has deserved at His hand ... Here being in death [*Sein im Tode*] becomes punishment, torment, outer darkness, the worm, the flame – all eternal as God Himself, as God Himself in this antithesis, and all positively painful because the antithesis in which God here acts cannot be a natural confrontation, but must inevitably consist in the fact that infinite suffering is imposed upon the creature which God created and destined for Himself, when God reacted against this creature as it deserves ... In Him God Himself suffers what guilty man had to suffer by way of eternal punishment' (CD III/2, 603; KD, 734).

[74] This calls for the incorporation within Barth's hamartiology of the sin of impatience – a topic on which, unfortunately, Barth writes very little (cf. CD IV/3.1, 406–7).

hope, as 'in His Word He waits for us to give Him the glory in faith …' (*CD* II/1, 421). 'If we suffer with Him in this hope, and we believe according to God's Word that we have to suffer with Christ in this hope, we can and may and must suffer in patience: answering His patience with our patience … with our waiting for redemption' (*CD* II/1, 422).[75]

How is Jesus Christ for us in the event of his passion? He is for us (1) as the one who from eternity is the patient one to the very depths of his being. He is for us (2 and 3) as the one who takes upon himself our sin of impatience in the fullness of its demonic power, suffering this reality for us in the patience of the Father. He is for us (4) as the one who in this work acted patiently in our place, honouring the patience of the Father. Scripture's bountiful witness to the divine patience as a perfection of God's being and its role on both sides of the cross gives us ample warrant for fruitful consideration of the role of patience in the atoning work of Christ, and specifically in the event of Holy Saturday.

But how is this relevant? Why proclaim Christ's work in this way? Although rejoicing in Christ's work suffices in itself, there are nevertheless implications that we do well to appreciate, only one of which I mention here. Sin is impatience and the mutilation it brings upon itself. We seek divinity when we determine for ourselves when God's kingdom or our own should come – when the time for our wishes to be fulfilled or our sufferings to end has arrived. We constantly refuse to give 'space and time' to God and others 'for the development of [their] existence [and plans]', bringing upon ourselves and others the destruction and mutilation which follow from burdening immaturity with what it cannot handle, forcefully implementing plans prematurely, or coming up with our own perverse alternatives when too much remains outside our control. Eve's impatience for the god-likeness God later proved to be so willing to give (Gen. 3.5; 2 Pet. 1.4), Abram taking Sarai's slave to beget the children of the covenant (Gen. 16.1–2), the accident we cause by driving impatiently, the rushed marriage regretted for decades, pushing our kids into competitive sports and advanced classes before they are ready … Christ bears these acts of impatience and the destruction they cause in himself, freeing us to relinquish our impatience.

---

[75] A significant benefit of my interpretation of the cross as an act of divine patience is that our suffering in patience can now be seen more clearly as an imitation and following-after of his suffering in patience. Christ's suffering for us in his crucifixion and death is the full demonstration of the divine patience and therefore the basis for our own patience in suffering. 'The quality of Jesus' death', as Lauber notes, 'determines the quality of Christian discipleship' (Lauber, *Barth on the Descent*, 6). As Barth's thought currently stands, we are to imitate Christ and be patient in our suffering precisely at the point where God's patience (and therefore presumably that of the incarnate Son as well) ended! This leaves us, discordantly, with no patience to imitate.

5

ATONEMENT AND SIN

An underlying awareness of the unity and diversity proper to God is fundamental to Barth's understanding of Christ's atoning work and the unity and diversity thereof. Developing this thesis, Chapters 2–4 explored the relationship between God's being-in-act, the doctrine of the Trinity and the doctrine of the divine perfections with that of the atonement. In this chapter, I turn to the relationship between hamartiology and the atonement in Barth's theology, which raises the question of consistency – am I exploring an important but essentially unrelated area of thought to my thesis (focusing as it does on the doctrine of God)? Why the doctrine of sin, as opposed to that of the resurrection, creation, Church or sacraments?

First, while turning to hamartiology may entail an abandonment or de-emphasis of theological ontology in some theological works, this is not at all true for Barth. His understanding of evil as 'nothingness' and his complex account of the doctrine of sin are thoroughly integrated and derived from his Christology and doctrine of reconciliation, which are themselves rooted (as we have seen) in the doctrine of God, such that Barth's doctrine of sin offers us what Barth himself understands to be a continued if indirect perspective on the relationship between the doctrine of God and Christ's atoning work. The knowledge of sin, he writes, is 'a specific variation of the knowledge of God', a knowledge of the God become flesh in which 'the knowledge of human sin is enclosed' (CD IV/1, 359, 389).[1] Our study of sin, in other words, is in line with my governing interest in the relationship between theology proper and the doctrine of the atonement, and its indirect perspective brings to light a number of themes and points which we might otherwise overlook.

---

[1] Hartmut Ruddies writes that sin 'existiert als confusio der Versöhnung' (Ruddies, 'Christologie und Versöhnungslehre', 179). It is a specific variation of the knowledge of God because it is a confusion or perversion of reconciliation – but when viewed from the standpoint of Christ's reconciling work it opens up yet further avenues for exploring that same work.

Second, Barth's treatment of sin provides particularly fruitful material for considering the unity and diversity of the atonement. First, he treats the doctrine of sin within that of reconciliation and in doing so offers us an extended opportunity to continue exploring our thesis. Second, his hamartiology brings to light important themes and aspects of Christ's saving work which are muted in the sections of the *CD* we have already covered, and which we would otherwise miss. Finally, the doctrine of sin has played an essential role in the development of the doctrine of the atonement throughout the history of the church (as that which Christ's work overcomes) in a way that sets it apart from the doctrines of the Church, sacraments and even (unfortunately) the resurrection.[2] For these reasons, the selection of the doctrine sin for this chapter is a strategic one, given both the nature and content of Barth's treatment and the trajectory of historical treatments of the doctrine.

In this chapter we will first survey the overall structure of Barth's account (as it spreads across volume IV of the *CD*), and then explore the implications of this material for the doctrine of reconciliation, focusing on the Christological unity of his hamartiology and several other loosely organizing features of his thought. As a concluding test case, we will explore the possibility of integrating the insights offered by René Girard into Barth's overall account of both sin and reconciliation.

Christological Knowledge of Sin[3]

Barth locates his doctrine of sin within that of reconciliation, treating it in three separate sections in *CD* IV/1–3, subsequent to his development of Christ's life, death and resurrection in each of those part volumes. *CD* IV/1, §60 treats the 'Pride and Fall of Man', *CD* IV/2, §65 covers the 'Sloth and Misery of Man', and *CD* IV/3.1, §70 examines the 'Falsehood and Condemnation of Man'. While it is well known that Barth understands

---

[2] One can read dozens of books on the atonement, including such a classic as Anselm's *Cur Deus Homo*, without getting even the slightest hint that the resurrection is an essential aspect of Christ's saving work. Sin, on the other hand, is a necessary feature of any theory of the atonement, as there is no impetus or necessity underlying Christ's work without that which he must overcome. I in no way wish to de-emphasize the role of the resurrection within the atonement, however, and in fact I find Barth's integration of the resurrection within reconciliation as an essential component of Christ's work to be one of his great contributions to the history of doctrine. Two of the best books I have found to offer such an integration are Dawson, *The Resurrection in Karl Barth* and Torrance, *Space, Time, and Resurrection*.

[3] For an excellent survey of Barth's hamartiology, see Matt Jenson, *Gravity of Sin: Augustine, Luther and Barth on 'Homo Incurvatus in Se'* (New York: T & T Clark, 2006), 130–87.

sin to be pride, sloth and falsehood, Barth's elaboration of this doctrine is exceptionally rich and diverse, involving an intricate and varied structure interwoven with an unusually dense concentration of passages of biblical exegesis.[4] As with the other doctrines explored in this book, my intent is to offer a general overview of the doctrine of sin so as to facilitate a discussion of its relationship with the doctrine of the atonement, rather than to give a truly comprehensive treatment of Barth's hamartiology.[5]

Barth unconditionally rejects knowledge of sin on any other basis than the self-revelation of God. This should come as no surprise – his rejection of natural theology includes, naturally enough, any basis of knowledge of our own sin apart from God's self-revelation. Barth writes:

> [Man] may understand and recognise that he is limited, deficient and imperfect. He may be aware of the problematic nature of his existence as man. But this does not mean even remotely that he is aware of his being as the man of sin, at odds with God and his neighbor and with himself ... The real evil in which man enmeshes himself and is enmeshed is only too active in the way in which he experiences and understands the inner conflict of his existence. (*CD* IV/1, 360–1)

We do not know of our sin through our own power and capacity to do so, no matter how well-tuned a conscience or how horrendous our personal experiences may be, for our sin is so extensive that even our understanding of sin is coloured irremediably by our sinfulness. To reiterate, 'the evil in which man enmeshes himself and is enmeshed is only too active in the way in which he experiences and understands the inner conflict of his existence' (*CD* IV/1, 361).[6]

---

[4] In fact, it stands with *CD* II/2 and *CD* III/1 as containing some of the densest concentrations of biblical exegesis in the *CD*. Barth tends to do exegetical work in proportion to the audacity of his theological claims. When he senses that he is forging new theological ground, as in his Christological reorientation of election and sin, he seeks to bolster his case in Scripture.

[5] The closest work we have to a comprehensive treatment of Barth's doctrine of sin is probably Wolf Krötke, *Sin and Nothingness in the Theology of Karl Barth*, trans. Philip G. Ziegler and Christina-Maria Bammel (Princeton, NJ: Princeton Theological Seminary, 2005). Alongside that, one would have to include: Jenson, *Gravity of Sin*. While both of these works are excellent, neither fills the lacuna in Barth scholarship when it comes to a definitive work on Barth's hamartiology. This is not at all to disparage either work, as neither aims to fill this particular gap. For a helpful article that places Barth's view in the context of other treatments of the doctrine of sin, see David H. Kelsey, 'Whatever Happened to the Doctrine of Sin?', 50, no. 2 (1993), 169–78.

[6] 'Barth's Christological determination of sin is not so much an attempt to dislocate "theological" from "empirical" reality, as an argument born of a sense that human persons are characteristically self-deceived ... Far from averting attention from evil as

The notions of sin that one may have, while they may in fact bear some proximity to the true nature of sin, 'quickly invade and color his conception of justification and then his understanding of the atonement ... But soon, in all probability he will no longer understand that there can be for him and for the race no atonement, no hope or peace, apart from the forgiveness and righteousness purchased for them by Jesus Christ in His death on the cross' (*CD* IV/1, 373). And even if the effects of a natural knowledge of sin do not always seem quite so insidious as that, they surely leave their mark on our understanding of Christ's work, directing our thoughts in wrong directions altogether or distorting our views through under- or over-emphasis of different aspects of Christ's work.[7]

'In opposition' to such a natural knowledge, necessarily tainted by that which it seeks to understand, Barth 'maintain[s] the simple thesis that only when we know Jesus Christ do we really know that man is the man of sin, and what sin is, and what it means for man', for:

> It is a matter of the knowledge of the one God who in His Word became flesh for us, and therefore of the knowledge of His truth in this one revelation, and therefore of the one indivisible knowledge of the Christian faith, the basis and subject of which is God in His atoning work and therefore God in Jesus Christ. The knowledge of sin is enclosed [*beschlossen*] in this knowledge. (*CD* IV/1, 389; *KD*, 430)

That is to say that, for Barth, a Christian understanding of the doctrine of sin places us firmly within the doctrine of the self-revealing and self-giving God who brings the fullness of his being to bear upon our sin, bringing sin to light, confronting it and doing away with it, so as to re-establish his fellowship with us, his covenantal partners. This is Barth's underlying point – he rejects a natural doctrine of sin not only because the nature of sin undermines our capacity to fulfil this task, but above all because our knowledge of ourselves and God is rooted not only in problems pertaining to our own constitution, but is rather dependent on God's own proper activity of self-revelation.[8]

---

fact, Christology is intended to furnish a means of clarifying our vision and dissolving our illusions about our own moral integrity' (John Webster, 'The Firmest Grasp of the Real: Barth on Original Sin', *Toronto Journal of Theology* 4, no. 1 (1988), 22–3).

[7] The basis for Barth's rejection of natural theology should be sufficiently familiar that I do not need to explore it here.

In this context, Barth is no less concerned about a philosophically based understanding of sin than he is about the 'irremediable danger of consulting Holy Scripture apart from the centre, and in such a way that the question of Jesus Christ ceases to be the controlling and comprehensive question', apart from which 'the Scripture principle will not stand very long' (*CD* IV/1, 368).

[8] This explains why Barth locates his doctrine of sin within his doctrine of reconciliation,

Thus, while the doctrine of sin is not itself a part of the doctrine of God,[9] it has its place in Christian theology solely in light of and in relation to the doctrine of God via that of Christology and reconciliation. It is the presence of the living God in the person and work of Christ which, for Barth, opens up the possibility and necessity of the doctrine of sin (and along with it the full spectrum of Christian doctrine). This is true because 'in the knowledge of sin we have to do basically and in general with a specific variation [*bestimmten Modifikation*] of the knowledge of God, of God as He has mediated Himself to man, and therefore of the knowledge of the revelation of faith' (*CD* IV/1, 359; *KD*, 397). That is to say, by turning to the doctrine of sin we are in fact exploring a 'specific variation' of the material covered in the previous chapters, the relationship between the being of God and the atonement, from the specific vantage point of that which is overcome by means of God's being in reconciliation.

Unpacking his thesis that Jesus Christ is the basis for the Christian doctrine of sin, Barth notes four decisive points. First, 'the existence of Jesus Christ is the place where we have to do with human sin in its absolutely pure and developed and unequivocal form', where it is divested of its 'equivocal appearance' and where the 'three moments of evil, rebellion against God, enmity with one's neighbour and sin against oneself' are equally and fully manifest (*CD* IV/1, 398). Second, Jesus, who 'revealed the reality of human sin ... is also the Judge who discloses its sinfulness' (*CD* IV/1, 400). Third, Jesus reveals sin 'as the truth of all human being and activity' (*CD* IV/1, 403). Finally, only in Jesus Christ do we know 'the significance and extent of sin, or in the words of Anselm: *quanti ponderis sit peccatum*' (*CD* IV/1, 407). Briefly, in Jesus Christ God deals with sin (1) completely, (2) as God

rather than prior to it. The situation is not one in which a familiar problem awaits an unknown or unexpected answer. Rather, the answer itself is what makes us aware of the problem in the first place. It is the mountain air that awakens us to the toxic and sickly city fumes we were so used to breathing. It is our adoption into a new family that shocks us into the realization of just how the destructive and hellish the family relations we thought normal truly were. Only the solution can bring light to this problem, for the problem is too near to us, too much a part of us, for us to be able to see it.

[9] In other words, Barth does not understand sin or evil to be an essential and permanent aspect of the being of God or of God's covenant, such as he finds Hegel to believe: 'the Christian dialectic of covenant, sin and reconciliation cannot therefore be subjugated at any point to a Hegelian dialectic of thesis, antithesis and synthesis ... Sin does not follow from creation and covenant. It is already negated and excluded by the will of God active in creation' (*CD* IV/1, 80). Similarly, although without reference to Hegel this time, Barth writes: 'any systematic co-ordination of God and sin is made quite impossible for the Christian by his knowledge of what took place there [at Calvary]' (*CD* IV/2, 400). Whether Barth's modified form of supralapsarianism is ultimately consistent with this understanding is an important question which would take us beyond the scope of the present inquiry.

and therefore as Lord and Judge, (3) in such a way as to free us from its grip on every aspect of our lives, (4) through an act (death and resurrection) apart from which sin could not have been fully manifest or dealt with in all its depth and implications. Each in its own way, these points further unpack Barth's view that the doctrine of sin can be explored only within the doctrine of Reconciliation, only as a response to the self-revealing and reconciling work of God in Jesus Christ. It is through God's intervention in the person and work of Jesus Christ that we come to understand sin precisely as that which confronts God and God seeks to overcome.

Sin and Nothingness

Barth confirms this line of thought in his treatment of evil, which, as he understands it, does not have its own proper essence and therefore does not contain within itself the resources for accounting for its diversity. 'It has the essence only of non-essence, and only as such can it exist' (*CD* III/3, 352). That 'nothingness' [*das Nichtige*] does exist, however, is clear, for 'nothingness is not nothing' (*CD* III/3, 349), and its reality is apparent from the fact that 'true nothingness is that which brought Jesus Christ to the cross, and that which He defeated there' (*CD* III/3, 305).[10] What then is evil or nothingness? It is an antithesis that 'has no substantive existence within creation … It is the antithesis which can be present and active within creation only as an absolute alien opposing and contradicting all its elements, whether positive or negative' (*CD* III/3, 302).[11] That is to say, 'nothingness "is", therefore, in its connexion with the activity of God.

---

[10] As John McDowell notes, Barth's reflections on evil in §50 'constitute notable steps that enable one to read volume IV … as, in some sense, §50's detailing and drama- tized expression. As such, Barth's much misunderstood and maligned negative and paradoxical depictions of evil need to be read as expressions disabling any simple *systematic theologizing of evil*. Put starkly, *das Nichtige* cannot and should not be theologically systematized since it is disruptive of grand theological schemes, and can best be portrayed through this form of "mythopoetic" discourse within the Christian grammar of God's-being-for-the-world-in-Christ' (John C. McDowell, 'Much Ado About Nothing: Karl Barth's Being Unable to Do Nothing About Nothing', *IJST* 4, no. 3 (2002), 319.

[11] 'Its quasi-reality is received in a relation of negation or privation of the 'good', a description approving of Augustine's post-Plotinian *Malum est privation boni* (*CD* III/3, 318), and is therefore the nullity that is only parasitical on, and not in any way identifiable with, the good that is 'reality' (or 'being') (*CD* II/2, 170–1)' (*ibid.*, 326–7). As Daniel Migliore writes, 'For Barth, the essence of sin is properly grasped only when it is seen as a countermovement against the grace of God … In its essence, sin is a refusal to live in right relationship with God and others as made known in the Word of God whose center is Jesus Christ' (Daniel L. Migliore, 'Sin and Self-loss: Karl Barth and the Feminist Critique of Traditional Doctrines of Sin', in *Many Voices, One God*, eds George W. Stroup and Walter Brueggemann (Louisville, KY: WJK, 1998), 146). Similarly, Allen Jorgenson writes that, 'in spite of the *sui generis* character of sin, it is

It "is" because and as and so long as God is against it' (*CD* III/3, 353): against it in the upholding of his creation for the sake of his fulfilment of the covenant through the person and work of Jesus Christ and therefore in the calling and vocation given to his covenantal partners. Lacking an essence, sin does not have a unity proper to itself, proper to its own essence – its unity consists in being that which God pours forth his own proper unity in diversity so as to resist and overcome it, for God does not 'deal with it incidentally but in the fullness of the glory of His deity', and 'is not engaged indirectly or mediately but with His whole being, involving Himself to the utmost' (*CD* III/3, 349).

While these are deep theological waters, my purpose is to bring to our attention one specific point: Barth's claim that 'nothingness "is" … [only] in its connexion with the activity of God'. To properly understand this thesis, we must examine it at two levels (having to do with the doctrine of creation and the doctrine of God). First, because creation has its basis only in the will and act of God, the complex diversity of sin and nothingness affecting the full spectrum of the created order likewise has its basis ultimately only in the will and act of God.[12] This will is not the same as God's creative will, for God gives neither an essence nor permanence to nothingness, but rejects and does away with it. Thus, while Barth clearly does not hold that God wills the existence of evil, the being of nothingness nevertheless has its ultimate basis only in the will and act of God, as that which assails, opposes, resists and offends him (*CD* III/3, 356). It can do this because 'God did not will to be God for His own sake alone, but that as the Creator He also became the covenant Partner of His creature, entering into a relationship with it in which He wills to be directly and primarily involved in all that concerns it' (*CD* III/3, 356). God wills to have a creature in fellowship with Himself, one which can cross 'the frontier from the one side, and [be] invaded from the other', thereby allowing nothingness to achieve actuality in the creaturely world (*CD* III/3, 350). In this way only God wills the existence of evil as nothingness.

Second, in having to do with God's act ('nothingness 'is' … [only] in its connexion with the activity of God'), we have to do with God's being

---

not autonomous and its reality depends on that which it opposes' (Allen Jorgenson, 'Karl Barth's Christological Treatment of Sin', *SJT* 54, no. 4 (2001), 448–9).

[12] 'Man is by the grace of God, the grace which appeared in Jesus Christ so that there is no place where he can be neutral to God, or act as his own master or an interpretation of his existence which is opposed to him' (*CD* IV/1, 402). This lack of 'neutrality' is vital for understanding the relationship between sin and the being of God. Sin is and can be only in direct confrontation of God and only on the basis of his own activity. Just as there is no neutral ground between us and God, there is no neutral ground between our sin and God which sin can occupy without relying upon his sustaining activity and without directly confronting him and his electing purposes. Cf. *CD* IV/2, 394, 434.

and therefore the unity-in-diversity proper to God's being which we have explored in the doctrines of the Trinity and divine perfections in Chapters 2–4. In his exposition of nothingness, Barth writes:

> When seen in the light of Jesus Christ, the concrete form in which nothingness is active and revealed is the sin of man as his personal act and guilt, his aberration from the grace of God and its command, his refusal of the gratitude he owes to God and the concomitant freedom and obligation, his arrogant attempt to be his own master, provider and comforter, his unhallowed lust for what is not his own, the falsehood, hatred and pride in which he is enmeshed in relation to his neighbor, the stupidity to which he is self-condemned, and a life which follows the course thereby determined on the basis of the necessity thus imposed. (*CD* III/3, 305)

The 'concrete form of nothingness' turns out to be a multitude of forms of sin. Why is this the case? While Barth does not say as much, I contend that the explanation is rooted finally and exclusively within the doctrine of God, for this multiplicity becomes apparent 'when seen in the light of Jesus Christ', and therefore in the light of the being of God present and active in him in the fullness of his divine perfections. The diversity proper to sin is derivative of the diversity of the fullness of God given to us in covenant fellowship and God's own fulfilment thereof.

In other words, the diversity of sin is a derivative of, or a counter-movement against, the diversity of God's own proper perfections. Because God wills to share his being and life with that which is not Himself, the counter-movement of sin has its basis solely in that activity, and can take the form only of a rejection and perversion of that which it was offered. The doctrine of sin is thus a specific variation of the doctrine of the divine perfections, a variation brought to light by God's pouring forth of his being 'by giving Himself in His Son, by Himself becoming a creature and as such taking on Himself the sin, guilt and misery of the creature' (*CD* III/3, 362). As Eberhard Busch writes, 'Barth did not want to present an isolated doctrine of sin ... It was to be directly incorporated into the doctrine of reconciliation and subordinated to it. Sin was thus strictly understood as a counter-movement against the action of God; as a contradiction ... against God's grace.'[13] Given the nature of the unity and diversity of the divine perfections that we have just seen, we could just as well rework this statement to include love, justice, omniscience and so forth.

This explains why Barth locates his hamartiology within the doctrine of reconciliation: 'in the knowledge of sin we have to do basically and in general with a specific variation of the knowledge of God, of God as He has

---

[13] Busch, *Karl Barth*, 378.

mediated Himself to man, and therefore of the knowledge of revelation and faith' (*CD* IV/1, 359). Because the work of reconciliation is accomplished by God's actualization of his own being to overcome that which opposes him (sin), God reveals both himself and sin in reconciliation. The source of our knowledge of sin (as that which is overcome) and our knowledge of God (as the one who overcomes sin) are thus inextricably and essentially related within the doctrine of reconciliation.

Sin as Pride, Sloth and Falsehood

Turning to the concrete exposition of the doctrine of sin, Barth offers a series of definitions of sin rooted in 'particular Christological standpoint[s]' (*CD* IV/1, 413). While a glance at the table of contents suggests that sin, according to Barth, is a matter of pride, sloth and falsehood, a careful examination of the relevant sections of the *CD* reveals an exceptionally rich account of sin characterized by a consistent Christological emphasis, flexible and shifting structure and pastoral sensitivity.[14] Our purpose in this section is to explore some of these features and to achieve a preliminary familiarity of the material content of Barth's treatment, which will then fund our further inquiry into the relationship between Barth's hamartiology and doctrine of reconciliation.[15]

Barth begins his doctrine of sin by dwelling on more general aspects of sin, which he then concretizes via his account of the triptych of pride, sloth and falsehood. 'The pride of man', Barth writes:

> Is a concrete form of what a more general definition rightly calls the disobedience of man and Christianity rightly and more precisely calls the unbelief of man ... It is true enough that unbelief is *the* sin, the original form and source of all sins, and in the last analysis the only sin, because it is the sin which produces and embraces all other sins. (*CD* IV/1, 414)

One might expect that Barth would engage sin as unbelief more fully, but he quickly transitions to pride as its concrete manifestation (*CD* IV/1, 417). Unbelief, we might say, is the heart or source of all sin, but simultaneously so general as to be unhelpful or insufficient in unmasking the specific character of sin, leading Barth to explore its concretions. Barth

---

[14] For instances of this pastoral sensitivity in his preaching, cf. Barth, *Deliverance to the Captives*, 30, 37.

[15] Our brief survey overlooks a number of significant aspects of Barth's hamartiology, such as Barth's denial of the traditional understanding of original sin. Cf. Webster, 'The Firmest Grasp of the Real'. On this topic, see the work of Henri Blocher which offers significant exegetical support for Barth's position on original sin (Henri Blocher, *Original Sin: Illuminating the Riddle* (Leicester: Apollos, 1997)).

prepares us for his exposition of sloth [*Trägheit*] in much the same way, by bringing 'what we have to say ... under a single common denominator, by saying that the existence of the man Jesus and the event of the direction of the Holy Spirit as issued by Him involve the shaming of all other men' (*CD* IV/2, 384). As he turns to consider sin as sloth, it is only 'from the standpoint presupposed in the deliberations of our first sub-section' on shame (*CD* IV/2, 403). Does this place shame and unbelief/disobedience on the same level? Evidently not, for 'even as sloth, sin is plainly disobedience. Again, this form obviously falls under the even more penetrating [*tiefer greifende*] definition of sin as unbelief', such that in this second section unbelief once again confronts us as the most penetrating definition of sin (*CD* IV/2, 405; *KD*, 454). Shame, in this instance, operates between unbelief and sloth in a manner unparalleled by a similar aspect of sin between unbelief and pride in *CD* IV/1. When Barth returns to the doctrine of sin a third time in *CD* IV/3.1, we might expect a further general account of unbelief as the 'central and universal definition' of sin (*CD* IV/1, 414). Surprisingly, however, Barth refers to it only tangentially within the triptych of 'unbelief, superstition and error [*Unglauben, Aberglauben und Irrglauben*]'.[16] Significantly, this would appear to undermine the likelihood that unbelief serves Barth in the capacity of a master-concept of sin, confusing the apparent structure of his account.[17]

Turning to the concretization of unbelief and shame, Barth explores sin under the three forms of pride, sloth and falsehood. 'The Pride of Man' is 'the human disorder which is the antithesis of the divine order of grace' (*CD* IV/1, 418). Whereas God 'becomes and is as we are ... we want to be God' (*CD* IV/1, 418), although typically 'under a powerful concealment in which we seek to be our own standard' (*CD* IV/1, 422). And in seeking to be god-like, we mistake the God for one who is 'a self-sufficient, self-affirming, self-desiring supreme being' (*CD* IV/1, 422).[18] Unlike the Lord

---

16 We are thus left with the possibility that unbelief is in fact the central or underlying sin in Barth's thought, though such a possibility is significantly mitigated by the fact that unbelief is virtually inconsequential to Barth's third and final treatment of the doctrine of sin. Whether we have in unbelief the chief sin which was somehow omitted in the final section, or whether we have a third and undeveloped triptych in unbelief, shame and falsehood is unclear. What is clear, however, is that Barth did not seem to be so interested in establishing a single aspect of sin as central to his treatment as to take the necessary steps to make such a move sufficiently clear to his readers. The unity of the doctrine of sin, I suggest, lies elsewhere.

17 Barth's treatment of falsehood is all the more surprising for its straightforwardness: while Barth moves from unbelief/disobedience to pride in *CD* IV/1, and unbelief/disobedience to shame to sloth in *CD* IV/2. *CD* IV/3.1 offers a far more direct and sustained treatment of falsehood without allusion to underlying or more general aspects of sin of which falsehood is a concretization.

18 Concealment [*Verdeckung*] is a particularly insightful and provocative theme throughout Barth's treatment of sin, in which he demonstrates a powerful and

who became servant, we seek 'the very opposite – the servant who wants to be Lord' (*CD* IV/1, 432). Unlike the Lord who bore our guilt and 'caused Himself to be judged' in our place (*CD* IV/1, 445), we seek 'to be [our] own judge instead of allowing that God is in the right against [us]' (*CD* IV/1, 445), such that even in our self-condemnation we set ourselves upon our self-made thrones. Unlike the God who became helpless in bearing our sin and guilt for us, the sinful man 'imagines of himself, and repeats to himself, that he can and will know how to help and save and liberate himself, giving himself a position and being, asserting and maintaining himself' (*CD* IV/1, 459).[19]

Barth balances his account of this 'heroic, Promethean form of sin' with a second form, that of 'sluggishness, indolence, slowness or inertia ... The evil inaction which is absolutely forbidden and reprehensible but which characterises human sin' (*CD* IV/2, 403). Evil not only takes the form of activity (pride) but of inactivity: sloth. In this form of sin, humankind 'wants to be left alone by the God who has made this man a neighbor with His distinctive freedom' (*CD* IV/2, 407). As sloth, sin is (1) 'stupidity' or 'that which the Bible describes and condemns as human folly' (*CD* IV/2, 411) – a 'strange but mighty and tumultuous and dreadful force [playing a leading role] in world history' (*CD* IV/2, 412). At the same time it is (2) isolation, 'in which we want to be alone instead of being those we already are in and by this One': fellows and neighbours and brothers of this One who is our 'Fellow and Neighbour and Brother' (*CD* IV/2, 433). In this we 'will that which according to His incarnation God does not will', and thus reject both the being of God and his call upon our lives (*CD* IV/2, 434). In antithesis to Christ's life as one 'long exaltation, purification, sanctification and dedication of the flesh', our sloth manifests itself (3) 'as a life of dissipation' (*CD* IV/2, 452). Finally, sloth takes the form of (4) 'look[ing] frantically [and] anxiously busying ourselves to snatch at life before we die', slothfully refraining from 'the grace of participation in the movement and exaltation which come from Jesus' (*CD* IV/2, 468).

Barth's treatment of sin in *CD* IV/3.1 consists of an extended examination of sin under the form of 'falsehood'. As truth encounters us 'in provoking identity with its Witness, Proclaimer and Revealer' (*CD* IV/3.1, 440), falsehood (1) 'cleav[es] their unity' and so 'tries to manipulate the truth and the true Witness' (*CD* IV/3.1, 441). As 'the true Witness is the

---

pastoral sensitivity to the complex and veiled presence of sin in everyday life, not at all dissimilar to the sensitivity demonstrated in (Ernst Troeltsch, *The Christian Faith: Based on Lectures Delivered at the University of Heidelberg in 1912 and 1913*, ed. Gertrud Le Fort, trans. Garrett E. Paul (Minneapolis: Fortress, 1991), 241–53).

[19] Although I omit this feature of Barth's analysis for the sake of brevity, he adds a layer of complexity to his overall account by noting at every step the 'concealment' of sin (cf. *CD* IV/1, 422).

man of Gethsemane and Golgotha' (*CD* IV/3.1, 441), falsehood (2) seeks to generalize and 'translate and reinterpret and transform it ... to appropriate and domesticate it' in a host of different ways (*CD* IV/3.1, 442). As God's Word 'approaches and invades us in this power, and ... claims us as those who are pledged to hear and obey', falsehood (3) obscures the 'encounter' of 'two partners who are from the very first and unchangeably unequal, namely, God and man', not by a flat denial so much as by reinterpreting and explaining it 'with the less unsettling notion of a continuous co-existence of the two' (*CD* IV/3.1, 444). Finally, as God meets us in his own proper freedom as 'loving Father and Lord, Friend and Helper', giving and requiring of us 'the freedom of one who belongs to the free God and is freed by him' (*CD* IV/3.1, 446) falsehood (4) either systematizes this confrontation or imagines its own foolish freedom.

According to Barth, humankind exists 'in the unity of [its] activity and being ... Man is what he does. And he does what he is' (*CD* IV/1, 492). Accordingly, he follows his discussion of pride, sloth and falsehood with a consideration of his state of being ('two sides of one determination').[20] First, he complements his treatment of 'the pride of man' ('what the sin of man is') with that of 'the fall of man' ('who and what the man is who commits sin') (*CD* IV/1, 478). In moving from pride [*Hochmut*] to fallenness [*Fall*], the latter term 'corresponds exactly to what we have learned to know as the essence of sin – the pride of man' (*CD* IV/1, 478). Barth elaborates his account of humankind's fall in three main points. First, 'the word of divine forgiveness' makes clear that 'man is God's debtor. He is a debtor who cannot pay' (*CD* IV/1, 484). Second, 'the fact that Jesus Christ died totally for the reconciliation of every man as such ... means decisively that this corruption is both radical and total' (*CD* IV/1, 492). Ours is, in short, a 'being in sin' [*sündig-menschlichen Dranseins*] (*CD* IV/1, 494; *KD*, 550). Third, in the mercy which God had on all men in the sacrifice of Jesus Christ, God 'concluded them all in disobedience' (*CD* IV/1, 501).

In keeping with the pattern developed in *CD* IV/1, Barth turns to consider the 'man of sloth', finding that 'the situation which we create ... is the misery of man in the sense of his exile as the sum of human woe' (*CD* IV/2, 483). This misery is (1) 'a sickness which can terminate only with the death of the patient' (*CD* IV/2, 485), as our liberation from it occurs 'only in the crucified Jesus' (*CD* IV/2, 485). As Christ is the new beginning, the misery of man is 'an endless circle' (*CD* IV/2, 490). Finally, as we are only genuinely free in Christ, our misery 'is the determination of our will as *servum arbitrium*' (*CD* IV/2, 494).

The life of falsehood, on the other hand, is one which 'chooses and draws down upon [itself] ... condemnation. To be condemned is to be judged, i.e., to be judged by God' (*CD* IV/3.1, 462). Falsehood makes 'the rash attempt

---

[20] Jenson, *Gravity of Sin*, 161.

to set up a situation between God and man in which Jesus Christ does not exist as the Mediator between them', in which, as a result, '[a man] conjures up the shade of this dead man and thus places himself under this threat' (CD IV/3.1, 464). This fantasy is no mere game, however: 'the moment God nails him to his fatal exchange of places, to his falsehood, to his cursing of himself, the sword will inevitably fall, his condemnation will become a present reality and he can only be lost' (CD IV/3.1, 465). As such, 'he lives in a subjective reality alien to and contradicting his objective reality', one that 'has no center' and therefore no 'periphery' or 'real co-existence', lacking 'any unifying force' (CD IV/3.1, 469–70).

From the very outset, then, we sense the complexity of Barth's account. First of all, the glaring asymmetry ensuing from the lack of a general form of sin underlying Barth's development of falsehood would seem to suggest that the framework of Barth's hamartiology is ultimately not what drives his complex account. Second, the triptych of pride, sloth and falsehood is preceded by unbelief and shame and then mushrooms out to include fall, misery and condemnation, such that the picture is always expanding. Finally, within Barth's account of any one of these aspects of sin, diversity is once again prominent in a new way as new aspects of sin quickly emerge. Rebellion, disorder and chaos (CD IV/1, 436), debt and guilt (CD IV/1, 484), and a host of other forms of sin come pouring out of the woodwork, such that the structure of the account appears to be more of a starting point for branching out than a rigid framework by which to comprehend and order Barth's ensuing exposition. What are we to make of this diversity and ultimately not very satisfying structure?

Sin and the Divine Perfections

Earlier I suggested that the doctrine of sin is a specific variation of the doctrine of the divine perfections. To secure a proper grasp of Barth's hamartiology, it is necessary to return to this point and explore its implications. Given the Christocentric foundation for Barth's doctrine of sin, we will misunderstand the order and structure of the latter inasmuch as we fail to keep the former firmly in mind. In other words, the unifying and ordering principle of the doctrine of sin is not immanent to that doctrine, but derivative from Christology, or more properly, the doctrine of the divine perfections. Or as Matt Jenson puts it, it is strictly 'a function of Barth's theocentrism'.[21] The Trinitarian unity in diversity of the divine perfections thus provides the key to understanding Barth's hamartiology.

Barth writes of his definition of sin as the pride of man that it 'is not exhaustive. In the later chapters on reconciliation it will be supplemented

---

[21] Ibid., 186. That theocentrism is perfectly compatible with Christocentrism in Barth's theology is amply evident in Jenson's chapter.

from other Christological standpoints. But even so, it denotes more than just a part of the content. Sin in its unity and totality [*Einheit und Ganzheit*] is always pride ... Sin ... in its totality [*Totalität*] is pride' (*CD* IV/1, 413; *KD*, 459). We are already familiar with the point that the basis for further supplementation is rooted in *Christological* standpoints. What is of particular interest here is Barth's expression 'in its unity and totality'. Recall that in *CD* II/1 Barth writes that every individual divine perfection 'which is to be affirmed of God can signify only the one [*Einzelne*], but the one which is to be affirmed of Him must of necessity signify also every individual [*jedes Einzelne*] trait and the totality [*Gesamtheit*] of all individual traits. Every distinction in God can be affirmed only in such a way as implies at the same time His unity [*Einheit*] and therefore the lack of essential discrepancy in what is distinguished' (*CD* II/1, 332–3; *KD*, 374).[22]

The unity and diversity of evil and sin is a variation of and dependent upon the unity and diversity of God's perfections with which it is in conflict.[23] Like the divine perfections, each form of sin defines sin in its unity and totality, though without being exhaustive.[24] And like the divine perfections, in which Barth moves from God's being-in-act to his loving freedom

[22] The terms *Ganzheit*, *Totalität* and *Gesamtheit* in these passages are synonymous. While Barth uses *Gesamtheit* to refer to the totality of God in this passage of *CD* II/1, later in the same volume he uses *Ganzheit* in a manner identical with our passage drawn from *CD* IV/1: God is 'free in His unity and totality [*Einheit und Ganzheit*] always to be present in one specific way according to His good-pleasure' (*CD* II/1, 473; *KD*, 532). Similarly, Barth writes that 'God's glory is also the fullness, the totality, the sufficiency, the sum of the perfection of God in the irresistibility of its declaration and manifestation' (*CD* II/1, 645; *KD*, 728), again using the term *Ganzheit*.

[23] As Cole notes, 'theologians use the concept of sin as a master concept to sum up the whole range of biblical ways of speaking of that state of being, those attitudes and actions displeasing to God, *which contradict his character* and sabotage the design for human flourishing (glory)' (Cole, *God the Peacemaker*, 68, emphasis added).

[24] For this reason, a good deal of caution is needed if we are to refer to any particular form or understanding of sin as having an overarching character, despite the fact that Barth himself offers a good deal of warrant for such a move.
    We can see just how seriously Barth resists elevating one overarching or basic sin, with what sincerity he takes each of sin's forms to define sin in its totality, in his freedom to write in the midst of World War II that 'there never was a people so sick as the German people today. It will surely be in a more pitiable state tomorrow than all those upon which it has brought so much distress' (Karl Barth, *The Church and the War*, trans. Antonia H. Froendt (New York: Macmillan, 1944), 44). To acknowledge the reality of sin as sickness rather than as guilt in a people that has brought such devastation upon oneself and others takes a profound appreciation of the unity in diversity of sin, such that one aspect of sin (particularly guilt, when considering those who have sinned against us) does not trump the others in an ultimately unchristian manner. That Barth has not minimized guilt in his emphasis on sickness is apparent in that he presupposes the mutual guilt of the Nazis and the rest of the world earlier in his letter (Barth, *The Church and the War*, 24–7).

to a much broader account, Barth's hamartiology moves from unbelief (and shame) to pride, sloth and falsehood (and fall, misery and condemnation), and from there to an ultimately much broader and more diverse account of sin. This relationship explains why certain aspects of Barth's structure seem to collapse in *CD* IV/3.1 – because ultimately the structure is of secondary importance. It also explains why Barth is so uninterested in finding a foundational sin and why diversity is so much more prominent in Barth's account than unity.

With this thesis clearly expressed, a number of Barth's statements appear in stark relief: 'In all its forms sin is man's perverted dealing with the stern goodness and righteous mercy of God addressed to him in Jesus Christ. It is their denial and rejection, their misunderstanding and misuse' (*CD* IV/3.1, 369); 'Sin as sin against the grace of God is falsehood as it is also pride and sloth' (*CD* IV/3.1 372); 'The light is still there, but quenched; the wealth as it slips away; the glory as it turns to shame; the purity to impurity; the joy to sadness ... It is the history of his impotent ignoring of the grace of God present to him' (*CD* IV/2, 488–9); 'Renouncing self-mastery [in their debauchery], they have rejected the lordship of God ... The habit of self-forgiveness spoils the taste for a life by free grace' (*CD* IV/2, 461). The key in each of these statements is relationship between the divine perfections and their rejection or perversion.

Sin 'is' only in connection with the activity of the divine perfections of God, deriving from thence its character and structure. Sin exists only in quenching, turning, moving, ignoring, renouncing, rejecting and otherwise offering a countermovement against the perfection of God in his covenantal activity. While Barth nowhere states as much, the divine perfections, actualized according to God's elective purposes in the person and work of Jesus Christ, form the ultimate basis for Barth's doctrine of sin. In this way, as Daniel Migliore notes, 'Barth offers an unmistakably theological description of sin in contrast to ways of speaking that are more or less reductionistic',[25] in which the abundance of the material development far exceeds that of the formal structure.[26]

Christological Knowledge of Sin and the Doctrine of the Atonement

My purpose in delving into Barth's hamartiology is strictly focused on his doctrine of reconciliation and, more specifically, for the resources within the doctrine of God to explore the unity and diversity of the doctrine of the atonement. While my venture into the doctrine of sin may seem to be an unpromising enterprise, in Barth's thought it proves particularly fruitful, due to his dogmatic location of hamartiology within the doctrine of

[25] Migliore, 'Sin and Self-loss', 146.
[26] For a sampling of this abundance, cf. *CD* IV/1, 398–9, 406, 414, 494; *CD* IV/2, 384, 390–1, 395, 410, 442, 486, 491, 772; *CD* IV/3, 372, 446, 456, 462, 464.

reconciliation, and more specifically within the doctrine of God. What then are the fruits of this exploration, the consideration of which in large part I have postponed until now?

We explored in the previous chapter the tremendous potential of the doctrine of the divine perfections for opening up new lines of thought with regards to the atonement. For example, while we are familiar with thinking of Christ's work in light of God's justice or mercy, there are fruitful and relatively unexplored avenues available within the doctrine of the atonement in light of a properly Christocentric account of such perfections as the divine wisdom, patience and omnipotence. But as we have seen in the present chapter, 'in the knowledge of sin we have to do basically and in general with a specific variation of the knowledge of God' (CD IV/1, 359) or, more specifically, in the knowledge of sin we have to do basically with a variation of the divine perfections as actualized in God's elective purposes. But if this is the case, if in our knowledge of sin we have a variation of the knowledge of God's perfections because it is precisely God's *self-revealing* work of reconciliation that gives us our knowledge of sin, then we likewise have in our knowledge of sin a variation of our knowledge of reconciliation (as in Chapter 4). *Just as the doctrine of the divine perfections encourages us to explore Christ's work in light of each of the perfections of the Triune God, Barth's doctrine of sin encourages us to a variation of this task, approaching Christ's work in light of the various aspects sin revealed in Scripture and given their definitive exposition in light of the cross.*[27]

For instance, given that 'the existence of the man Jesus and the event of the direction of the Holy Spirit as issued by Him involve the shaming of all other men' (CD IV/2, 384), Barth contends that Jesus consented to '[man's] situation, to bear his shame, to be put to shame in his place on his behalf, thus removing man from the situation which contradicts His election and love and creative will, divesting him of his shame and clothing him with His own glory' (CD IV/2, 384). While such statements strewn throughout the CD may be easy to overlook, my hope is to give reason to pause and consider the full significance of such claims. In effect, Barth has just offered us a condensed recapitulation of the four-fold 'for us' of CD IV/1, §59.2 ('The Judge Judged in Our Place'), from the standpoint of shame rather than guilt. Where (1) Christ took our place as Judge he takes our place as the glorious one who shames us; where (2) he took our place as the judged, he is the one shamed; where (3) he was judged in our place, he was shamed in our place; and where (4) he acted justly in our place, he removes our shame and clothes us with his own glory (CD IV/1, 273; CD IV/2, 384). Shame, in other words, while it may not be as thoroughly developed in Scripture as

---

[27] It is interesting to note that Fiddes accounts for the unity in diversity of the atonement via the multiple understandings of the human predicament/sin (Fiddes, *Past Event and Present Salvation*, 5–13).

the role of guilt, is in principle a fully satisfactory standpoint for exploring the work of Christ, and one that thereby opens up new theological and pastoral possibilities for the Church.[28]

Shame, however, is only one of numerous possibilities. In the span of just a few pages of the *CD*, and in more or less detail, Barth refers to sin as unbelief, hatred, frivolous encroachment and usurpation, illegitimate attempt to control its object, subservient and obsequious sloth, unreason, ignorance of God, lack of wisdom, folly, stupidity, vanity, senility, mediocrity, unteacheableness and indifference (*CD* IV/2, 405, 410). Of course it is not the case that any 'bad' word that we can think of unlocks the key to a new aspect of Christ's saving work. We must carefully sift the deluge of terms Barth unleashes to refer to sin, developing them according to the biblical witness in the light of its centre in the person and work of Jesus Christ, and only on that basis use them in such a way as to explore the possibilities with regards to Christ's saving work. But the resources here are immense for increased understanding of Christ's work, for as Cole notes, 'Scripture has a multitude of descriptors of sin … the semantic field for 'sin' in the Hebrew Bible [alone] contains no fewer than fifty terms.'[29]

In other words, by considering the doctrine of the atonement in light of the doctrine of God, we can see how the doctrine of sin is not simply its own discreet doctrine among the various loci of the Christian faith. Rather, the doctrine of sin is an essential facet of the inter-related doctrines of God and

---

[28] In effect, in doing this Barth anticipates the recent work of Joel Green and Mark Baker (and that of Norman Kraus upon whom they rely) on shame and the doctrine of the atonement (Baker and Green, *Recovering the Scandal*, 153–70; C. Norman Kraus, *Jesus Christ Our Lord: Christology from a Disciple's Perspective* (Scottdale, PA: Herald Press, 1987)). This is not to suggest, of course, that the concept of shame was unknown in studies of the atonement prior to this. Martin Hengel, for example, offers an excellent treatment of the role of shame and humiliation in the practice of crucifixion in the ancient world (Martin Hengel, *Crucifixion in the Ancient World and the Folly of the Message of the Cross*, trans. John Bowden (Philadelphia, PA: Fortress, 1977)).

While Barth would surely question the underlying approach to culture that permeates their book, their appropriation of the role of shame within the biblical portrayal of the cross, Christ's vicarious experience of ultimate shame on the cross, his exposure of false shame and removal of alienation are all themes which resonate with Barth's own thought. The really important thing to note, however, is that the biblical witness to the doctrine of sin and the being of God funds (rather than supports) Barth's appropriation and understanding of shame, such that cultural sensitivities played no obvious or normative role in his appropriation of shame (as they do in Baker and Green), and the likelihood is accordingly reduced that culture will not only open the door to, but domesticate, our understanding of shame. It is important to recognize, though, that Baker and Green do in fact seek to safeguard against such a danger, allowing a biblical understanding to critique a cultural understanding of shame (Baker and Green, *Recovering the Scandal*, 162, 68).

[29] Cole, *God the Peacemaker*, 68.

atonement, offering us yet another hermeneutical approach within Scripture and the history of theology by which to explore new standpoints of Christ's saving work. That is to say, while reflection on the divine perfections or the efficacy of Christ's death and resurrection may guide our thought in certain directions, the Scriptural witness (and theological reflection) concerning sin may further enrich this process, opening our eyes to other divine perfections and aspects of the efficacy of Christ's work which we may otherwise miss. For according to Barth, sin is that which we know of only inasmuch as it is overcome by Christ's saving work as he brings the divine being to bear against it.

The pastoral possibilities latent within such an approach are immense – for it is here that we see so clearly how Christ's saving work bears on hurt, pain and sin. While the different divine perfections provide the foundation for the different theories of Christ's saving work, implicit within those theories are the different understandings of sin corresponding to the divine perfections emphasized within those theories. And inasmuch as we learn to emphasize the diversity proper to sin in light of Christ's atoning work, we equip ourselves to think through our own sins and those of others in light of who Christ is and what he has done for us, unleashing the power of the cross. Inasmuch as we reduce sin to guilt or disobedience or some other 'favourite' aspect, we both deprive ourselves of vital theological resources for bringing Christ's work to bear on sin in its many forms, or inadvertently use aspects of sin and Christ's work in those situations which prove to be less fitting and therefore less beneficial.

Unifying Factors and the Doctrine of the Atonement

We have seen that Barth offers a Christologically ordered treatment of sin that is exceptionally rich in content, varied in structure, and ultimately derives its basis and form from the doctrine of the divine perfections. This relationship between the divine perfections and the various forms of sin is sufficient in and of itself to provide ample material for our consideration. In fact, however, we have only begun to explore the unity of Barth's hamartiology. While the Christocentric and ultimately theological (i.e. doctrine of God) foundation for the being of sin is, of course, the ultimate and primary basis for Barth's account, he also develops a second unifying feature throughout his account, which plays a significant if modest role in his hamartiology.[30] This bears not only on Barth's hamartiology, but also (and more significantly for my thesis) upon our understanding of the unity

---

[30] Another line of inquiry that I choose to omit here has to do with the role of the *munus triplex* in Barth's thought and that of others as a unifying scheme for the doctrine of the atonement.

and diversity of Barth's treatment of the atonement. In this second major section of the chapter I will explore the 'three moments of sin', and then consider their implications for the unity and diversity of the doctrine of the atonement.

A Looser Organizing Feature: The Three (or Four) Moments of Sin

Barth writes that sin 'consists always and everywhere in trespass against God and fratricide … And it is always and everywhere true that in so doing he becomes guilty of self-destruction, of treachery against his own nature as given by God and created good' (CD IV/1, 398).[31] Sin, in other words, consists of 'the three moments of evil, rebelling against God, enmity with one's neighbor and sin against oneself' (CD IV/1, 398). Barth's use of the three moments of sin in CD IV/1 is slight, however, and it is in the next part-volume (CD IV/2) that the role of this concept comes fully into its own. Barth also slightly revises the three moments, writing that 'we are confronted by man's refusal (1) in his relationship with God; (2) in his relationship with his fellow-men; (3) in his relationship with the created order; and (4) in his relationship with his historical limitation in time' (CD IV/2, 409), such that the third moment from CD IV/1 has now been expanded into two moments.[32]

Barth integrates these four moments into his fourfold account of sloth, considering sloth in each of these four moments, and within each of these four steps considers the role of the other three moments as well (CD IV/2, 409, 432, 452, 467), resulting in a four-fold treatment of each of the four moments. For instance, the second form of sloth has to do with our relationship to our neighbours: 'the royal freedom of this one man consisted and consists in the fact that He is wholly the Fellow-man of us His fellows', but we 'remain in our isolation and seclusion and self-will and unwill-ingness, and therefore in our latent or patent hostility, in relation to them; in a word, in our inhumanity' (CD IV/2, 433). Further incorporating the 'four moments' into his thought, Barth then allows this second moment to play itself out in relation to the other three moments, noting how it includes our endangered bond with God (441ff.), collapses 'the structure and order of his human nature as the soul of his body' (443ff.), and 'extends to human life as characterized by its limited temporal duration' (444ff.). The net effect of this manoeuvre is an exceptionally rich and multi-faceted account of sin.

Unfortunately Barth does not continue the pattern initiated in CD IV/1 and greatly expanded in CD IV/2, and so far as I can tell does not mention

---

[31] Cf. McKnight, A Community Called Atonement, 22–3.

[32] In doing so he draws upon the material of CD III/2, expanding the third moment (from CD IV/1) to include the two themes of §§46–7 (Man as Soul and Body, and Man in His Time), thus pulling his anthropology firmly within the orbit of his doctrine of reconciliation and therefore his hamartiology as well.

the three (or four) 'moments' of sin in *CD* IV/3.1. Clearly this avenue is relatively narrow in terms of exploring the unity of Barth's hamartiology. However, it contributes to our understanding of the complex structure of Barth's argument while bringing to light a vital component of Barth's doctrine of the atonement: namely, the ontological spectrum impacted by this event, as Christ's reconciliation alters not only the God–human relationship, but also the intra-human and human–rest-of-creation relationships. This foray into the doctrine of sin, in other words, gives strong warrant for expanding the diversity of Barth's account of Christ's reconciling work.

Since for Barth hamartiology has its place only within the doctrine of reconciliation, the moments of sin must necessarily have their place only within corresponding and underlying moments of reconciliation.[33] Because each of the elements or aspects of the doctrine of sin have their place only inasmuch as that which is opposed and overcome by the work of Christ, any aspect of hamartiology necessarily has its counterpart within the doctrine of reconciliation as that which opposes and overcomes it. Therefore, just as there are three moments of sin, so the reconciling work of Christ restores our relationship not only with the Triune God, but also with our neighbours and with our very selves. While Barth does not refer to these various moments in his development of the atonement proper (*CD* IV/1, 157–357), his hamartiology affords us the opportunity, or rather demands the responsibility, of reading such a framework back into this account despite its omission. Essentially, Barth's hamartiology provides a firm foundation for understanding Christ's reconciling work as bearing on an ontological spectrum, touching the created order, self, family, community, institutions, nations, the angelic (and demonic) order, and the relations between these.

The key to such an enterprise is to consistently develop each of these aspects of reconciliation Christologically, in which Jesus' relationship to each of these aspects of reality provides the governing framework for consideration. Equally important is the commitment to understand the substitutionary death of Jesus Christ not merely as bearing the sin and guilt we have before God, but also as bearing the sin, guilt and death that affects so many different aspects of the created order. Admittedly, Barth does not explore these vital aspects of the doctrine of reconciliation as fully as we might hope,[34] particularly since liberation theologians in the

---

[33] By 'moments of reconciliation' I mean something rather different than McKnight's 'atoning moments'. Cf. McKnight, *A Community Called Atonement*, 50–78.

[34] As George Hunsinger writes in an exceptional essay, 'Barth would have something important to learn from [liberationists]. While it is certainly true that one can find passages in Barth's theology where the radical political imperatives of the gospel sound forth, it is also true that these imperatives are often muffled by the extraordinary expanse of other themes which he so prodigiously sets forth (Hunsinger, *Disruptive Grace*, 55). Cf. the dissertation written under Hunsinger's supervision: Hieb, 'The

last several decades have alerted us to this need through their consistent demand that we apply Christ's work on the cross to the situation of the poor and oppressed.[35] To his credit, however, Barth establishes the systematic foundation for such an extension of his thought in such a way that its incorporation is a fulfilment of his thought, a matter of bringing Barth's abbreviated exposition (despite its length) to its natural conclusion. Thus, while Barth did not consciously develop his doctrine of reconciliation according to the lines we are now pursuing, it must be said that Barth may in fact go a good deal further in this direction than many would suppose. In the remainder of this section we will consider some of these developments, particularly the relationship of reconciliation to the social/political sphere, angelic/demonic order, and creation generally.

Barth's development of Christ's reconciliation as a social reality (the second moment of sin) occurs largely at the political level. As Joseph Bettis writes, 'Barth's mature theology … leads directly, inevitably and necessarily to radical political ethics', a necessary consequence of 'any theology which would be true to its responsibility to speak honestly and truly about the living God'.[36] On the basis 'of the fact that the Son of man came to seek and to save the lost',[37] Barth's radical political ethic leads him to reject a merely spiritual message of justification, which by its 'exclusive emphasis upon the Kingdom of God, forgiveness of sins and sanctification' would cease 'to seek or find any entrance into the sphere of these problems of human justice'.[38] Rather, he demands that we 'concentrate first on the lower and lowest levels of human society', which include not only 'the poor, the socially and economically weak and threatened', not only 'certain classes and races but, supremely, of that of women'.[39] This socio-political work is by no means incidental to Barth's theology.[40] While the connection is most evident in Barth's hamartiology, and must be retrospectively worked into

Liberating Reconciliation of the Cross: Atonement for Sin and Liberation from Suffering in Karl Barth's "Theologia Crucis"'.

[35] Boff, *Passion of Christ*; Carlos Bravo, 'Jesus of Nazareth, Christ the Liberator', in *Systematic Theology: Perspectives from Liberation Theology*, eds Jon Sobrino and Ignacio Ellacuría (Maryknoll, NY: Orbis, 1996), 118–21; Gustavo Gutiérrez, *A Theology of Liberation: History, Politics, and Salvation* (Maryknoll, NY: Orbis, 1973), 145–87; Moltmann, *The Crucified God*.

[36] Joseph Bettis, 'Political Theology and Social Ethics: The Socialist Humanism of Karl Barth', in *Karl Barth and Radical Politics*, ed. George Hunsinger (Philadelphia, PA: Westminster Press, 1976), 161.

[37] Karl Barth, *Community, State, and Church: Three Essays*, trans. H. M. Hall, G. Ronald Howe and Ronald Gregor Smith (Garden City, NY: Doubleday, 1960), 173.

[38] *Ibid.*, 104–5.

[39] *Ibid.*, 173, 75.

[40] For a delightful book on the history of Barth's political involvement, see Frank Jehle, *Ever Against the Stream: The Politics of Karl Barth, 1906–1968* (Grand Rapids, MI: Eerdmans, 2002).

his account of the atonement, it is amply evident that such integration is at the core of his thought: that the work of Jesus Christ with its corresponding vocation for humankind is a social reality, and that Christ's death and resurrection were intended not only to reconcile us to God but to each other – a reality with profound social and political implications.

When it comes to the third moment of sin (its relationship to the created order), Barth offers scant reflection on the bearing of the doctrine of reconciliation upon the created order generally.[41] He refers to the third moment of sin as being our 'relationship with the created order' (CD IV/2, 409), but then specifies that order as being that between the body and soul. While this reflection (particularly centred on the resurrection of Jesus Christ) could be a platform for further inquiry, he leaves us with few resources for considering the relationship between Christ's death and resurrection and biblical passages such as Paul's claim that 'creation waits with eager longing for the revealing of the sons of God', and that it 'was subjected to futility ... in hope that the creation itself will be set free from its bondage to corruption and obtain the freedom of the glory of the children of God. For we know that the whole creation has been groaning together in the pains of childbirth until now' (Rom. 8.19–22).[42] Earlier in the CD, Barth wrote that '[man's] Creator has given him precedence ... over his immediate but very different fellow-animals within the one dwelling place', proceeding to add that 'man's salvation and perdition, his joy and sorrow, will be reflected in the weal and woe of this animal environment and company ... As an attendant, the animal will participate with man ... in the covenant, sharing both the promise and the curse which shadows the promise' (CD III/1, 177–8). Unfortunately, Barth offers us no more than the tiniest morsel in this regard. Neither does he re-appropriate his concept of creation as the 'external basis of the covenant' (CD III/1), exploring how the fulfilment of the covenant impacts its external basis. Hopefully the current interest in theology and ecology will provide the impetus for a development of Barth's thought in this direction.[43]

Turning to another consideration, Barth's moments of sin regrettably

---

[41] In a somewhat related criticism, see:Clifford Green, 'Freedom for Humanity: Karl Barth and the Politics of the New World Order', in *For the Sake of the World: Karl Barth and the Future of Ecclesial Theology*, ed. George Hunsinger (Grand Rapids, MI: Eerdmans, 2004), 102–4.

[42] Somewhat along these lines, Barth briefly states that in 'the third day a new life of Jesus begins; but at the same time on the third day there begins a new *Aeon*, a new shape of the world' (DO, 122). Disturbingly, however, he elsewhere responds to the question of whether there is 'a "Fall" of the outer world as well as a Fall of man?' by saying: 'I am not sure. I am not ready to say that there is a "fallen creation". I would not deny it, but I cannot affirm it' (Barth, *Table Talk*, 46). Questions about a 'fallen creation' may account for the minimal attention Barth pays to 'redeemed' or 'reconciled creation'.

[43] My thanks to Brandon Frick, whose unpublished manuscript ('Barth and Non-Human

do not include our bondage to Satan and the powers and principalities which are so important in the biblical witness (one thinks, for instance, of the Gospel of John and the Epistles to the Ephesians and Colossians).[44] As John Webster notes, Barth compensates for this lack 'in paragraph 78, published posthumously as part of *The Christian Life*. Here Barth has a remarkable section on "the Lordless Powers" released by the human person in alienation from him or herself'.[45] One need not wait that long, however, to see that Barth firmly incorporates the role of the devil into Christ's saving work, even if he does not do so via the 'moments of sin' as perhaps he should have done. Here it behoves us to turn to Barth's remarkable exposition of the temptation stories bracketing Jesus' life: the temptation in the wilderness and in the Garden of Gethsemane.

In the wilderness temptation narrative, Satan, the one 'to whom the world belongs', approaches Jesus 'with the counsel, the suggestion, that he should not be true to the way on which He entered in Jordan, that of a great sinner repenting; that He should take from now on a direction which will not need to have the cross as its end and goal' (*CD* IV/1, 261–2).[46] Unsuccessful in this temptation, the devil 'departed from him until the decisive moment' (Lk. 4.13) – which Barth takes to be the events of Good Friday (*CD* IV/1, 264).[47] While it is true that 'in this world Satan can have only the power which is given and allowed him as he is powerfully upheld by the left hand of God', the will of Satan is nevertheless identical [*identisch*] with that of God in this occasion (*CD* IV/1, 267–9; *KD*, 295). On Golgotha, 'the enemy who had been repulsed as the tempter' exercised 'by divine permission and appointment the right, the irresistible right of might', for the fact 'that the deceiver of men is their destroyer, that his power is that of death, is

---

Creatures: Animal Ethics and Natural Theology') led me to some of Barth's key passages on this topic.

[44] Much has been made of this aspect of the atonement in the past 90 years, particularly since the publication of Aulén, *Christus Victor*. Many of the works in this trajectory, however, operate with a significantly demythologized account of Satan. Cf. Girard, *I See Satan*; Gunton, *The Actuality of Atonement*; Ray, *Deceiving the Devil: Atonement, Abuse, and Ransom*; Weaver, *The Nonviolent Atonement*. For one theologian who tends to eschew this trend (of an overly demythologized Satan), see: N. T. Wright, *Jesus and the Victory of God* (Minneapolis, MN: Fortress, 1996), 443–74.

[45] Webster, 'The Firmest Grasp of the Real', 26.

[46] This passage is particularly noted in: Bakker, 'Jesus als Stellvertreter', 41ff.

[47] Interpreting Satan as being actively involved in the events of Good Friday indicates just how committed Barth is to the *Christus victor* theme. Von Balthasar, for example, takes a more minimal approach than that of Barth. Cf. Balthasar, *Mysterium Paschale*, 107. Strangely, however, there is no mention of Gustaf Aulén's work in the *CD* (Gunton, *The Barth Lectures*, 206). Barth wonders, however, 'whether it is advisable to try to work out systematically our thinking in this direction. What is clear is that a place should be found for this group of images and the particular truth which it represents' (*CD* IV/1, 274).

something that had to be proved true in the One who was not deceived, in order that it might not be true for all those who were deceived, that their enmity against God might be taken away from them, that their curse might not rest on them' (CD IV/1, 271–2). With as strong an affirmation as one could wish of the traditional *Christus Victor* theme, Barth concludes:

> Satan uses his power to overwhelm Jesus, and he succeeds, but his power loses its subjects, for the world and men escape him once and for all, and it ceases to be power over them, an impassable gulf being opened between him and the world ruled by him, between him and the ἁμαρτωλοι, deceived by him. He Himself is impressed into the service of the will of God as fulfilled in the suffering and death of Jesus. (CD IV/1, 272)[48]

We get a sense of how Barth uses this line of thought when he argues in his 'Letter to Great Britain from Switzerland' that because 'the world in which we live is the place where Jesus Christ rose from the dead', it 'is not some sinister wilderness where fate or chance holds sway, or where all sorts of "principalities and powers" run riot unrestrained and rage about unchecked'. Christ has 'completely disarmed those "principalities and powers".'[49] More provocatively still, Barth writes that as a result of Christ's resurrection, 'the rebellious angelic powers … will be forced into the service and the glorification of Christ.' For 'to them, too, His work is relevant' – while they are not justified by Christ as we are, it does seem 'to have some connection with human justice. For what seems to be meant … is that in Christ the angelic powers are called to order and, so far as they need it, they are restored to their original order. Therefore any further rebellion in this realm can, in principle, only take place … within Christ's order, in the form of unwilling service of the Kingdom of Christ.'[50] Clearly Barth has an extensive and lively understanding of Christ's reconciliation as a defeat of Satan and the rebellious angelic powers.

To consolidate these reflections, we will return to Barth's 'moments' of sin. Barth clearly offers an account of the atonement that extends far beyond a spiritual reconciliation of the sinner with God. Reconciliation and therefore the sin which it overcomes is not simply a spiritual reality between the sinner and God, but simultaneously and necessarily one that pertains to the social aspects of reality and the internal being of the sinner. I have sought to develop these various aspects of Barth's thought in a variety of ways in order to unpack the cosmological spectrum impacted by Christ's atoning work. Unfortunately, however, Barth does not include within this spectrum

---

[48] Cf. Barth, *Deliverance to the Captives*, 39.
[49] Barth, *This Christian Cause*, 32–3.
[50] Barth, *Community, State, and Church*, 116–17.

a robust account of the role of the created order in the atonement, although he does offer what turns out to be a quite robust account of the angelic/demonic order. Should we supplement these lacking emphases, the result, I suggest, would be what we might loosely call the 'five moments' of reconciliation: Christ's atoning work (and the corresponding hamartiology) as it bears on our relationship with (1) God, (2) the angelic realm (including both angels and demons), (3) our neighbours, (4) our selves, and (5) the created order as a whole.[51]

But this consolidation, this emphasis on the diversity of the created order or the cosmological spectrum affected by Christ poses a question for my thesis. Is the unity and diversity of the work of Christ rooted in the being of God or in the diversity proper to the created order? The two standpoints would seem to suggest quite different strategies with regard to approaching the doctrine of reconciliation. In reality, the two are not at all opposed, when one takes into consideration that God is the sole basis of the created order (*creatio ex nihilo*). The diversity proper to creation is not something foreign to God which he must address through Christ, but rather has its basis in his own being, which he then brings to fulfilment through Christ. In other words, the diversity within creation, like the diversity within the doctrine of reconciliation, ultimately has its basis within the being of the creator God. In Jesus Christ, the Triune God elects to share his being and life with his creature, such that Jesus Christ is fully God, fully man, Lord over the angelic orders, neighbour of all humankind, and a part of God's created order. In this properly theological and christological unity lies the basis for the unity of the 'moments' of sin.

Approaching the doctrine of reconciliation from the standpoint of the being of God is therefore not in the least in competition with an approach which takes its starting point from the diverse aspects of creation affected by Christ's saving work, although the former approach is theologically more sensitive to the dogmatic shape of theology and ultimately offers a broader range of resources towards understanding the doctrine of reconciliation.

Summary

Because Barth locates his hamartiology within his doctrine of reconciliation, developing it at length throughout volume IV of the *CD*, the former affords us a significant retrospective look at the latter, while simultaneously opening up new lines of inquiry that had been insufficiently developed. In the first part of the chapter, we explored the Christological and ultimately theological (doctrine of God) unity underlying the doctrine of sin and its immense

---

[51] I say 'loosely' because there is nothing intrinsically complete about these five levels. While Barth gives reason for us to affirm these five, there could very well be others.

diversity in Barth's account. In parallel to the previous chapter, we explored how this affords us yet another vantage point from which to approach Christ's saving work – using the biblical witness to sin as a way of appropriating and utilizing yet more dimensions of Scripture's witness to the work of Christ. In the second section of the chapter, we considered the various 'moments of sin', and how these provide a significant enrichment of our project, alerting us to the breadth of the created order reconciled by Christ's work. While Barth himself does not make systematic use of this point, it is not only consistent with his theology but opens our eyes to a number of ways in which Barth in fact follows through with this line of thought.

Test Case: Girard and the Theology of Reconciliation

As in the previous chapters, we conclude by examining a concrete application of the thesis just developed. Specifically, I will explore the possibility of appropriating René Girard's work on the doctrine of atonement to see whether, via its understanding of sin as envy, it might offer us resources for yet a fuller understanding of Christ's saving work.[52] I choose Girard because his proposal is one of the few contemporary options to offer constructive resources for those theologians critical of traditional theories of Christ's work. While his account requires expansion, his grasp of the anthropological 'moment' of sin (as being against one's neighbour) as envy, when properly filled out to incorporate the other moments, guides us to a fuller understanding of Christ's work.

According to René Girard, society is constantly on the brink of self-destruction. Our inclination to imitate others ('mimetic desire'), good and natural in and of itself,[53] easily mutates into envy, for the 'imitation of the neighbor's desires engenders rivalry' and the rapid escalation of hostility, in which we perceive that our neighbour can possess the object of her desire (whether tangible or not) only at our own expense or loss.[54] Such conflicts constantly threaten to tear society apart in a pattern of violence and revenge. The unique thing about such mimetic conflicts, according to Girard, is that they tend to be opportunistic: at advanced stages they 'are easily drawn to another scandal whose power of mimetic attraction is superior to theirs', such that one scandal is substituted for a new and more powerful and prestigious one, until finally 'the most polarizing scandal remains alone on the stage ... when the whole community is mobilized against one and the

---

[52] Relating the world of Girard and Barth is not unheard of. Cf. Schwager, 'Der Richter wird gerichtet', 139.
[53] Girard, *I See Satan*, 15.
[54] *Ibid.*, 10.

same individual'.[55] This process of mimetic substitution is a vital one for the survival of the community, such that the crisis of war of '*all against all*' is transformed 'into a war of *all against one*'.[56]

At this climactic point, Satan reveals his astonishing power of 'expelling himself and bringing order back into human communities'.[57] At the very height of mimetic conflict, and 'in order to prevent the destruction of his kingdom, Satan makes out of his disorder itself, at its highest heat, a means of expelling himself': he 'persuades the entire community, which has become unanimous, that this guilt [of a single, random and indefensible victim] is real'.[58] By expelling and destroying this sacrificial victim or 'scapegoat', 'the crowd finds itself emptied of hostility and without an enemy ... Provisionally, at least, this community no longer experiences either hatred or resentment toward anyone or anything; it feels *purified* of all its tensions, or all its divisions, of everything fragmenting it'.[59] Satan restores the semblance of peace to the community, so that his reign can continue. So while rivalry and conflict naturally escalate, Satan diffuses them by casting himself out, by uniting the mass against an innocent victim, or one 'suitable to receive the blame for society's ills, regardless of their actual innocence',[60] because their murder will not demand an act of reprisal by another segment of that society. In this way the tension of rivalry is temporarily gathered together and expelled by the community – a 'sacrificial theory of social cohesion', as Hunsinger calls it.[61] The community thus 'sleep[s] the sleep of the just', and Satan forestalls 'the total destruction of his kingdom'.[62] The community, finding that the scapegoated victim actually achieved the miracle of peace, divinizes the victim and celebrates the event in the form of sacrifices, thereby 'regulating a "sacrificial crisis" that recurs periodically'.[63]

This cycle, while present in every culture, is likewise veiled in every culture, such that one never finds a conscious understanding or exposure of this reality. Only through painstaking exploration and reading between the lines in the poets of ancient cultures was Girard able to piece together this thesis. The exceptions, of course, are the Scriptures of the Jewish

---

[55] *Ibid.*, 23.

[56] *Ibid.*, 24.

[57] *Ibid.*, 34.

[58] *Ibid.*, 35.

[59] *Ibid.*, 36.

[60] George Hunsinger, 'The Politics of the Nonviolent God: Reflections on René Girard and Karl Barth', in *Disruptive Grace: Studies in the Theology of Karl Barth* (Grand Rapids, MI: Eerdmans, 2000), 22.

[61] *Ibid.*

[62] Girard, *I See Satan*, 37.

[63] Hans Urs von Balthasar, *Theo-Drama: Theological Dramatic Theory*, trans. Graham Harrison, Vol. 4: The Action (San Francisco, CA: Ignatius, 1988), 303.

and Christian faiths.[64] Although this is true to a certain extent in the Old Testament, according to Girard this mimetic cycle is explicitly and resoundingly revealed in the New Testament in the life and death of Jesus Christ. Only here do we find the perspective of the victim and the questions: (1) is the victim in fact guilty, and (2) who will throw the first stone? And, more importantly still, only in the resurrection are we confronted with the undeniable fact that Jesus was an innocent victim and that in the community which followed him the cycle of mimetic violence was not only confronted and exposed but reversed.[65] This is the atonement Jesus Christ accomplishes: fully casting out Satan by rendering the cycle impotent through exposure. With the irrefutable vindication of a single victim, the question is unleashed upon the world of whether each and every victim might not be innocent, such that the power of Satan's mimetic cycle collapses.

At first glance, there is much to critique in Girard's thesis. He ravages the Old Testament, admitting that much of it speaks of a God wholly unlike the Christian God. His position ultimately offers no real solution to the problem of sin, for in unveiling Satan he admits that in so doing, and as Satan can no longer 'expel' himself, he now unleashes himself fully[66] – 'these mechanisms continue in our world usually as only a trace, but occasionally they can also reappear in forms more virulent than ever and on an enormous scale'.[67] Within atonement studies, it seems evident that Girard's position is merely a demythologized and therefore exemplarist account of *Christus victor* in

---

[64] Hunsinger, 'The Politics of the Nonviolent God', 24.

[65] The resurrection is of immense significance for Girard – it is the 'power superior to violent contagion' necessary 'to break the power of mimetic unanimity …' It is the 'spectacular sign of the entrance into the world or a power superior to violent contagion' (Girard, *I See Satan*, 189). If we properly emphasize the role of the resurrection in Girard's thought, it is not longer possible, as in Gregory Love, to suggest that for Girard 'it is thus *the suffering of the victim* – the abnegation of power to resist violation – that has the saving effect' (Gregory Anderson Love, 'In Search of a Non-Violent Atonement Theory: Are Abelard and Girard a Help or a Problem?', in *Theology as Conversation: The Significance of Dialogue in Historical and Contemporary Theology*, eds Bruce L. McCormack and Kimlyn J. Bender (Grand Rapids, MI: Eerdmans, 2009), 205). For Girard the suffering of Jesus as the victim is simply a standard part of the mimetic cycle of violence. It is the resurrection and that which it reveals which has the saving effect. Accordingly, I think that the feminist critique of Girard quite misses the point.

The role of the resurrection in *I See Satan Fall Like Lightning* also suggests the development in Girard's thought. While previously it was thought that Girard's was a 'closed system' that denied a historical resurrection, this no longer seems to be the case. Cf. Balthasar, *The Action*, 308; Hunsinger, 'The Politics of the Nonviolent God', 26–7.

[66] Girard, *I See Satan*, 185.

[67] Balthasar, *The Action*, 308; Girard, *I See Satan*, 158; Heim, *Saved from Sacrifice*, 263–4.

which the work of Christ amounts to little more than what it teaches us.[68] Finally, one might argue that his work ultimately stems from his literary/ cultural studies,[69] with only a thin theological veneer attached, and one focused almost exclusively on theological anthropology at that. But while these criticisms are significant, they miss the power of Girard's thesis and touch on points which are accidental to his argument and could in principle be altered (although he and his proponents may be loath to do so).[70]

The key to appropriating Girard's thought lies in appreciating the limits he sets for his project: 'the present book can define itself as ... an *apology* of Christianity rooted in what amounts to a Gospel-inspired breakthrough in the field of social science, not of theology'.[71] While he does occasionally make slightly bolder statements,[72] the gist of Girard's project is to develop the anthropological insight of the Gospel in such a way that is not at all antagonistic toward but rather inseparable from its theological point – a project he explicitly roots in the double nature of Jesus Christ.[73] The question we ought to ask, given Girard's aim, is not whether he advances an account of the work of Christ which is in and of itself sufficient or orthodox, but rather whether Girard has uncovered a significant aspect of the work of Christ which belongs in a full account. The answer to this much more charitable question is yes, and the key, once again, has to do with anthropology.

As we saw in our account of Barth's hamartiology, there is a number of 'moments' of sin, which necessarily correspond to 'moments' of Christ's reconciliation. One of these 'moments' operates at the social level of reality – sin against neighbours and the reconciliation thereof. There is every

---

[68] As Hunsinger writes, 'what Girard offer is an essentially "Pelagian" solution to an inherently "Augustinian" problem. All that is needed ... is for the victimage mechanism to be revealed for what it is' (Hunsinger, 'The Politics of the Nonviolent God', 28).

[69] René Girard, *Violence and the Sacred* (Baltimore, NJ: Johns Hopkins University Press, 1977).

[70] Cf. Hunsinger, 'The Politics of the Nonviolent God', 29. Many of the claims Girard makes concerning Satan, the Old Testament and other theological matters are in fact not central to his thesis, and are amenable to significant adaptation. Put differently, while it is true, as Hunsinger says, that 'Girard too often comes across in his writings as a champion of hermeneutical excess', we only stand to gain by not over-reacting to this excess, but rather looking past it to see the valid insight within it (Hunsinger, 'The Politics of the Nonviolent God', 25). My purpose here is not to give a pure represen- tation of Girard's thought, but rather to draw from his work a contribution to the Christian faith that is nevertheless recognizably rooted in his own insights.

[71] Girard, *I See Satan*, 3. Cf. pp. 105, 137, 141, 150.

[72] *Ibid.*, 150, 82.

[73] 'The anthropological revelation is not prejudicial to the theological revelation or in competition with it. It is inseparable from it. This union of the two is demanded by the dogma of the Incarnation, the mystery of the double nature of Jesus Christ, diving and human' (*ibid.*, 190).

reason to presuppose that Girard's anthropological insight into the Gospel may in fact bring some clarity to Scripture's witness to this specific moment and, in doing so, open our eyes to the other moments that relate to it. As this is merely a brief test case at the conclusion of the chapter, I will leave to the side the details of Girard's exposition of the biblical account of sin as envy, focusing rather on sketching a broader theological framework for his account that will, I hope, lend further plausibility to the significance of his insight.[74]

Girard's first and decisive move is his account of human sin as envy which then leads to violence and murder. Drawing on our thesis from the first section of this chapter, we ask: does envy provide us with a vantage point within the doctrine of sin to develop a unique theory of the atonement? I believe it does, although here I can afford only the briefest summary. Jesus comes to us as the Lord who does not envy but is self-giving, exposing us as those who envy God's lordship and wish to be our own lords that our own will might be done (Mt. 6.10), as the ones who, if we could, would kill God but instead kill his prophets (Acts 7.52), as the ones who, wishing to be gods, are threatened by similar claim to deity by our neighbours and enviously seek to rise above them in violent conflict (whether passively or aggressively), as the ones who see the created order as on occasion for envy and strife. But Jesus does this as the one who 'though he was in the form of God, did not regard equality with God as something to be exploited' (Phil. 2.6), but gave himself for us, who 'emptied himself, taking the form of a slave' (Phil. 2.7), who does not sacrifice others for himself but vice versa. In coming to us, he enters our world of envy and takes upon himself the envy of the world and the death that is its ultimate fruit – 'even death on a cross' (Phil. 2.8).[75] But in doing this, he is exalted by the Father, passively

---

[74] With regard to the biblical support for Girard's position, I commend, *ibid.*, 7–46; Raymund Schwager, *Must There Be Scapegoats? Violence and Redemption in the Bible*, trans. Maria L. Assad (San Francisco, CA: Harper & Row, 1987). To facilitate some readers' interactions with Girard, I also suggest without further elaboration that Girard's conflation of Satan and the cycle of mimetic violence is not essential to his thesis. In other words, this cycle may be one of the many tools Satan uses.

[75] While Girard himself eschews a substitutionary understanding of this aspect of Christ's work, in which the Father wills Christ to die in our place, attributing this to violence, in principle Girard has all the necessary resources to account for a good kind of violence, just as there is a good kind of mimetic contagion. Von Balthasar makes a similar point, writing: 'cannot the Cross of Jesus also be read as a "sacrifice," that is, in the sense of a self-surrender? Girard has no hesitation in saying Yes. But only on condition that we maintain the abyss between this latter self-surrender and the old ritual sacrifice, which is intended to placate a god who requires violence' (Balthasar, *The Action*, 307). Cf. p. 10. But as we have seen in previous chapters, there is no difficulty at all in developing a substitutionary or sacrificial account of Christ's death which eschews the placation of a god requiring violence. Along these lines see also Boersma, *Violence*. While Girard's point stands for satanic sacrifice, it seems to leave

receiving that which envy aggressively attempts to seize: the 'name that is above every name' (Phil. 2.9), the name into which we have been baptized (Acts 2.38). In this he constitutes us anew, setting forth a model and giving us the vocation to imitate him, to enter a cycle of redemptive mimesis in which that which is coveted (1 Cor. 12.31) leads now to life rather than death.[76]

Such a framework offers several significant developments to Girard's thesis. First, it facilitates the growth of the theological aspects of his thesis by placing the anthropological point within a theological framework, seeing envy in light of God's condescension and self-humiliation (Phil. 2.5–11). Second, it offers resources to develop his thesis in a more substitutionary direction, wherein Christ not only exposes our jealousy and envy and the mechanism by which we deal with it, but also bears our envy and its consequences, lending an objective aspect to Girard's more subjective approach.[77] Most importantly, though, I believe that it alleviates the tension some might feel with regard to a potentially reductionist interpretation, overly emphasizing the anthropological aspect of the cross. A strong way to respond to reductionist interpretations is to offer a fuller framework which vindicates and honours their respective insights, availing ourselves thereby of 'subjects that current theologians, even the most orthodox, have a tendency to neglect'.[78] While the above sketch does little more than raise such a possibility, I hope that it does so in such a way as to commend the work of René Girard to those might otherwise tend to dismiss him, as well as suggest the strengths of the thesis we developed in this chapter on sin.

As it stands, is Girard's account sufficient? 'Is salvation simply a matter of cessation of scapegoating', and was Christ's death and resurrection intended merely to expose the cycle of mimetic violence? With Vanhoozer, 'I think not'.[79] However, properly interpreted, Girard makes a vital contribution to the doctrine of the atonement, when it is born in mind that this contribution is primarily at the anthropological level of the gospel. Barth's hamartiology and its relationship to the doctrine of reconciliation gives us the resources to take these insights and fill them out in a fuller theological framework, such that they can play their vital role.

---

ample room for a Trinitarian construal of sacrificial or substitutionary atonement as developed in Chapters 3 and 4 of my book.

[76] Heim, *Saved from Sacrifice*, 236–51.

[77] Schwager attempted this unsuccessfully in Schwager, *Must There Be Scapegoats*, 208–9. Von Balthasar also finds his attempt unsuccessful (Balthasar, *The Action*, 312).

[78] Girard, *I See Satan*, 192.

[79] Vanhoozer, 'Atonement in Postmodernity', 390.

6

A TEMPLE THEORY OF THE
ATONEMENT

The death and resurrection of Jesus Christ, by which God reconciles us to himself, is a rich and complex event. We do well to honour and rejoice in this diversity, in the abundance of ways in which Jesus' death and resurrection overcame our sinful condition so as to bring us into fellowship with the triune God. The burden of this book has been to explore the resources within the doctrine of God for such a task: appropriating the fullness of Christ's saving benefits by means of a sustained reflection on the relationship between Christ's reconciliation and the doctrines of the Trinity, divine attributes, and sin. It is my contention that the unity and diversity proper to God's triune being and his divine perfections provides the decisive standpoint from which to appreciate and embrace the unity and diversity of Christ's saving work.

One of the dangers attending such a thesis is that it might become overly abstract, only loosely connected to the biblical witness and the concrete development of the doctrine of the atonement in the history of the church, lacking thereby the necessary traction in precisely those areas in which it seeks to have the greatest impact. For this reason I concluded Chapters 3–5 with brief test cases considering the implications developed therein for specific aspects of Christ's saving work. While these test cases ensure that to some extent we thwarted the imminent danger of abstract irrelevance, they were necessarily brief and only lightly connected to the scriptural witness.

Accordingly, the purpose of this chapter is to develop the atoning work of Christ from a single standpoint and in close relationship to the biblical witness, in such a way as to indicate more fully the resources implicit within the vision painted in the preceding chapters – offering thereby something much more along the lines of a full meal (although not, perhaps, a multi-course feast as might be found in a monograph devoted to the subject). Leftovers will not do, however – if my thesis is as significant as I believe it to be, something new is called for. That is, while exploring and revising well-worn paths within the history of the doctrine of the atonement is a significant and worthwhile task, I will attempt to advance a relatively undeveloped aspect of Christ's saving work.[1]

Specifically, I will explore Christ's atoning work from the standpoint of God's omnipresence. As we saw in Chapter 4, *the doctrine of reconciliation must honour the Trinitarian oneness and multiplicity of the perfections of God by witnessing to the role of the divine perfections in their distinct individuality and in their inter-relatedness.* To test this thesis, which in many ways is the central claim of my argument, it seems fitting to select a divine perfection which at first glance is particularly ill suited to that of the atonement (e.g. omnipresence). Should such a venture prove fruitful, it will go some way toward lending credibility to my thesis. To accomplish this task, I offer in what follows a brief survey of the history of the doctrine and the relevant biblical material, building toward a constructive conclusion, modelled loosely after the pattern of Barth's fine-print sections characteristic of his *CD*. This survey will guide us into a consideration of the Old Testament tabernacle/temple and the New Testament Church as the special locus of God's presence with his people, especially emphasizing the substitutionary work of Christ resting at the foundation of these themes.

Omnipresence in the History of Doctrine

Throughout the history of the Church, theologians have noted that Scripture speaks of God as one who is present everywhere: 'Where shall I go from your Spirit? Or where shall I flee from your presence? If I ascend to heaven, you are there! If I make my bed in Sheol, you are there!' (Ps. 139.8). Along these lines, for example, we see John of Damascus' statement that 'God, then, being immaterial and uncircumscribed, has not place. For He is His own place, filling all things and being above all things, and Himself maintaining all things.'[2] Anselm writes that 'the supreme essence is what supports, overtops, encloses and pervades all other things',[3] and confesses to God: '[You are] not in place or time but all things are in

---

[1] A truly new theory within the theological scene is, of course, an exceptionally rare and typically unfortunate event. My work builds on that of others and is for that reason not 'new'. However, I have been unable to find a similarly developed account of Christ's work that pulls together the elements I here consider. Allusions to this trajectory abound, however, as seen, for instance, in references by N. T. Wright to Christ's fulfilment of the temple in himself and see footnote 79 on page 163, Vanhoozer, 'Atonement in Postmodernity', 397–8.

[2] John of Damascus, *Exposition of the Orthodox Faith*, eds Philip Schaff and Henry Wace, trans. S. D. F. Salmond (Grand Rapids, MI: Eerdmans, 1983), I.xiii.15.

[3] Anselm, 'Monologion', in *The Major Works*, eds Brian Davies and G. R. Evans (New York: Oxford University Press, 1998), 26.

You. For nothing contains You, but You contain all things'.[4] Similarly, Thomas Aquinas writes that 'God is in all things by His power inasmuch as all things are subject to His power; He is by His presence in all things, as all things are bare and open to His eyes; He is in all things by His essence, inasmuch as he is present to all as the cause of their being.[5] The Reformed theologians continue this line of thought, with Francis Turretin, for instance, affirming that

> God may be said to be present with all things in three modes: (1) by power and operation; (2) by knowledge; (3) by essence … He is said to be everywhere by his power because he produces and governs all things and works all things in all (Acts 17.28). He is present with all by his knowledge because he sees and beholds all things … Finally, he is everywhere by his essence because his essence penetrates all things and is wholly by itself intimately present with each and everything.[6]

Isaac Dorner writes that '[God] must therefore be *in* all, yet not captivated by it. That is the meaning of the expression: Everywhereness, or Omnipresence'.[7] Heinrich Heppe cites Polan, arguing that 'God's *immensitas* is the essential attribute of God, through which the divine essence is signified as not being limited, circumscribed or bounded by any place, but as penetrating and filling places one and all everywhere and being present to all things (Polan II, 12)'.[8]

Probing a little more deeply, however, one finds that the picture is somewhat more complex than a straightforward affirmation of God being present to all things, or all things being in him. Augustine, while noting that God fills the heavens and the earth, writes of 'something much more remarkable … [that] although God is wholly present everywhere, He does not dwell in everyone'. For 'by the presence of His divinity God is everywhere, but [He is] not everywhere by the grace of His indwelling'.[9] Peter Lombard writes that 'God, existing ever unchangeably in himself, by presence, power, and essence is … in every place without being bounded', but then proceeds to note that 'he exists more excellently in holy spirits and

[4] Anselm, 'Proslogion', in *The Major Works*, eds Brian Davies and G. R. Evans (New York: Oxford University Press, 1998), 98.
[5] Thomas, *Summa Theologica*, I.8.2.
[6] François Turrettini, *Institutes of Elenctic Theology* (Phillipsburg, NJ: P & R Publishing, 1992), I.197.
[7] I. A. Dorner, *A System of Christian Doctrine* (Edinburgh: T & T Clark, 1880), I: 240–1.
[8] Heinrich Heppe, *Reformed Dogmatics: Set Out and Illustrated from the Sources*, ed. Ernst Bizer, trans. G. T. Thomson (London: Allen & Unwin, 1950), 67.
[9] Augustine, 'Letter 187: On the Presence of God', in *Selected Writings* (New York: Paulist, 1984), 410, 22.

souls, namely indwelling through grace; and most excellently in the man Christ, *in whom the fullness of the divinity dwells corporally*, as the Apostle says'.[10] In short, theologians note both a 'general' and 'special' manner of God's presence, or a presence 'through essence' and a presence 'through grace'.[11] 'God, although he is essentially and entirely in all, is nonetheless said to be more fully in those in whom he dwells, that is, in whom he is in such a way that he makes them his temple.'[12] The difference between this general and special mode of presence, according to Lombard, lies in the fact that in the latter God shares his blessings and in grace dwells with those who are with God in such a way that they can 'enjoy him and see him as he is', and know and love him.[13] Drawing out the implications of such a view, Turretin notes that 'God is far off from the wicked (as to the special presence of his favor and grace), but is always present with them by his general presence of essence'.[14] In other words, God's presence is a complex reality, allowing for special and more intimate forms of presence, or even distance and rejection.

Barth is particularly sensitive to the interrelationship between these two aspects of God's omnipresence. 'As the One He is … He is present to everything else, to everything that is not Himself but is distinct from Himself' (*CD* II/1, 461). Immediately, however, he specifies the nature of this presence, noting that it includes both remoteness and proximity – a fact that he roots in the togetherness and distinction existing within the eternal triune being of God (*CD* II/1, 468). God's omnipresence includes the remoteness or space necessary for the existence of God's creature, and the sovereign proximity in which God coexists with his creature as its Lord (*CD* II/1, 463). This presence, moreover, is the differentiated presence of the living God who is free to interact with his creatures in a variety of ways, in individual and distinct cases, according to his covenantal purposes. What distinguishes Barth from many theologians is the particular way in which he orders God's general and special presence (his general presence to all that is, and his special presence with his chosen people). While the tendency in the theologians cited above is to begin with the former and then turn to the latter, Barth reverses this order, via his doctrine of election, in which the covenant is the internal basis of creation and creation is the external basis of the covenant (*CD* III/1). He writes: 'Space is the form of creation in virtue of which, as a reality distinct from God, it can be the object of His love'

---

[10] Peter Lombard, *The Sentences*, trans. Giulio Silano (Toronto: Pontifical Institute of Mediaeval Studies, 2007), I.202.

[11] *Ibid.*, I.202, 06.

[12] *Ibid.*, I.204. Lombard draws on Augustine's *On the Origin of the Soul* and *On the Presence of God*, as well as Blessed Gregory's commentary on the Song of Songs, in making this point.

[13] Ibid., I.204, 06.

[14] Turrettini, *Institutes*, I:200.

(*CD* II/1, 465); and more clearly still: 'we are forced to say that according to the order of biblical thinking and speech it is this special presence of God which always comes first and is estimated and valued as the real and decisive presence' (*CD* II/1, 477–8). This special form of his presence, the internal basis of creation, 'is His presence in His Word ... in Jesus Christ' (*CD* II/1, 483). Accordingly, 'if the dwelling of God in Jesus Christ is the fulfillment, the constant factor, to which every other dwelling of God attested in the Old and New Testaments can stand only in the relationship of expectation or recollection, this dwelling of God stands out again above every other' (*CD* II/1, 484).[15] For Barth, God's presence everywhere is for the sake of and ordered towards his fundamental concern of being present to his creation in the person and work of Christ – in this special form of his presence.

Thus, while there may be a strong (and largely philosophically motivated) inclination in certain theological streams to treat God's omnipresence straightforwardly as God's being present everywhere throughout his creation, an equally strong trajectory demands that we attend likewise if not foremost to the diversity within the modes of God's presence in his creation, attending to his special presence in the Church and his altogether unique presence in Jesus Christ. Barth in particular would have us reverse this order, such that God's presence in Jesus Christ is the basis for the fellowship he has with his people in fulfilment of the covenant, for the sake of which he created the heavens and the earth.

From this glance at the history of doctrine, then, several different themes emerge which call for further inquiry, particularly as we keep in mind the role that God's omnipresence plays in the doctrine of the atonement. First, while the ubiquity of God's presence is commonly acknowledged, the more pressing need is to account for the diverse modes of God's presence in his creation, focusing particularly on his presence in Jesus Christ and therefore and on that basis within the Church. Second, whatever conclusions we come to in exploring this first theme, a biblical theology of God's dwelling presence should play a vital role, especially as it focuses on the role of the tabernacle/temple.[16] Most of the theologians mentioned above at one point

[15] Cf. Eleonore Stump's similar point, made from a philosophical perspective: 'Minimal personal presence is a prerequisite for closeness; and when the closeness between persons is great enough ... they will be able to be present to each other in the stronger sense of *being present*' (Eleonore Stump, 'Presence and Omnipresence', in *Liberal Faith* (Notre Dame, IN: University of Notre Dame Press, 2008), 62. The minimal form of presence is 'foundational' in that it is a prerequisite, though the stronger form of presence is teleologically primary.

[16] N.T. Wright notes that 'there are three aspects of the Temple and its significance', namely: 'the presence of YHWH, the sacrificial system, and the temple's political significance' (Wright, *Jesus and the Victory of God*, 406–7). For the purposes of this chapter we will focus only on the first of these, although the second and third aspects are valid and would need to be incorporated into a fuller account. Because I do not

or another broach this subject in their account of omnipresence – for the two are so deeply intertwined in the Bible that such a step is nearly inevitable. Finally, such inquiry must attend to the unique and decisive role of the person and work of Jesus Christ. Here, however, we venture somewhat into uncharted territory, for we must compensate for a rather glaring lacuna within studies of God's omnipresence/presence, both theological and biblical: the nearly unanimous silence (within this particular theological locus) with regards to Jesus' cry from the cross – 'my God, my God, why have you forsaken me?' (Mt., 27.46; Mk., 15.34). We now turn, then, to consider the canonical witness to the (omni)presence of God, emphasizing the role of the tabernacle/temple.

Biblical Theology of the Divine Presence Part 1: The Temple

Scripture witnesses to God as one who is present to all his creation, as one whose presence cannot be escaped. God is the creator of heaven and earth (Gen. 1–2), who cannot be contained by the highest heavens (1 Kgs. 8.27). His influence is not limited by location as is that of other gods (Num. 23), and he cannot be escaped in Sheol (Ps. 139.8) or the depths of the sea (Jon. 2). However, the Bible is not particularly concerned in such abstract thoughts about God. Rather, such claims occur in the context of and are specifically related to the special presence of God with his creatures. The God of the Bible is the God who seeks to dwell with his creatures, to be in fellowship with them and only as such and toward this end is he the creator God who is present to his entire creation.

Genesis 1–3 establishes the theme of God's presence in Scripture, preparing us for its development in the theology of the tabernacle/temple. The Garden of Eden was where 'God would "walk with" the first man and woman in the evening breeze' (Gen. 3.8), and was in fact 'the first archetypal temple in which the first man worshipped God'.[17] G. K. Beale contends that the

---

explore this second aspect in particular, I devote less attention to the Letter to the Hebrews than might otherwise be expected, as much of its material concerning the tabernacle/temple focuses on its sacrificial dimension.

[17] G. K. Beale, *The Temple and the Church's Mission: A Biblical Theology of the Dwelling Place of God* (Downers Grove, IL: InterVarsity Press, 2004), 66. In this chapter I do not pursue an important line of thought regarding the Temple's relationship to creation, Eden and cosmology as a whole. Beale's work is particularly strong in this area. See also R. E. Averbeck, 'Tabernacle', in *Dictionary of the Old Testament: Pentateuch*, eds T. Desmond Alexander and David W. Baker (Downers Grove, IL: InterVarsity Press, 2003), 816–18; Timothy C. Gray, *The Temple in the Gospel of Mark: A Study in its Narrative Role* (Tübingen: Mohr Siebeck, 2008), 180–97; Wright, *Jesus and the Victory of God*, 205.

whole cosmos, in fact, was created 'to be his great temple in which he rested after the creative work. Nevertheless, his unique revelatory glory did not fill the entire earth yet, since it was his intention that this goal be achieved by his human vice-regent, whom he installed in the garden sanctuary to extend the cultic boundaries of God's presence worldwide.'[18] Scripture thus establishes from the very beginning God's special presence in the form of a temple and fellowship with humankind.

While the theme of God's special presence is implicit in the creation narratives of Genesis, it reaches full stride in the account of the Exodus, the encounter with God at Sinai and the building of the tabernacle. Leading the Israelites out Egypt, the Lord went before them in a pillar of cloud and fire (Exod. 13.21) – a guide, defence and a visible sign of his presence. Upon reaching Sinai, the Lord descended such that 'his glory dwelt on the mountain [וַיִּשְׁכֹּן כְּבוֹד־יהוה עַל־הַר]' (Exod. 24.16), in a thick cloud and in fire (Exod. 19.9, 18, 20), giving Moses the law which the people were to obey so as to be to him a 'priestly kingdom and a holy nation'. In that law, the Lord gave to Moses the pattern for a tabernacle which the people were to build so that the Lord might 'dwell in their midst [בְּתוֹכָם וְשָׁכַנְתִּי]' (Exod. 25.8).[19] Solidifying God's purpose of dwelling with his people and thus tying together the Exodus, Sinai and the tabernacle, the Lord says: 'I will dwell [וְשָׁכַנְתִּי] among the Israelites, and I will be their God. And they shall know that I am the LORD their God, who brought them out of the land of Egypt that I might dwell among them [בְּתוֹכָם לְשָׁכְנִי]; I am the LORD their God' (Exod. 29.45–6).[20] At the conclusion of the book of Exodus, when the tabernacle had been built and all had been made ready, 'the cloud covered the tent of meeting, and the glory of the Lord filled the tabernacle' (Exod. 40.34), marking the dwelling presence of the Lord with his people just as it had at Sinai. Thereafter the theme of God's covenant presence with the people of Israel plays a dominant role throughout the Pentateuch.

Before we turn to the continuation of this theme in the building of the temple, two further points are in order. First, the Pentateuch looks beyond the Lord's dwelling in the tabernacle (a theme often spoken of in terms of the presence of the glory of the Lord [Num. 14.10]), anticipating a time when 'all the earth shall be filled with the glory of the Lord' (Num. 14.21)

---

[18] Beale, *The Temple*, 227.

[19] This emphasis on dwelling [שָׁכֵן], along with several other themes, leads Averbeck to conclude that the tabernacle was 'a sort of moveable Sinai' (Averbeck, 'Tabernacle', 824).

[20] On the structure and contents of the tabernacle, see *ibid*. Like the early Christians, I focus in this chapter on the theology of the temple, reflecting on its structure only inasmuch as it is theologically significant (as in the case of the function of the veil). Cf. I. Howard Marshall, 'Church and Temple in the New Testament', *Tyndale Bulletin* 40, no. 2 (1989), 222.

– in short, a time when the whole earth will be a tabernacle.[21] In effect this further integrates the themes already covered with the Garden of Eden. 'I will place my dwelling in your midst ... And I will walk among you [וְהִתְהַלַּכְתִּי בְּתוֹכְכֶם], and will be your God, and you shall be my people' (Lev. 26.11–12). Just as God walked [הִלֵּךְ] in the garden (Gen. 3.8), and the task of Adam and Eve was to expand that garden over the whole earth,[22] so Leviticus and Numbers anticipate the time when the Lord will walk among his people in such a way that his glory covers the whole earth. Second, it is significant to note that while the Lord dwells in the tabernacle, he does so freely. He dwells in the midst of the camp (Num. 5.3), but comes down and departs from the tabernacle (Num. 12.4–9), refrains from going into battle with the Israelites (Num. 14.39–45), and later in the historical books his glory is said to have departed from Israel (1 Sam. 4.21–2). While the tabernacle (and later the temple) is vital for the people of Israel, the Lord was always understood to dwell in the tabernacle in such a way as to allow for both his presence and his absence, such that the emphasis was on the tabernacle only in light of the prior and decisive activity of the Lord.[23] The tabernacle cult, that is, never had any validity or significance apart from the underlying activity and presence of the Lord.

Turning to the temple in Jerusalem, we find that it 'was the permanent form of the mobile tabernacle ... the two are so closely related that, for all intents and purposes, they are functionally identical'.[24] Like the tabernacle after which it was patterned,[25] the temple was a place for the Lord to dwell in forever (1 Kgs. 6.13, 8.13) and upon its completion, 'when the priests came out of the holy place, a cloud filled the house of the Lord, so that the priests could not stand to minister because of the cloud; for the glory of the Lord filled the house of the Lord' (1 Kgs. 8.10–11; cf. Exod. 40.33–4 and 2 Chr. 7.1–2). The temple thus sums up the purpose behind the Exodus (Exod. 29.45–6), the moveable form of Israel's experience on Sinai (the tabernacle), and ultimately God's creative purposes for the Garden of Eden.

One passage especially calls for further exploration with regards to the temple: Solomon's prayer of dedication (1 Kgs. 8.22–53; cf. 2 Chr. 6.12–42). In this prayer, Solomon asks: 'But will God indeed dwell [יֵשֵׁב] on the earth? Even heaven and the highest heaven cannot contain you, much less this house that I have built!' (1 Kgs. 8.27). Will God do this? Can he do this? Must he do this? These questions have no force in the face

---

[21] Beale, *The Temple*, 166. Cf. Timothy R. Ashley, *Numbers* (Grand Rapids, MI: Eerdmans, 1993), 260.

[22] Beale, *The Temple*, 83.

[23] The same relationship obtains, in other words, between God's presence and his temple as his presence and creation as a whole. Cf. 1 Kgs 8.27.

[24] Beale, *The Temple*, 293.

[25] Averbeck, 'Tabernacle', 218.

of the history of God dwelling with his people. Rather, such questions give
way to Solomon's petition: 'regard your servant's prayer and his plea' (1
Kgs. 8.28), in which he firmly establishes both God's general and special
presence, rooted in the grace or freedom of God. While heaven is the Lord's
dwelling place [יֵשֵׁב] (1 Kgs. 8.49), he nevertheless dwells in the temple, for
upon the completion of Solomon's prayer the glory of the Lord, the sign of
his presence, filled the temple (2 Chr. 7.1–2). While the fire coming down
on the temple was a powerful manifestation of God's presence, Solomon's
prayer offers helpful resources for understanding God's dwelling presence
in temple, and answering the question: given that God is present everywhere
in creation, what might his presence in the temple actually mean?

According to Solomon, for God to dwell in the temple is for his eyes and
his heart to be there [עֵינַי וְלִבִּי שָׁם] (1 Kgs. 9.3; 2 Chr. 7.16), for his eyes
to 'be open night and day toward this house', and for him to 'hear the plea
of your servant and of your people Israel when they pray toward this place
… [and to] heed and forgive', when they sin (1 Kgs. 8.29–30). The pattern
of hearing and forgiving when Israel sins and repents, particularly in the
immediate context of repeated affirmations of God's steadfast love [חֶסֶד]
(1 Kgs. 8.23, 2 Chr. 5.13, 6.14, 6.42, 7.3, 7.6), draws heavily on one of
the most decisive revelatory events in the Old Testament, wherein the Lord
reveals his name to Moses while restoring his covenant with Israel after
the debacle of the golden calf.[26] 'The Lord, the Lord, a God merciful and
gracious, slow to anger, and abounding in steadfast love and faithfulness,
keeping steadfast love for the thousandth generation, forgiving iniquity and
transgression and sin, yet by no means clearing the guilty, but visiting the
iniquity of the parents upon the children and the children's children, to the
third and the fourth generation' (Exod. 34:6-7).[27] What does it mean for the
Lord to dwell in his temple? It means that the temple is the locus of God's
self-revealing and covenant-fulfilling activity (even in the face of human
sin), as he sees, hears and responds to his people.[28]

Eventually the Babylonians captured Jerusalem, plundered the temple (2
Kgs. 24.10–13), and burned it (2 Kgs. 25.9; Jer. 52.13). Although rebuilt by
Ezra, the temple failed to achieve its former splendour or to be inhabited by
the Lord as it had been in the past and Israel (still largely in exile) longed for

---

[26] Brevard S. Childs, *The Book of Exodus* (Philadelphia, PA: Westminster Press, 1974),
611–12.

[27] 'It appears that vv. 6-7 are Yahweh's full name, which, in the composite Torah, he has
been progressively revealing to humanity and Israel … It is also a description, so that
the word *šēm* bears both its literal meaning, "name," and its extended meanings of
"nature" and "reputation".' William H. Propp, *Exodus 19–40* (New York: Doubleday,
2006), 609.

[28] The Psalms continue to emphasize the theme of God's seeing, hearing and responding
from his temple. For instance, God sees (Ps. 11.1–5) and hears (Ps. 18.6) from his
temple, and sends help from his sanctuary (Ps. 20.2).

its restoration and all that this would entail. At stake in the destruction of the temple, as Psalm 74 makes amply clear, is the covenantal commitment of the Lord (vv. 20, 22). Will the Lord cast off his people forever, or will he remember his dwelling (vv. 1–2)? As Wright explains:

> When Israel finally 'returned from exile', and the Temple was (properly) rebuilt, and reinhabited by its proper occupant – this would be seen as comparable with the making of the covenant on Sinai. It would be the betrothal of YHWH and Israel, after their apparent divorce. It would be the real forgiveness of sins; Israel's god would pour out his holy spirit, so that she would be able to keep the Torah properly, from the heart, it would be the 'circumcision of the heart' of which Deuteronomy and Jeremiah had spoken. And, in a phrase pregnant with meaning for both Jews and Christians, it would above all be the 'kingdom of god'. Israel's god would become in reality what he was already believed to be. He would be King of the whole world.[29]

But how was the temple to be rebuilt and inhabited? How will the Lord 'come to his temple' (Mal. 3.1)?

Beale contends that according to the New Testament the Church is 'the actual beginning fulfillment of the end-time temple prophesied in the Old Testament,' as seen, for instance, in the allusion of 1 Corinthians 3 to Mal. 3.1–2 and 4.1.[30] 'Do you not know that you are God's temple and that God's Spirit dwells in you? If anyone destroys God's temple, God will destroy that person. For God's temple is holy, and you are that temple' (1 Cor. 3.16–17; cf. 6.19). The church is thus the fulfilment of the temple envisioned in the Old Testament. In the letter to the Ephesians, we find the claim that:

> you are citizens with the saints and also members of the household of God, built upon the foundation of the apostles and prophets, with Christ Jesus himself as the cornerstone. In him the whole structure is joined together and grows into a holy temple in the Lord; in whom you also are built together spiritually into a dwelling place for God. (Eph. 2.19–22)

As if the direct reference to the temple were not enough, the point is reinforced with the building imagery and above all the claim that we are a dwelling place [κατοικητήριον] for God.[31] 1 Pet. 2.4–10 continues to develop

---

[29] Wright, *The New Testament and the People of God*, 301.
[30] Beale, *The Temple*, 253.
[31] Cf. Exod. 15.17, 2 Chron. 30.27 and Ps. 75.3, for the Septuagint's use of κατοικητήριον in a manner relevant to the present thesis.

this line of thought, referring to Christ the cornerstone and referring to his addressees as 'living stones' who are to let themselves 'be built into a spiritual house, to be a holy priesthood, to offer spiritual sacrifices acceptable to God through Jesus Christ'. Peter's letter, this passage in particular, is developed 'in the motif of the historic Babylonian exile in order to identify his readers with the OT promises of deliverance', reaching even 'further back into Israel's history to the time of the exodus' so as to draw 'from the language of the covenant that constituted Israel as God's chosen nation',[32] all of which coalesces to highlight Peter's statement that the church is a spiritual house, or temple.[33] The church is the fulfilled temple.

The eschatological vision at the end of the book of Revelation gathers these themes together, further cementing the significance of the temple within the canon. While John 'saw no temple in the city' (Rev. 21:22), the temple nonetheless plays a vital role in this final vision of the Bible, for the city's temple 'is the Lord God the Almighty and the Lamb' (Rev. 21:22), the 'glory of God' (the sign of his presence filling the tabernacle/temple) fills the new Jerusalem with its light (Rev. 21.11, 23), and it is 'the home [σκηνὴ] of God ... among mortals', where 'He will dwell [σκηνώσει] with them' and 'they will be his peoples, and God himself will be with them' (Rev. 21.3). There is and can be no physical temple in this city, for the city is itself the holy of holies.[34]

> The reality of God dwelling with his people has arrived, and the need for copies of the original has passed. The city with its cubical dimensions (Rev. 21.16–18) reflects the dimensions of the holy of holies, and ... the Lord God the Almighty and the Lamb are its temple (Rev. 21.22). In this final reference to the temple in the NT canon the categories of temple are submerged in the vision of God and the Lamb, in whose presence the saints experience the fulfillment of the promise of God, to dwell with his people forever (Rev. 22.1–5).[35]

---

[32] Karen H. Jobes, *1 Peter* (Grand Rapids, MI: Baker Academic, 2005), 158–9.

[33] The temple of Israel is commonly referred to as the house of the Lord. Cf. Exod. 23.19, Deut. 23.18, 1 Kgs 8.17–20. While the 'spiritual house' could also refer to the people as a whole (as in the 'house of Israel' in Lev. 10.6 and 22.18), the reference to stones and priesthood in the near vicinity seems to favour Jobes' point that 'the Christian community is portrayed as a temple, implying that now it – not a literal stone building – is the place of God's earthly dwelling by the Holy Spirit, a place of true worship and of acceptable sacrifice' (*ibid.*, 148). Cf. Peter Thomas O'Brien, *The Letter to the Ephesians* (Grand Rapids, MI: Eerdmans, 1999), 212.

[34] R. Larry Overstreet, 'The Temple of God in the Book of Revelation', *Bibliotheca Sacra* 166 (2009), 460–2.

[35] G. N. Davies, 'Tabernacle, Sanctuary', in *Dictionary of the Later New Testament and its Developments*, eds Ralph P. Martin and Peter H. Davids (Downers Grove, IL: InterVarsity Press, 1997), 1156.

In this final vision the Lord God the Almighty and Jesus Christ the Lamb are the temple, the saints are its pillars and God dwells with his people in fulfilment of His creative purposes. The theme of the temple as the fulfilment of God's creative purposes has reached consummation.

Biblical Theology of the Divine Presence Part 2: God's Absence

The biblical theme of God's presence becomes far more complex, however, when we note that in and of itself and apart from the activity of God the tabernacle/temple theme is of little or no interest in the biblical witness. The Bible is clear that the temple has no power over God, no efficacy apart from his good pleasure, and ultimately derives its meaning and significance solely from the antecedent will of God. Jeremiah warns the men of Judah: 'Do not trust in these deceptive words: "This is the temple of the Lord, the temple of the Lord, the temple of the Lord"' (Jer. 7.4), for the temple itself does not bind God to the men of Judah and therefore offers no ultimate power or safety. Rather, God binds himself freely to the temple, on the condition that the men of Judah walk in the way of the Lord. T. F. Torrance explains:

> The sacrificial and liturgical acts were regarded as *witness* and only witness to God's own action and appointment. The real agent in the Old Testament liturgy is God himself. God is not acted upon by means of liturgical sacrifice. Liturgical sacrifice rests upon God's self-revelation and answers as cultic sign to God's own word and action, which is the thing signified.[36]

The sacrificial and liturgical system, in short, has its meaning only within the antecedent and foundational will of God – a point that applies equally to the temple. The temple itself is a gift of God and therefore not something which of itself binds or constrains God in any way other than that which he might freely determine for himself. Because of this, a theology of the temple is meaningful and significant only inasmuch as it focuses upon the temple *indirectly* as God's chosen mode of presence with his covenant people. But this, in turn, means that we must include within a theology of the temple a theology of what we might rather loosely call God's absence or abandonment, for this theme is just as vital to a full understanding of God's relationship to the temple as that of his presence.[37]

---

[36] Torrance, *Atonement*, 18–19.

[37] Up to this point I have not significantly departed from the delightful work of Beale, *The Temple*. While space likely plays a significant factor in this omission, Beale's lack of reflection on God's absence or abandonment throughout his book may stem from

A good place to begin considering this theme may be the role of the veil in the tabernacle/temple – a subject to which we will return later in the chapter. The purpose of the veil was to separate the holy place [הַקֹּדֶשׁ] from the most holy [קֹדֶשׁ הַקֳּדָשִׁים], the latter containing the ark of the testimony (Exod. 26.33–4). The separation is vital, for the 'holiness' in question is that of God, and death awaits the one entering this holy place improperly (Exod. 28.35, 43). While God's presence in the tabernacle and specifically in the most holy place is a matchless blessing, it is likewise an unparalleled threat or danger. The veil of the tabernacle serves to protect the priests from entering the presence of God and perishing as a result, recalling the role of the limits set for the people at Mount Sinai, set up lest the people touch the mountain and die, lest they break through to see God and perish (Exod. 19.12, 21). It was the task of the Levites to guard the temple to protect the Israelites (Num. 1:53, 3:38), and precautions were set up such that those carrying the holy things of the temple would not touch them and die (Num. 4:15-20; cf. 2 Sam. 6:5-19) – a reality keenly felt by the people (Num. 17.12–13). In short, the presence of the Lord was an exceptionally dangerous blessing – the blessing being a knife's edge with a chasm on either side. Even in instances when no particular sin or deviance was intended or good was meant, coming into the presence the Lord under any but the most strictly delineated conditions meant death to the trespasser.[38] The wonder, in fact, is that anyone could meet with God and still live (Deut. 5.22–7).[39]

While this theme establishes the danger immanent in God's presence, it only introduces us to what we might call the dreadful side of God's presence; for although the Old Testament is concerned to prevent the death of the people as a result of coming into improper contact with God's presence, it is even more concerned that the people not abandon God, incurring thereby God's abandonment. The choice, as Moses puts it, is between 'life and prosperity, death and adversity' (Deut. 30.15): if Israel obeys God, then life, prosperity and blessing will be theirs (Deut. 30.1–10,

focusing too much upon the theme of the temple itself, rather than what I consider a more proper emphasis: examining the temple indirectly as the mode of God's presence with his people. Keeping the question of God's purposes somewhat more to the foreground throughout the consideration of this theme highlights the darker side of this theme (one that is quite prominent throughout Scripture), the theme of God's absence. To be fair, however, it is worth noting that even Barth mentions the negative side of God's presence only once in his consideration of the divine omnipresence (*CD* II/1, 476).

[38] Along these lines, Adam Neder writes: 'If God were to reveal himself directly to sinful human beings apart from the veil of creaturely media, there could be only one result: the total annihilation of the sinner' (Neder, *Participation in Christ*, 4).

[39] The concern that nothing with a blemish enter through the veil lest it profane God's sanctuaries (Lev. 21.22) is a comparably minor theme. The much more pressing concern is that the people not die as a result of coming into God's presence improperly.

16); but if they disobey, if their hearts turn away, if they forsake him, their lot will be curses and death (Deut. 28.20, 30.17–18). Unfortunately, the history of Israel is that of forsaking the Lord. As the Lord foresaw (Deut. 31.16–18), they forsook him and devoted themselves to whoredom (Hos. 4.9–10); they forsook him repeatedly by making offerings to other gods and worshipping them (Jer. 1.16; 2.13–19; 9.13–16; 16.11; 17.13; 19.4; 22.9).

Scripture draws upon a rich and varied range of terms and expressions to depict the Lord's response to Israel's whoring ways. One of the primary concepts[40] used in this description is עָזַב of which 'the basic meaning is "leave",' wherein 'a person or a being conceived with personal character-istics removes itself from an object, dissolving thereby its connections with that object'.[41] When used in the context of the creator God's covenantal relationship with his people, 'leaving' or 'forsaking' takes on a wider and immensely significant range of meaning, as we see in the latter part of Deuteronomy. The Lord tells of the curses and destruction that he will send if the people forsake him (Deut. 28.20), and although he promises to be with, and not to forsake, Joshua and Israel, he prophesies of a time when they will forsake him, breaking his covenant, and he in turn will forsake them: 'they will forsake me [וַעֲזָבַנִי], breaking my covenant … My anger will be kindled against them in that day. I will forsake them [וַעֲזַבְתִּים] and hide my face from them; they will become easy prey, and many terrible troubles will come upon them … On that day I will surely hide my face on account of all the evil they have done by turning to other gods' (Deut. 31.16–18).

The Psalms are particularly fruitful for exploring the meaning of this concept, given their utilization of poetic repetition for the development of concepts. 'Forsaking' is a matter of God failing to help and hear one's need (Ps. 21), hiding his face, turning away in anger and casting off (Ps. 27.9), being 'far from [us]' (Ps. 38.21), or 'abandoning' his heritage (Ps. 94.14). Those who are forsaken among the dead are like those 'counted among those who go down to the Pit … who have no help … like the slain that lie in the grave, like those whom [God] remember[s] no more, for they are cut off from [his] hand;' it is a matter of being 'put … in the depths of the Pit, in the regions dark and deep', where the wrath of God lies heavy (Ps. 88.4–7). The enemies of the Psalmist say: 'Pursue and seize that person

---

[40] By no means do I intend to suggest that this is the key, central or only way to express God's reaction to sinful Israel. It is simply one of the important trajectories in Scripture, which bears a particularly close relationship to the temple theme we are following here. That said, however, it is worth noting that according to Wright, 'the return of YHWH to Zion, and the Temple-theology which it brings into focus, are the deepest keys and clues to gospel christology' (Wright, *Jesus and the Victory of God*, 652).

[41] E. Gerstenberger, 'עָזַב', in *Theological Dictionary of the Old Testament*, eds G. Johannes Botterweck and Helmer Ringgren (Grand Rapids, MI: Eerdmans, 1977).

whom God has forsaken, for there is no one to deliver' (Ps. 71.11). In short, abandoning or forsaking is a complex reality (rooted in God's covenantal purposes) spanning personal and social, temporal and eternal realities, while ultimately centring on the relationship of God to the one who is forsaken.

The fact that forsakenness is frequently alluded to in face of persecution from enemies is significant (e.g. Ps. 27.11–12; 38.19–20), for the Old Testament does not see Israel in a neutral or normal position in which life is basically good unless God either blesses them (which is very good) or curses them (which is very bad). Rather, Israel is hedged around by enemies seeking to destroy her. The alternatives are either God's saving presence or Israel's total destruction.[42] In other words, for God to leave or forsake Israel, for him to hide his face, to be far away, for him to hold back from offering help, is for him to sign Israel's death warrant, to abandon her to Sheol, to the pit (Ps. 16.10). To be cast out or cut off from the presence of God or from that of his people is, quite simply, to die (Gen. 3.23–4, 4.14; Exod. 12.15, 30.33, 31.14–15). And because these are mutually exclusive alternatives, God's forsaking or 'casting off' (Ps. 71.6–11 ties these concepts together) is a matter of his wrath, of renouncing his covenant (Ps. 89.38–9). In short, for God to remove his presence or to leave and forsake his people is for him to act in wrath by abandoning them to Sheol, renouncing his covenant, handing them over to be destroyed by their enemies.[43] And it is precisely this constellation of themes that we find as the content of God's threats in Lev. 26.14–45, Num. 32.15, Deut. 28.15–68 and 1 Kgs. 9.5–9. God's presence ultimately means the fulfilment of his covenant with an obedient people thriving under his blessing, while his leaving or forsaking

---

[42] Calvin was right on target when he wrote that 'our happiness consists in our cleaving to God, and … on the other hand, there is nothing more miserable than to be alienated from him' (John Calvin, *The Epistle of Paul the Apostle to the Galatians, Ephesians, Philippians Colossians, Thessalonians, Timothy, Titus and Philemon*, trans. William Pringle (Grand Rapids, MI: Baker, 1979), 154, 75, 81–3).

[43] J. M. Hamilton ties in this consideration with a reflection on the nature of God's (omni)presence: 'Since texts testify to the wicked actually experiencing the angry presence of Yahweh (Ps. 68.1–2; 78.66; 83.15, 10; 139.19), we must conclude that this withdrawal [of God's presence] is relational rather than physical. That is, wicked covenant-breakers do not escape God's presence; rather, instead of his face shining on them, they experience him pursuing them in justice' (J. M. Hamilton, 'Divine Presence', in *Dictionary of the Old Testament: Wisdom, Poetry and Writings*, eds Tremper Longman and Peter Enns (Downers Grove, IL: IVP Academic, 2008), 118).

John Yocum's attempt to offer a different reading of Psalm 22, on the basis that 'the details of suffering described in the first half of the psalm relate to treatment by others, and the apparent refusal of God to intervene', does little to distinguish God's lack of intervention from his wrath in the mind of the Israelite (John Yocum, 'A Cry of Dereliction? Reconsidering a Recent Theological Commonplace', *IJST* 7, no. 1 (2005), 76).

entails an equally complete collapse of that people – ruin and destruction at the hand of his wrath.[44]

Again and again we see God forsaking his people, casting them out of his presence and allowing them to fall into destruction at the hands of their enemies. 'Like Adam, Israel sinned and was cast away from God's presence and out of the land. At the same time God withdrew his presence from their temple (Ezek. 9:3; 10:4, 18–19; 11:22–23). The same thing happened to restored Israel in AD 70, when the Romans destroyed Jerusalem and the temple, though God's presence had long since left that temple.'[45] And until Yahweh returns and saves Israel once and for all, 'the great story is not yet complete, is still full of ambiguity' and the cycle of abandoning and returning continues.[46]

Temple Theory of the Atonement

With these reflections in place, we have in some measure established both the significance of the theme of God's (omni)presence in Scripture, as well as the canonical framework for exploring the work of Christ from this vantage point. In other words, the preceding material has served us in a preparatory capacity, and we now turn in earnest to the heart of the matter: the person and work of Christ as the one whose substitutionary work fully incorporates within itself the meaning and function of the temple. In order to set forth this material adequately, we will consider (1) a temple Christology, (2) a temple theory of the atonement, and conclude (3) with a consideration of the implications thereof.

---

[44] It is worth noting that Moses promises to Joshua and Israel that God will not forsake them (Deut. 31.8). This promise, I think, is best understood within the broader context of Deuteronomy 27–32, such that it means that God, for his part, and as long as they are obedient, will not abandon his people. It is a conditional promise in which God will certainly be faithful not to forsake them, as long as they also are faithful. This fits with Ps. 9.10, 37.35, Zech. 1.3 and a host of other passages which claim that God will not forsake the righteous or those who seek him, or that he will return to those who return to him. Although God will not forsake his people of his own accord, he demonstrates himself to be more than willing to disinherit them and establish a new line so as to complete his covenantal purposes. Cf. Exod. 32.10, 33.3–5; Num. 14.11–19, 16.20–5, 41–50. It also points to the gratuity of God's new covenant where he not only guarantees his own faithfulness but that of his people (cf. Jer. 31, Ezek. 34–7).

[45] Beale, *The Temple*, 117.

[46] Wright, *The New Testament and the People of God*, 217.

Temple Christology

The purpose of this section is to explore the Scriptural testimony to the fact that Jesus Christ was himself the fulfilment of both the old and the new temples – the consummation of the tabernacle/temple of the Old Testament and the inauguration of the new temple prophesized in the Old Testament and written of in the New. John tells us that 'the Word became flesh and lived among us, and we have seen his glory, the glory as of a father's only son, full of grace and truth' (Jn. 1.14). Two aspects of this statement demand our close attention. First, the phrase 'became flesh' is a translation of σκηνόω a word which means 'to tent' or 'to tabernacle'.[47] For the Word who is God (Jn. 1.2, 1.18, 20.28) to 'tabernacle' with us is for him to fulfil the Old Testament prophecies concerning the temple and God dwelling with his people. As Paul Hoskins notes, 'In the Septuagint of Zechariah 2:14 and Ezekiel 43:9, one finds an appealing linguistic parallel to John 1:14b: κατασκηνώσω ἐν μέσῳ ("I will dwell among")'.[48] In these passages, the Lord promises once again to dwell in the midst of his people, to return to Judah and once again to choose Jerusalem. In this regard Ezekiel in particular emphasizes the temple, though both he and Zechariah draw richly upon the covenantal blessings the Lord had made in the past. By drawing on these passages, John suggests that Jesus Christ is himself the tabernacle/temple – the fulfilment of God's promises of being present with his people.[49]

If the significance of the word σκηνόω insufficiently establishes such a connection, John's affirmation that we have seen thereby 'his glory [δόξαν]' should make it all the more likely, for throughout the Old Testament the Lord's 'glory' is the manifestation of his presence. When the tabernacle was completed, the 'cloud covered the tent of meeting, and the glory of the Lord [δόξα κυρίου] filled the tabernacle' (Exod. 40.34 LXX). Likewise, after Solomon dedicated the temple, 'the glory of the Lord [δόξα κυρίου] filled the house of the Lord' (1 Kgs. 8.11 LXX). Just as God's indwelling presence in the tabernacle/temple of old was accompanied by the filling of the temple

---

[47] 'This *logos* comes to *makes its tabernacle with us*: the phrase 'and dwell among us' in Jn. 1.14 is in Greek *kai eskenosen en hemin*, which echoes the language of Sirach 24.8, 10, with *skene* being both the Greek for 'tent' or 'tabernacle' and also, interestingly, an apparent cognate of the Hebrew *Shekinah* itself' (*ibid.*, 414).

[48] Paul M. Hoskins, *Jesus as the Fulfillment of the Temple in the Gospel of John* (Milton Keynes: Paternoster, 2006), 118. Hoskins also draws connections to Exod. 29.45 and 1 Kgs. 6.13.

[49] Hoskins notes that (in the Gospel of John) Jesus replaces and fulfils the temple, in such a way that 'some measure of continuity exists between him and the Temple. It is possible to speak of Jesus as the "true Temple"'. This, in conjunction with the discontinuity (inasmuch as Jesus 'surpasses or transcends' the Old Testament patterns and prophecies), leads Hoskins to describe Jesus' relationship to the temple as being 'typological' (*ibid.*, 182).

with his glory, so when God tabernacles with us in the person of the Word, we behold his glory, for Jesus Christ is the temple of the Lord. As Yves Congar notes, 'the new and decisive event which had come to pass in Jesus Christ had, at one and the same time, replaced – and so made redundant – and fulfilled all the modes of God's presence among his people, by his Word and by his Glory ... in his Tabernacle or his Temple'.[50]

With this strong affirmation in place, we proceed to other passages in the Gospels that also use these categories. In John 2, for instance, Jesus tells the Jews: 'Destroy this temple, and in three days I will raise it up.' While the Jews took this as a reference to the temple in Jerusalem, John clarifies: 'he was speaking of the temple of his body' (Jn. 2.19–21).[51] In a similar vein, we find in Matthew that 'something greater than the temple is here' and Jesus calls himself the 'cornerstone' (Mt. 21.42) – a theme made much of in the Epistles. To some of these more direct statements, we should add that Jesus bypassed the Temple in certain ways, fulfilling its role in himself. Along these lines he offered forgiveness, called for repentance, and 'offered membership in the renewed people of the covenant God' without reference to the temple or the cultic system revolving around it.[52] Somewhat like the Essenes, who seemed to have seen themselves (at least temporarily) as an 'alternative' Temple, the gospels portray Jesus as one who is the true temple, fulfilling in himself the purpose (and fate) thereof.[53]

Turning to the Epistles, we find the remarkable passages in Colossians which state that 'in him all the fullness of God was pleased [εὐδόκησεν] to dwell [κατοικῆσαι]', and that 'in him the whole fullness of deity dwells [κατοικεῖ] bodily' (Col. 1.19, 2.9). Wright suggests a helpful connection: 'We might note the allusion to Temple- and Shekinah-theology in 19a/b (cf. 2.9, and Eccl. 24.3–12), where the "fullness" of God is "pleased to dwell" in Christ, as in Psalm 67.17 (LXX)',[54] a verse referring to 'the mount that God desired [εὐδόκησεν] for his abode [κατοικεῖν], where the LORD will reside forever [κατασκηνώσει εἰς τέλος]'. Much like the prologue to the Gospel of

---

[50] Yves Congar, *The Mystery of the Temple: Or the Manner of God's Presence to His Creatures from Genesis to Apocalypse*, trans. Reginald F. Trevett (London: Burns and Oates, 1962), 132.

[51] Hoskins examines two other passages in John (in addition to those which we have just touched on), which he finds to offer compelling testimony that Jesus was in fact the new temple: Jn. 1.51 and 4.20–4 (Hoskins, *Jesus as the Fulfillment of the Temple in the Gospel of John*).

[52] Wright, *Jesus and the Victory of God*, 257.

[53] Wright, *The New Testament and the People of God*, 205.

[54] N. T. Wright, *The Climax of the Covenant* (Minneapolis: Fortress, 1992), 117. Beale makes the same connection, suggesting that 'Paul applies the psalmist's reference to God dwelling in Israel's temple to God now dwelling in his Son, apparently as the expression of the latter-day temple in which God's presence fully resides' (Beale, *The Temple*, 267).

John, the epistle to the Colossians sees Jesus as the fulfilment of the Old Testament's expectation for a new and eternal temple. He is the permanent locus of the presence of God and of the fellowship of God with his people. It was in part for this reason that 'instead of the Temple, the geographical and theological centre of Judaism, the early Christians spoke of Jesus as the one who had embodied the living presence of the creator [God], and of his own spirit as the one who continued to make that [God] present in the lives and assemblies of the early church'.[55] Jesus was the new temple, and the Christians were part of this building through the work of his Holy Spirit.

Temple Theory of the Atonement

The New Testament understanding that Jesus is the new and eternal temple includes within itself an understanding of his mission, firmly binding together Jesus' person and work. In short, Jesus came in order to complete in his life and death both the final destruction of the old temple, and the eternal fulfilment of the promised new temple. As Wright puts it, '[Jesus] believed … that he himself was the bearer of Israel's [and therefore the temple's] destiny. He was the Messiah, who would take that destiny on himself and draw it to its focal point'[56] – a destiny involving both destruction and fulfilment. Drawing on the work of earlier chapters, we ask once again: 'Cur Deus homo?' In the trajectory established in the first half of this chapter and the three-fold substitutionary work developed in Chapter 4, we answer that (1) just as Jesus came as the Judge, so he came as the true temple – the one in whom God was present; (2) just as he was the one judged, so he suffered the abandonment of the old temple; (3) and just as he acted justly in our place, so he fulfilled the role of the temple by being, receiving and proclaiming the glorious presence of the Lord.[57]

1. Jesus Christ Came as the True Temple

Jesus comes to us as the true temple, the one in whom God is present with us, the one who shares with us the presence proper to the triune life of God. Just as 'the former priests were many in number, because they were prevented by death from continuing in office' (Heb. 7.23), and just as the sacrifices for sins had to be made again and again, so, in a fashion, the temple itself was several in number, built again and again (Garden of Eden, Sinai, the Tabernacle, Solomon's Temple and the Second Temple), for it was neither permanent nor perfect. In Jesus Christ we have neither a copy nor a shadow (Heb. 8.5), but the true tabernacle, the true temple: the original pattern and now final and perfect dwelling of God, that He might thereby be present with

---

[55] Wright, *The New Testament and the People of God*, 368.
[56] Wright, *Jesus and the Victory of God*, 594.
[57] I pattern this section of the chapter after *CD* IV/1, 273ff.

his people as the covenant God, walking with them and they with Him. To adapt Barth's statement, Jesus Christ is 'the true, and essential and original' temple (*CD* IV/1, 275), the one who 'is at once the essence and fulfillment of all other [temples] but also that which replaces [them] and makes [them] superfluous' (*CD* IV/1, 276), the one who came that God might dwell with us. Just as Jesus comes as the judge, so he comes as the true temple, the locus of God's special presence. And it is because this is the case, because he is the true temple of God, that he is qualified for the work which he came to do.

The will of God was to tabernacle, to be present with his people, to share the presence he had with himself in eternity with us his creatures. But the presence of God amidst a people intent on hiding, rebelling and fleeing his presence can mean nothing but death for that people when the one from whom they flee is the maker of heaven and earth, the covenant God of Abraham, Isaac and Jacob. As we saw earlier, life is not 'neutral' – it is hedged in by enemies and death. To flee the presence of the Lord is to be an outcast and die of exposure in the wilderness or at the hands of one's enemies. In coming as the true temple, Jesus ensured that the time of hiding and fleeing would come to an end, and that the threats and promises of the Lord throughout the Old Testament would be fulfilled – for with the coming of the true temple all false, adulterous and perverted temples must collapse into rubble. For 'if God does not meet us in His jealous zeal and wrath … then He does not meet us at all … That man is not abandoned in this way, that God is really gracious to him, is shown in the fact that God confronts him in holiness' (*CD* II/1, 366), abandoning and yet uniting us to himself in Jesus Christ, the true temple. The climax of God's covenantal purposes had come. In one way or another, the old temple which had forsaken the Lord and prostituted itself out to other gods would be destroyed and along with it all who abandoned the Lord.

In the decisive coming of the presence of the Lord, destruction of the god-forsaking temple had to happen, for nothing can withstand God's presence, and under no conditions could it be avoided. The only question was: how this would happen – how would this destruction take place? But it would happen – the time of humankind fleeing and forsaking the Lord while he broke out now in wrath and then in mercy had come to an end. God was fulfilling his original purpose to be present with his people. But the presence of the Lord, as we have seen, as ambiguous: it means destruction for those who forsake God just as much as it means salvation for those who cling to him. And who has not forsaken the Lord, the true temple?

2. Jesus Christ Is the One Who Was Abandoned and Forsaken in the Place of the Old Temple

Wright suggests that 'as would-be Messiah, Jesus identified with Israel; he would therefore go ahead of her, and take upon himself precisely that fate, actual and symbolic, which he had announced for nation, city, and Temple'.[58] Of course Jesus' announcement was not merely his, but drew on the trajectory throughout the Old Testament in which the mercy and patience of God were in continuous tension with his wrath and righteous anger, and his threats and acts of abandonment and destruction were always tempered by promises of a day to come when God's blessing would once again be upon the people of Israel. Jesus identifies with Israel, and the temple in particular, in such a way as to take upon himself the fate of the God-forsaking temple announced throughout the Old Testament and most recently by Jesus himself (Mt. 24.2, Jn. 2.19). We find this aspect of his substitutionary work most clearly proclaimed in the Gospels, at the scene of Christ's crucifixion: in Jesus' cry of dereliction (Mt. 27.46; Mk. 15.34: 'My God, my God, why have you forsaken me?') and in the tearing of the temple veil (Mt. 27.51; Mk. 15.38; Lk. 23.45).[59]

Of the many strange and difficult passages in Scripture, Jesus' cry of dereliction might well be the most shocking of all. The beloved Son with whom God is well pleased (Mt. 3.17, 17.5), the Word become flesh, living among us and revealing to us the glory of God (Jn. 1.14), he who is one with the Father (Jn. 10.30, 17.11, 21), the one who taught his disciples to pray: 'Our Father …' (Mt. 6.9) … this one cries out to his Father: 'if it is possible, let this cup pass from me; yet not what I want but what you want' (Mt. 26.39), and upon the answer to this prayer in the form of the offered cup of his suffering and death cries out: '"Eli, Eli, lema sabachthani?" that is, "My God, my God, why have you forsaken me [με ἐγκατέλιπες]?"' (Mt. 27.46). Surely this cry offers one of the most abrasive confrontations of everything we think we know about God. How can the incarnate Word of God, he who is favoured by God and one with the Father be abandoned and forsaken by him? How can he who is God's presence with us have the special presence of God's blessing revoked, so as to feel God's crushing and wrathful absence?

As is well known, Jesus' cry draws from the opening lines of Psalm 22: 'My God, my God, why have you forsaken me? Why are you so far from helping me, from the words of my groaning? O my God, I cry by day, but you do not answer; and by night, but find no rest.'[60] But what are

[58] Wright, *Jesus and the Victory of God*, 608. In keeping with this statement, Beale notes that 'the destruction of Israel and her temple, however, was the mere outward expression of the judgment that had already taken place in Christ's death, resurrection and at Pentecost' (Beale, *The Temple*, 214).

[59] A third theme, which I will not explore in this chapter, is that of the darkness preceding Jesus' cry (Mt. 27.45; Mk. 15.33). Several references to 'outer darkness' in the Gospel of Matthew (Mt. 8.12, 22.13, 25.30) strongly suggest that this is a way of speaking about hell. Cf. Richard Bauckham, *Jesus and the God of Israel: God Crucified and Other Studies on the New Testament's Christology of Divine Identity* (Grand Rapids, MI: Eerdmans, 2009), 259.

[60] Bauckham notes that while Mark draws heavily on the psalms of lament in general,

we to make of this reference? To hone in on one Gospel for a moment, Holly Carey argues convincingly that Mark draws heavily on Psalm 22 throughout the passion narrative, and that there is good reason to think Mark's readers were prepared to appreciate the larger context of the psalm (which speaks of the vindication of the suffering servant).[61] But does interpreting Jesus' cry in light of the vindication at the conclusion of Psalm 22 and in conjunction with the theme of Christ's vindication throughout the Gospel[62] give sufficient grounds for us to claim that 'the Markan Jesus has not been abandoned by God in the sense that the presence of God has left him altogether', and that instead 'these phenomena suggest that the "abandonment" of Jesus refers to his helpless situation at the hands of his enemies'?[63] Precisely at this point our study of what I have called the 'dreadful side' of the temple theme bears significant fruit.

While Carey's argument that we must hold the whole of Psalm 22 in mind is well made, there are two significant weaknesses in her argument. First, despite her efforts to the contrary she allows the conclusion of the psalm to overwhelm its introduction, such that the abandonment in question seems to become rather inconsequential in her account.[64] Second, the dichotomy she poses between falling into the hands of one's enemies and suffering the loss of the presence of God runs against the grain of the Old Testament understanding of God's presence. As we saw earlier, the Old Testament eschews a vision of life as a neutral reality which can then be blessed or cursed by the presence or absence of God respectively. Rather, life is continually under siege, under the threat of death and only God's presence can save us. For God to hide his face, to be far away, for him to hold back from offering help, is to sign our death warrant, to abandon us to Sheol; and because these are the mutually exclusive alternatives, God's forsaking is a matter of his wrath. The idea that God could be present to Jesus and yet

---

Jesus' use of Psalm 22 echoes 'the most extreme of the situations in the psalms of lament: those in which the psalmist not merely fears abandonment by God, but experiences it as realized fact' (Bauckham, *Jesus and the God of Israel*, 256–7).

[61] This is the argument of: Holly J. Carey, *Jesus' Cry from the Cross: Towards a First-Century Understanding of the Intertextual Relationship Between Psalm 22 and the Narrative of Mark's Gospel* (New York: T & T Clark, 2009). Against this, see Bauckham, *Jesus and the God of Israel*, 255.

[62] Carey, *Jesus' Cry from the Cross*, 45–69.

[63] *Ibid.*, 163.

[64] While the term 'inconsequential' may seem rather harsh, it is appropriate. If the plight of Jesus' situation refers to his 'helpless situation at the hands of his enemies', as Carey suggests, then in fact Jesus makes for a remarkably poor and uninspiring martyr, whose prayer in the Garden of Gethsemane pales in comparison to similar prayers offered by saints and pagans alike before their deaths at the hands of their oppressors.

Admittedly, the whole tone of her book argues against such a dichotomy. Unfortunately, however, the conclusion of her argument ran somewhat against the grain of the book as a whole.

hand him over to his enemies is utterly foreign to the Old Testament and the theology of the Psalms from which Jesus draws in crying out this prayer.

While Carey's argument still stands that we must interpret the cry of Jesus in light of the psalm as a whole, this begins by fully honouring the first two verses, which speak of the forsaking of the psalmist by God. What does it mean for Jesus to cry out that he is forsaken by God? It means that God is abandoning him into the hands of his enemies, and letting him fall down into Sheol; that he has removed his covenantal blessings from Jesus and ultimately is casting Jesus away from himself as an object of his wrath.[65] From another angle, Cranfield makes the same point: 'the cry ought to be understood in the light of [Mark] xiv.36, II Cor. v. 21, Gal. iii.13. The burden of the world's sin, his complete self-identification with sinners, involved not merely a felt, but a real abandonment by his Father. It is in the cry of dereliction that the full horror of man's sin stands revealed.'[66] Jesus' cry of dereliction signifies the wrath and curse of God poured out on him. God's wrath burns hot against him and consumes him (Exod. 32.10), brings disaster on him (1 Kgs. 9.8–9), makes him a byword (2 Chr. 7.20–1), abandons him into the hands of his enemies (Jer. 12.7), does to him as he did to Shiloh (Jer. 7.14–15), and delivers his power to captivity and his glory to the hands of his foes (Ps. 78.61).[67] In short, the Lord has spurned and rejected him, and is full of wrath against his anointed, renouncing his covenant and defiling his crown (Ps. 89.38–9). Jesus has borne 'humanity's alienation from God',[68] the 'sin which separates man from God' (*CD* IV/3.1, 390), such that in him the temple (we might say the same of creation and humanity) lies in ruins, deprived of the presence of the creator God and his glory, deprived of his covenant blessing and with it the only source of life and salvation. He who was the temple of God, the presence of God with us, now fulfils the demise and destruction of the temple in himself, as he dies abandoned by God, in such a way as 'God has never forsaken, and does not and will not forsake any man as He forsook this man', turning 'against Him as never before or since against any' (*CD* IV/3.1, 414).

---

[65] Bauckham similarly notes the wide range of meaning of forsakenness in the Psalms. Cf. Bauckham, *Jesus and the God of Israel*, 256–7.

[66] C. E. B. Cranfield, *The Gospel According to Saint Mark* (Cambridge: Cambridge University Press, 1963), 458. Cranfield makes two points in this passage, the second of which I return to later in the chapter.

[67] Ps. 78.59–63 fills out both this event and our understanding of what it means for God to forsake: 'When God heard, he was full of wrath, and he utterly rejected Israel. He forsook [וַיִּטֹּשׁ; ἀπώσατο] his dwelling [מִשְׁכַּן; σκηνήν] at Shiloh, the tent [אֹהֶל; σκήνωμα] where he dwelt [שִׁכֵּן; κατεσκήνωσεν] among mankind, and delivered his power to captivity, his glory [καλλονὴν] to the hand of the foe. He gave his people over to the sword and vented his wrath on his heritage. Fire devoured their young men, and their young women had no marriage song.'

[68] Gunton, *The Barth Lectures*, 115.

It is vital to keep in mind, however, the Trinitarian framework (Chapter 3) for this event. While it is true that the Father forsook the incarnate Son who had taken upon himself the nature and role of the old temple, it is equally necessary to affirm that it was the one God who took upon himself and bore within himself this abandoning and forsaking according to the diversified mode of his being as Father, Son and Holy Spirit. The problem was not, strictly speaking, between the Father and the Son. Rather, the problem was how God was to love his people and tabernacle with his people, given their sin, given their forsaking of him. God takes upon himself (in the person of the Son) the condition and fate of the old temple, so as to deal with it within and by means of the resources within His own proper life as the triune God, so as to bear its abandonment and destruction within Himself so as to spare the temple and His people that eternal fate. Only the triune God can bear this abandonment within Himself without destroying Himself, so as to be with us as the one He is without destroying us in the process. Only in this way can the triune God tabernacle with us.

Both Matthew and Mark[69] continue the theme of God's abandonment of Jesus as the abandonment of the temple by noting the tearing of the veil in the temple.[70] Most commentators hold, as Beale notes, 'that the "veil of the temple was torn in two" in verse 51 [of Mt. 27] is a direct result of his death in verse 50'. His further contention, however, that 'the temple veil was a part of the temple, so that its tearing symbolically represented the destruction of the temple' is the subject of a great deal of debate.[71] Timothy Geddert, for instance, lists some 35 different interpretations of this passage![72] For our purposes, we will focus on a two-fold line of thought, in keeping with two of the most significant functions of the temple veil.[73]

---

[69] I am aware that each of the Gospels approaches its subject matter from a distinct perspective, such that each contains nuances the others might lack. For this reason care is needed when moving between Gospels in an account of the theme of the temple. Nevertheless, my purpose is to sketch a canonical vista of this theme. I have sought, however, to use different Gospels studies in awareness of these tensions, so as to not import the nuances of a specific Gospel into the argument of another.

[70] The connection of Jesus' cry and the tearing of the veil 'is supported by the presence of the conjunction κα, at the beginning of Mark 15.38, which suggests a linking of the two verses. This is in contrast to the presence of the disjunctive δὲ at the beginning of Mark 15.37, which indicates a subtle distancing from 15.36, and another δὲ immediately following in 15.39' (Carey, *Jesus' Cry from the Cross*, 167).

[71] Beale, *The Temple*, 189.

[72] Timothy J. Geddert, *Watchwords: Mark 13 in Markan Eschatology* (Sheffield: Sheffield Academic Press, 1989), 141–4. Daniel Gurtner offers a far more detailed account of scholarship, both contemporary and ancient, on this passage (Daniel M. Gurtner, *The Torn Veil: Matthew's Exposition of the Death of Jesus* (New York: Cambridge University Press, 2007), 1–28).

[73] Most scholars concede that the veil in question is the one separating the holy place from the most holy place (Exod. 26.31–3).Cf. Gurtner, *The Torn Veil*, 59–60, 62, 69.

As we saw earlier in the chapter, this veil had a separating function for two reasons: (1) it marked off a distinct place in which the presence of God could dwell, filling it with his glory, and (2) it established a boundary, protecting the Israelites (priests included) from coming into the presence of God under any but the strictest conditions, lest they be struck down and killed. In short, the presence of God was both an immense blessing and a tremendous danger. In keeping with this two-fold function, in the present section we will explore the meaning of the tearing of this veil in light of Jesus Christ's substitutionary work as the temple which is abandoned and destroyed, while in the next section we will explore its revelatory meaning from the standpoint of Jesus Christ as the one who is the new and eternal temple of God's presence for us.

As suggested earlier, the presence of the Lord is exceedingly dangerous. While it means life to the oppressed, it just as easily means death to the sinner. While it certainly may be the case that one of the effects of 'the demise of the old temple' was 'the release of the divine presence from the holy of holies'[74] in the positive sense of the saving divine presence extending beyond these confining boundaries, it behoves us to honour the relevant elements in due order, lest we jump too hastily to the 'release of the divine presence' as if this were an unambiguously good event. Recall that when the divine presence was released among the Israelites, it meant death in great numbers (Exod. 33.5; Lev. 10.2). What we need is not the simple release of the divine presence, but a new temple, a new form of the presence of God. And in needing a new temple (and the fulfilment of the divine promises), we need the destruction of the old temple (and the fulfilment of those divine promises as well). We need the fulfilment of both God's saving presence and his abandoning and destructive presence, both of which were prophesied throughout the Old Testament and in the ministry of Jesus.

In the tearing of the temple veil, therefore, we first see the destruction of the temple, the demise of that which distinguished the temple from any other building – the destruction of the sacred space where God was to meet with his people. Because God abandoned the temple and it now lay empty, there was no need to safeguard the 'holy of holies' from the priests: there was no more danger that they might enter the presence of God improperly, for his presence had departed. The tearing of the veil indicates the end of the primary purpose of the temple: to provide a sacred space for the indwelling presence of the Lord and the manifestation of his glory. The downfall of the temple has been decisively inaugurated. God's wrath is manifest in the destruction not only of the temple but of everything it symbolized: life,

---

[74] Beale, *The Temple*, 193. Similarly, Gurtner writes that 'the rending of the veil depicts the cessation of its function, which I have argued is generally to separate God from people. Its rending then permits accessibility to God in a manner not seen since Genesis 3' (Gurtner, *The Torn Veil*, 138, 88–9).

salvation, covenant and, above all, the complete satisfaction and fruition that only comes from the saving presence of God amongst his chosen people.

What then does the tearing of the veil mean, within this line of thought? It means that God has removed his presence, or rather unleashed it in the form of abandonment and judgement. In this dialectic of presence and absence we return to the theme of omnipresence, for the removal of God's presence or his act of abandonment does not create a purely secular space in which God is not present. Rather, God's withdrawal or forsaking is identical with the act of his wrath, of destruction. Jesus, fulfilling in himself the demise of the old temple, bears in himself the abandonment of God or, what is the same thing, the judging and wrathful presence of God as he destroys the temple. The tearing of the veil in the temple is that hideous sacrament of this event: the outward manifestation of God's invisible wrath, as the temple now stands desolate, awaiting the final outward manifestation of its inner fate in the fulfilment of Christ's prophecy that is to come in 70 AD. Rather than destroying the people of his covenant by unleashing his destroying presence among them as he had done at Sinai and elsewhere, God took upon himself the nature and fate of the old temple, bearing his own destructive presence in himself, so as to save those upon whom it would otherwise fall. To adapt Wright's point, Jesus 'was dying as the rejected [temple] … as the representative [temple], taking Israel's suffering upon himself' and in this way went 'ahead of her … tak[ing] upon himself precisely that fate, actual and symbolic, which he had announced for the nation, city, and temple'.[75]

3. In the Place of the Old, Jesus Was the True Temple

Finally, just as 'Jesus Christ was just in our place' and 'in our place He has made a perfect sacrifice' (*CD* IV/1, 281), so too, as the perfect temple, he awaits, receives and proclaims the indwelling presence of the Lord. Like the tabernacle/temple in the Old Testament, Jesus received and was filled with the presence of the Lord – in the form of the Holy Spirit.[76] The Spirit was upon him as a child (Lk. 1.15, 80), and at his baptism the Spirit descended on him in the form of a dove (Mt. 3.16; Mk. 1.10; Lk. 3.22),[77] with John in

---

[75] Wright, *Jesus and the Victory of God*, 570, 608.

[76] Graham A. Cole, *He Who Gives Life: The Doctrine of the Holy Spirit* (Wheaton, IL: Crossway, 2007), 149–71. The Holy Spirit, of course, is not the only way in which Jesus is the locus of God's presence with us, for he himself is Emmanuel, God with us (Mt. 1:23, Jn. 1.1, 1.18, 20.28), as Barth notes at the opening of *CD* IV/1. But that Jesus is God with us in not merely a Christological statement about the person of the Eternal Son, but rather a statement about the triune God – for the whole triune God is present with us in Jesus Christ, according to the diverse modes of his being. And the Son is incarnate in such a way as to be filled with the presence of God not only by his very nature as the incarnate Son, but also in the power of the Holy Spirit.

[77] A possible connection along these lines is to note that just as the Spirit descended

particular noting that the Spirit remained on him (Jn. 1.32–3). Throughout his ministry he was filled with and led by the Holy Spirit (Mt. 4.1; Mk 1.12; Lk. 4.1, 14–18). Just as the temple was filled with the presence of God, so Jesus Christ was filled with the Holy Spirit.

Gathering up this material into our theme, we see that the connection between the indwelling of the Spirit and the temple is a significant one. We see in 1 Cor. 3.16: 'Do you not know that you are God's temple and that God's Spirit dwells in you?' Gordon Fee notes that 'the word used (*naos*) refers to the actual sanctuary, the place of the deity's dwelling', a point that, when noted in conjunction with Paul's statement that 'God's spirit dwells [οἰκεῖ] in you', ties together the themes of the temple and Spirit quite closely, as the Spirit is the mode of God's activity by which he builds and sustains the new temple. Furthermore, Fee notes that 'it is possible, though by no means certain, that the imagery also had eschatological overtones for Paul', such that 'the present experience of the church as the place where the (eschatological) Spirit dwells would thus be the restored temple of Ezekiel's vision (chaps 40–8), where God promised 'to live among them forever' (43.9)'.[78] Working backwards from this Pauline vantage point, we can see how the Spirit's indwelling of Jesus is in fact Jesus' fulfillment of the role of the true temple: just as the Spirit dwelling in us is what makes us to be God's temple, so the Spirit dwelling in Christ is what makes him the temple in which we are included through the ongoing work of the Spirit.

While Jesus was filled with and guided by the presence of God through the Holy Spirit, he also proclaimed the presence of the Lord and glorified God – two active or personalized forms of the passive function of the Old Testament temple. A significant amount of Jesus' proclamation revolves around the presence of the kingdom of God (cf. Mk 1:15). 'The phrase … carried unambiguously the *hope* that YHWH would act … within history, to vindicate Israel'. This vindication would be the result of Israel's God becoming king, such that 'the whole world … would at last be put to rights', by his coming 'in his power and rul[ing] the world in the way he had always intended'.[79] Put differently, the kingdom of God was a matter of the creator of heaven and earth being present to his creation in the way in which he had

---

[καταβαῖνον] on Jesus at his baptism (Mt. 3.16), so in the Septuagint God descends [καταβεβηκέναί κατέβη καταβαῖνον] to Mount Sinai and the tabernacle/temple throughout the Old Testament (Exod. 19.10–25, 24.16, 34.5; 2 Chron. 7.1–3).

78 Gordon D. Fee, *The First Epistle to the Corinthians* (Grand Rapids, MI: Eerdmans, 1987), 146–7. Later, Fee notes that 'through the phenomenon of the indwelling Spirit, Paul now images the body as the *Spirit's* temple, emphasizing that it is the 'place' of the Spirit's dwelling in the individual believers' lives. In the same way that the temple in Jerusalem "housed" the presence of the living God, so the Spirit of God is "housed" in the believer's body' (Fee, *The First Epistle to the Corinthians*, 246).

79 Wright, *Jesus and the Victory of God*, 203.

always intended. Jesus not only embodied but proclaimed that presence, in a way that the old temple could only mutely and passively foreshadow.

Proceeding, just as the tabernacle/temple was filled with the glory of God, so Jesus actively glorified his Father, a theme highlighted throughout the Gospel of John, where it is found in conjunction with the theme of God's presence: 'Father … glorify [δόξασόν] your Son so that the Son may glorify [δοξάσῃ] you … I glorified [ἐδόξασα] you on earth by finishing the work that you gave me to do. So now, Father, glorify [δόξασόν] me in your own presence [παρὰ σεαυτῷ] with the glory [δόξῃ] that I had in your presence [παρὰ σοί] before the world existed' (Jn. 17.1–5). Just as the temple 'housed' the glory of the Lord, so now Jesus both is the glory of God and glorifies the Father. In this work of glorification, he anticipates his return to the Father, the glorious presence within God's triune life which was the antecedent basis within God's being for that which he shared with us through Jesus Christ.

Finally, as Jesus received and proclaimed the presence of God as the new and perfect temple, so he waited and hoped for the presence of God, learning even this by patience and suffering.[80] It is at this point that we can return to the overall context of Psalm 22, now that we have firmly established the meaning and significance of Jesus crying out its first lines.[81] For in fact the hope with which the Psalm ends has a vital place in understanding Christ's work.[82] In this psalm, the sufferer anticipates how he 'will tell of [the Lord's] name to my brothers and sisters; in the midst of the congregation I will praise you', how he will recount that God 'did not despise or abhor the affliction of the afflicted; he did not hide his face from me, but heard when

---

[80] Just as Hebrews affirms that 'although he was a Son, he learned obedience through what he suffered', so we might say that although he was God's tabernacling presence with us, he learned to wait and hope for God's presence through what he suffered.

[81] The key is to affirm both elements in this psalm, without allowing one to trump the other. Along these lines, see Calvin's claim that 'the first verse contains two remarkable sentences, which, although apparently contrary to each other, are yet ever entering into the minds of the godly together. When the Psalmist speaks of being forsaken and cast off by God, it seems to be the complaint of a man in despair; for can a man have a single spark of faith remaining in him, when he believes that there is no longer any succour for him in God? And yet, in calling God twice his own God, and depositing his groaning into his bosom, he makes a very distinct confession of his faith (John Calvin, *Commentary on the Psalms*, trans. William Pringle (Grant Rapids, MI: Baker, 2009), I.357). At a general level, Barth makes a similar point regarding the unity of Jesus being abandoned and loved by God, in regards to the coronation of the royal man through his passion (*CD* IV/2, 252), and when he writes of the cry of dereliction that 'it is at once the death-cry of the man who dies in Him and the birth-cry of the man who comes to life in him' (*CD* IV/3.1, 413).

[82] The beginning of the Psalm is equally significant, however, for 'the doubled expression ["my God, my God"] is found nowhere else, and serves … to emphasize the psalmist's personal relationship with God and his persistence in addressing God as "my God" even when abandoned by God' (Bauckham, *Jesus and the God of Israel*, 258).

I cried to him' (Ps. 22.22–4). Nowhere else in the Psalms 'is this [assurance of deliverance] ... more emphatically and extensively represented than in Psalm 22.'[83] Similarly, we find Jesus in Gethsemane calling out to his Father in the midst of his anguish (Mt. 26.39), and in Luke we find him crying out from the cross: 'Father, into your hands I commend my spirit' (23.46). These tokens of Jesus' intimacy with the Father, when combined with Jesus' firm belief in his resurrection on the third day, coalesce to give us every reason to hold that in the midst of Jesus' experience of the Father's abandonment he did not, for his part, abandon or forsake his Father, but trusted in him, commending to him his spirit and awaiting his vindication.[84] Just as the temple was utterly passive and had no power or claim upon the Lord but could only wait for the manifestation of his presence, so Jesus Christ, as the true and eternal temple, trusted and awaited the vindicating presence of the Lord, even in the midst of his experience of utmost abandonment and forsakenness. Without in any sense minimizing Jesus' God-forsakenness, therefore, we can agree with Cranfield that 'the cry ... marks the lowest depth of the hiddenness of the Son of God – and so the triumphant *tetelestai* of Jn xix. 30 is, paradoxically, its true interpretation'.[85]

Just as the cry of dereliction has two dimensions, so too does the tearing of the veil. While 'the rending of the veil signifies in the first place the end of the former system of worship' (with the 'end' in this case being a wrathful and complete destruction at the hand of God), so it also 'signifies ... that access to the true Holy of Holies is henceforth free', in the sense that the temple through which we now enter God's presence is no longer of the Israelite temple of stone, but the temple which is Christ, through his Holy Spirit.[86] As long as the nature of both the danger of God's presence and the mode of its current manifestation through the work of the Holy Spirit are properly established, we have every reason therefore to agree with those who emphasize that the tearing of the veil is a revelatory or freeing act,[87] ushering in a new era of God's saving presence with his people.

---

[83] *Ibid.*, 259.

[84] In this chapter, as in the book as a whole, I do not explore the relationship of the resurrection to the doctrine of the atonement – a pragmatic decision determined by the scope of the project, although one that ultimately means that my project is intrinsically incomplete. Cf. Beale, *The Temple*, 190.

[85] Cranfield, *Mark*, 458–9.

[86] Congar, *Mystery*, 143.

[87] 'The revelatory interpretation of the tearing of the Temple curtain is also consonant with the other Markan use of the verb *schizein* ("to rip"), which occurs at Jesus' baptism' (Joel Marcus, *Mark* (New York: Doubleday, 2000), 1067). Cf. Gurtner, *The Torn Veil*, 174–6. Within this line of thought, however, it is important to note with Bauckham that in this shift the presence or revelation of God is not generalized but relocated: 'it transfers the place of God's presence from its hiddenness in the holy of

A Retrospective Glance

Was it worth taking the time and effort to explore the work of Christ from the standpoint of God's (omni)presence? Of making theories of the atonement there is no end, and multiplication for its own sake is of little benefit. Such effort either should further some aspect of the church's theological understanding and/or strengthen its ability to fulfil its vocation, or it should be discarded. What then might be some of the theological and practical benefits of this chapter? The foregoing material offers what I see to be three material benefits to the church: (1) its use of the Old Testament in fulfilling its theological task (particularly concerning the doctrine of the atonement), (2) integrating the role of the Church into Christ's atoning work and (3) its contribution to our understanding of the nature of sin.

It is generally conceded that studies of the doctrine of the atonement tend to draw relatively little from the Old Testament. The exception which proves the rule is an occasional interest in the Israelite sacrificial system. While outcries at different times emerge seeking to anchor theology more firmly in the concrete world of the Old Testament,[88] my sense is that these fall on deaf ears not so much because of the message itself, but rather because of the lack of compelling work on the doctrine of the atonement emerging from careful study of the Old Testament witness which significantly expands or challenges our understanding of that doctrine. While the path of the sacrificial system is well trod (though by no means a major thoroughfare), other trails mark that lush country, waiting to be followed so as to show forth the vistas to which they will guide us. Exploring the atonement from the vantage point of the tabernacle/temple draws on a mass of biblical data from both the Old and New Testaments which typically plays little or no role in an account of Christ's work, thus further integrating Scripture as a whole with the Lordship of Christ and thereby paving the way for a fuller and more well-rounded proclamation of Christ's saving work by the church.

A second benefit of this approach is the manner in which the doctrine of the atonement naturally blossoms into ecclesiology. Whereas one can study many a work on the doctrine of penal substitution or *Christus Victor* without receiving the impression that God had a vested interest in a people rather than individuals, a 'temple' theory of the atonement exudes the

holies to the openly godforsaken cross of the dead Jesus' (Bauckham, *Jesus and the God of Israel*, 267).

[88] See, for instance, Robert Jenson's claim that early on 'Christian theology of the cross made two paired errors', the second of which 'was to sever the cross from its *past*, in the canonical history of Israel ... The inherited theories [of the atonement] discuss the Crucifixion in essential abstraction from Israel's history' (Jenson, 'On the Doctrine of the Atonement', 101–2). The first error has to do with cutting off the cross from the resurrection.

corporate nature of God's covenantal purposes from start to finish.[89] It was the people of Israel, and now the Church composed of both Jews and Gentiles, which was the focus of Jesus' mission. Jesus Christ, the true and eternal temple, is the locus of God's presence with his people. Atonement in this sense is much closer to its original meaning, at-one-ment,[90] in which the goal is bringing unity of fellowship to God and his people.

Continuing with our reflection on the 'third article', this standpoint for viewing Christ's work also offers far more resources to the church for integrating the doctrine of the Holy Spirit within that of the atonement, for it is the Spirit's indwelling in Christ by which he is the new temple, and it is through the repetition of this fact by the indwelling of the Spirit in believers that they are made to be part of the temple.[91] While this leaves a great deal of material to be examined (Christ's claim in Jn. 16.7 comes readily to mind: 'if I do not go away, the Helper will not come to you. But if I go, I will send him to you'), the connection between atonement, pneumatology and ecclesiology (as in Eph. 2.11–22) seems to be a particularly close and fruitful one from this angle.

Finally, a temple theory of the atonement has the potential to emphasize certain aspects of our sinful condition which we might otherwise tend to suppress or ignore, opening up significant new lines of pastoral application.[92] Jesus, coming to us as the fulfilment of the temple, as the one in whom God seeks to be present to us in the realization of his covenantal purposes, exposes in us the desire to flee from the presence of God: to flee and abandon him. As the one who enters the 'Far Country' to tabernacle with us,[93] Jesus exposes us as the ones who like Adam and Eve hide from the presence of the Lord (Gen. 3.8), like the Israelites beg God to leave them alone (Exod. 14.12) and like Jonah seek to flee from God's presence and vocation (Jon. 1.3). 'Enslaved to sin', we 'cannot take up another attitude towards God but that of escape from him, be it only by denying him, which

---

[89] Cf. McKnight, *A Community Called Atonement*, 9–14, 88.

[90] 'From *at one*, as the etymologists remark, *to be at one*, is the frame as *to be in concord*' (Johnson, 'To Atone').

[91] Vanhoozer writes along these lines that 'the saving significance of Christ's death consists in making possible God's gift of the Holy Spirit. The 'wonderful exchange' is thus not economic but thoroughly eschatological: *Jesus gives his body and blood for us, and in return we receive his Spirit* ... Jesus' death both creates and cleanses a new temple, the people of God' (Vanhoozer, 'Atonement in Postmodernity', 398–9).

[92] A recent spate of books rightly demands such incorporation into studies of the atonement. Cf. Brown, *Cross Talk*; Mark Driscoll and Gerry Breshears, *Death by Love: Letters from the Cross* (Wheaton, IL: Crossway, 2008).

[93] 'Man has not fallen lower than the depth to which God humbled Himself for him in Jesus Christ' (*CD* IV/1, 480–1).

is also a manner of hiding from him',[94] or by 'employ[ing this] truth ... in the evasion of its attack and seizure of control' (*CD* IV/3.1 436).

And in doing this Jesus likewise awakens us to ways in which we hide physically, emotionally and otherwise from the presence of others. For we cannot separate these two dimensions (hiding from or forsaking God and hiding from and forsaking others), for just as the second greatest commandment is like the first, so there is a likeness in the human realm to our desire to flee the presence of God.[95] Jesus opens our eyes to everyday abandonment, whether it be in the form of the student in class whose desperation for attention is so intense as to drive away those who otherwise might befriend her, or those few rare friends who can really help us by saying that most needed, painful and unwanted truth. And he awakens us to the bondage accompanying the state of abandonment – the slavish seeking of acceptance (from God and our neighbours) or the equally rigid refusal to invest oneself in relationships and pursuits for the fear of failing and incurring further rejection. He frees us by bearing of our abandonment and embracing us as his own, freeing us to live amidst the world's threats of failure, mediocrity and abandonment, without fear that we will ever be abandoned by him.

Conclusion

Why pursue new aspects of the atonement, such as the 'temple theory of the atonement' sketched here? The first and decisive reason, apart from any perceivable benefit to the theologian or the Church, is the simple fact that Scripture witnesses to Christ's saving work in a variety of ways, and it is the vocation of the Church to seek to understand these. We simply are not at liberty to select our favourite themes or passages of Scripture at the expense of others. Whether certain veins of thought with regard to the atonement and other subjects in Scripture may be incompletely developed or less well attested is neither here no there as far as the Church is concerned – its business is to appropriate and understand these to the best of its ability, trusting to the Lord that in the end they will prove fruitful in the Church's worship and ministry.

As we have seen, however, there are a number of readily perceivable benefits to a temple theory of the atonement: (1) its integration of significant portions of the Old Testament into a discussion in which they

---

[94] François Wendel, *Calvin: The Origins and Development of His Religious Thought* (New York: Harper & Row, 1963), 216.

[95] Cf. George Hunsinger, Justification and Justice: Toward an Evangelical Social Ethic. In *What Is Justification About? Reformed Contributions to an Ecumenical Theme*, edited by Michael Weinrich, and John P. Burgess. Grand Rapids, MI: Eerdmans, 2009.

are not normally relevant; (2) the integration of the doctrines of ecclesiology, pneumatology and soteriology are all considerable factors to be considered; and (3) the pastoral relevance of thinking about sin in light of abandonment. It is important to note, however, that our awareness of such benefits, while important, is strictly secondary. Our vocation is to love and submit to God's self-revelation in Scripture, allowing it to guide our thought as it will. The implications will follow, just as following the second greatest commandment follows from the first.

7

CONCLUSION

We conclude where we began: with Paul's decision 'to know nothing among [the Corinthians] except Jesus Christ and him crucified' (1 Cor. 2.2). Paul is able to say this because for him 'Jesus Christ and him crucified' is at the very centre of God's creative and redemptive purposes, fundamentally changing every aspect of life. But how do we come to share in Paul's vision? How can we come to see Christ's death and resurrection as such an all-encompassing reality that we can read the whole Old Testament in its light, use its resources to think through tensions and difficulties in a marriage or the workplace, and find our own identity so firmly in Christ that our deepest fears, shame and guilt no longer have power over us? Christ came to reconcile all things to God, 'all things, whether on earth or in heaven' (Col. 1.20) – but is our understanding of Christ's work so broad that we can really see 'all things' in its light? And if not, what should we do?

The answer, quite simply, is that we must renew our commitment to understanding the Scriptural witness to Christ's reconciling work, appropriating all the riches we have in that abundant account – for the Bible contains a manifold description of the atonement, if one has the eyes to see it. But there's the rub – do we have the eyes to see or the theological equipment necessary to reap this harvest? Or are we so beholden to certain theological assumptions and questions or favourite biblical passages that we unwittingly compromise ourselves in this regard? Are we so dedicated to a theory of our choice that we are unable to truly embrace other understandings of Christ's work? Mere lip-service simply will not do in this case! Are we so familiar with certain (apparently) key passages or (debatably) central themes that we are neither able nor interested in doing the work to mine Scripture for other (relatively) obscure or (supposedly) peripheral or (allegedly) less developed themes? The risk is that of an imbalanced diet in which the Church suffers from varying degrees malnutrition and seeks to compensate by sustaining itself from a menu other than that offered in Scripture – in short, junk food.

In recent years, however, the church has been coming to grips more fully with the plurality of the biblical witness to the work of Christ, and has sought to address the question of the unity of the atonement. Some seek to order Christ's work such that one element provides the framework for the others. Many use anthropological, cultural and linguistic lines of thought to account for the different elements of the biblical witness and the theories built upon them. Others seek conceptual frameworks to explain the plurality (e.g. the traditional *munus triplex*). While these approaches have a number of strengths, they are also troubling for two different reasons. First, although I do not defend this conviction in depth here, I do not find these approaches offer satisfactory accounts of the unity of Christ's work. All too often the unifying structure flattens out the biblical and historical material, leaving me dissatisfied. Second, it is deeply troubling that these approaches tend to lack sustained reflection on the God who was, in Christ, reconciling all things to Himself. The doctrines of the Trinity and divine perfections make guest appearances here and there – particularly in certain well-worn roles (did the Father punish the Son? What is the relationship between God's love and wrath?) – but rarely are the doctrines themselves and as a whole brought to bear upon the relevant issues as the stars of the show.

The burden of this book has been to constructively appropriate Karl Barth's theology to show that intentionally and consistently approaching the doctrine of the atonement from the vantage point of the doctrine of God (Trinity and perfections) provides the necessary framework and resources for embracing the unified diversity of Jesus' saving work. For it is the subject of this act that is utterly decisive for comprehending the meaning (and unity and diversity) of the act's effects. Because it was God that was in Christ accomplishing this work, the key to this work is precisely the God who was accomplishing it: the triune God in the fullness of his divine perfections in the fulfilment of his covenantal purposes. Reading Scripture from this perspective gives us the eyes to see the riches that we have in Christ, so as to know, with Paul, nothing but Jesus Christ and him crucified – and in knowing this to know all things.

Chapter 2 paved the way for this approach, establishing the way that in Barth's theology God is the living God, and as such the one who decides to share his being – his life – with us. But as this living one, God chooses to adopt a course in which his history with us has a centre: the person and work of Jesus Christ, and above all his death and resurrection. For this reason we focus our theological and biblical reflection on this one complex moment, and it is at this point that the whole biblical witness to God's self-revelation comes together to form a full and unified picture. In short, when we look at Jesus Christ we see God bringing the fullness of his divine life to bear upon us and our sin, in fulfilment of his covenantal purposes. Chapter 3 considered more thoroughly who this living God is: Father, Son and Holy Spirit. The doctrine of the Trinity, we found, provides the resources for seeing how God can take up our sinful human condition within himself so as to deal with it by means of the resources proper to himself, without being either unfaithful to himself or destroying us in the process. Simultaneously, it provides the foundation within God for that which he seeks to share with us through his atoning work: fellowship.

Chapter 4 delved into Barth's understanding of the perfections of God, drawing on the previous chapter to see how the doctrine of the Trinity shapes that of the divine perfections. With those reflections in place we explored the role of the doctrine of the divine perfections within that of the atonement. My thesis in this chapter, which in many ways is the heart of this book, is that the doctrine of the divine perfections demands that we seek to understand Christ's work from the standpoint of the biblical witness to each of the divine perfections, in accordance with the unified diversity in which God's perfections exist in the divine life. Put differently, every theory of the atonement necessarily relies on one or more divine perfections in its construal of our sin and Christ's saving work. Intentionally exploring the biblical account of the divine perfections with an eye towards how these might provide new standpoints from which to view Christ's work greatly expands our view of the atonement. Chapter 5 recapitulated this thesis from the vantage point of the doctrine of sin (as sin is comprehensible only in light of the divine perfections which it distorts in some way), meanwhile affording us the opportunity to explore the role of other potentially unifying features of the atonement within Barth's thought.

In Chapter 6 I offered a test case so as to corroborate my thesis by developing a relatively new theory of the atonement from the vantage point of the divine (omni)presence – a 'temple theory of the atonement'. The purpose of this exercise was to indicate just how fertile is the soil offered by my appropriation of Barth's thought, by testing it with what at first glance would not seem to be an overly promising question: what is the result of approaching Scripture's witness to the work of Christ from the standpoint of the divine (omni) presence? The result was a relatively new understanding of the atonement that appropriates a mass of biblical material not normally associated with this doctrine, makes excellent use of Jesus' cry of dereliction and the tearing of the temple veil, and is pastorally relevant through the account of sin to which it gives rise (abandoning or forsaking both God and others).

Should my thesis prove compelling, there are two different directions in which we could proceed. First, with regard to the thesis itself there are certain structural elements that are left largely undeveloped. For instance, to limit the scope of the book, I almost entirely omitted a treatment of the doctrines of the Holy Spirit and of the resurrection. An important step towards continuing to extend this thesis is to incorporate these two dogmatic loci. Both require extensive explanation and development, for, traditionally, works on the doctrine of the atonement reflect little if at all on the role of the Holy Spirit and Christ's resurrection. My own decision to postpone the consideration of these questions was largely due to the fact that I thought it impracticable to offer a focused treatment of my own thesis in conjunction with exploring these two loci (given how undeveloped they are in discussions of the doctrine of the atonement), despite their great significance.

The second route is of a far more practical nature for the Church. On the basis of our understanding of the unity of the atonement, the responsibility of the Church is to engage in a sustained effort to re-appropriate old views, familiarize itself with foreign perspectives, and develop new standpoints of Christ's saving work, harvesting the abundant riches we have in Christ's saving work. We can fulfil this task in several different ways, all of which ultimately cohere through the normative role of Scripture. First, we must explore our Christian heritage, seeking to understand and appropriate the resources bequeathed to us by our spiritual fathers and mothers. Irenaeus, Athanasius, the Cappadocian Fathers, John of Damascus, Anselm, Bernard of Clairvaux, Lombard, Aquinas, Luther, Calvin, John of the Cross, Theresa of Avila ... if we approach their works with an eye for new standpoints from which to appreciate the saving work of Christ, more often than not we will be rewarded. All were saturated with Scripture and versed in the tradition, and many have creative interpretations of the work of Christ yet to be fully appreciated.

Not only does my thesis provide an impetus for further historical study – it provides us with greater resources for going about this task charitably. Given the complex and multi-faceted understanding of the work of Christ (and the sin which he overcomes), all of which is rooted in the unified diversity of God's own being, we have several different vantage points from which to appreciate incomplete or faulty accounts of the atonement with which at first glance we might be inclined to disagree. For instance, relatively few today find the work of Socinus, Grotius, Schleiermacher, Kant or Hegel concerning the atonement to be compelling. But might they cue us in to some aspect of our sin, Christ's work, or God's being which could be constructively appropriated for the benefit of the Church? And could we not then draw on that insight, fill it out properly, and ultimately benefit thereby? Instead of accepting or rejecting theories wholesale, in other words, the above appropriation of Barth's thought allows for a more nuanced evaluation of theories of the atonement, or an increasingly charitable hermeneutic, which is free to draw on the strengths of others. The more we see Christ's work as a rich and complex (although unified) event, the greater resources we have to embrace the work of others which is different from our own.

Second, we should engage in a similar effort with regard to the experiences and reflections of the global church today. At times this effort will prove disappointing, for the evangelization of many countries in the past was so successful as to import our own understanding of Christ's work wholesale. For this reason, missionaries with whom I correspond rarely report an understanding of the cross other than penal substitution among the people they work with – the doctrine taught them by missionaries. While penal substitution is a vital part of Scripture's witness to Christ, there are other aspects to his work, which other cultures may be uniquely positioned to perceive in Scripture. We therefore have a responsibility and great opportunity to learn from the church in other cultures, as their experiences and sensitivities facilitate their appreciation of certain elements of the Scriptural witness concerning Christ's work to which we may be more or less blind.

Finally, we must approach Scripture with new eyes, for it is thence that the church throughout the centuries and in other parts of the world today derives the diversity of its unified message and by it that it tests and approves its teaching. How then are we to approach Scripture anew? This is first and foremost a question of mindset: our goal is to find therein an abundance of resources by which to understand, proclaim and apply the saving benefits we have in Christ – an abundance which is rooted in the unified diversity proper to God, which he brings to bear upon our sinful condition in Jesus Christ. This perspective alone will radically expand our understanding of Christ's saving work. More practically, we are to read the Scriptures in such a way as to become sensitive to the different divine perfections, aspects of our sin, characteristics of salvation (exodus, freedom, knowledge, life …) and different biblical themes (temple, law, marriage, city, family, adoption …), seeking to draw connections between these which might develop into aspects of Christ's saving work.

In other words, rather than going solely to those passages that speak most clearly about Christ's atoning work, we might also read Scripture with an eye to the divine perfections, asking how these relate to Christ's work. Or we might look at some of the key themes in Scripture, asking how these might relate to the atonement. For instance, we might notice that marriage is an important theme throughout Scripture, ranging from Adam and Eve to the adultery of Israel (think of Hosea and Gomer), and later Paul's view of the Church as the bride of Christ. Does the biblical development of this theme guide us to an understanding of God's character (e.g. purity, glory and faithfulness) and our own sin (e.g. idolatry, defilement, shame and faithlessness)? And, if so, are there passages that directly or more subtly might help us understand how these come together in light of Christ's death and resurrection? And what has the church done with these themes throughout the centuries? Questions such as these will open our eyes to the riches we have in Christ's atoning work. For this reason alone such a pursuit is worthwhile – to understand Christ's work more deeply and thoroughly, that we might be all the more filled with thanksgiving.

But there is another benefit accompanying this project, for the better we come to know our Lord the better we come to know ourselves – both who we are in him and who we were without him. Our understanding of Christ's work, therefore, will pay rich dividends as we apply this understanding to sin, pain and need – our own and that of others. The pastoral implications are immense, as we become more and more adept at connecting our sins and those of others to the different aspects of Christ's saving work. Surely sin is a matter of guilt and death. But the manifold work of Christ opens our eyes to far more aspects of sin, so that we can relate more and more of our own struggles and those of others, our lust, shame, triviality, sloth, impurity, faithlessness and impatience to the work of Christ. Cultivating our awareness of this diversity will enable us, as Brown puts it, to become increasingly 'adept pastoral "poets" of the cross'.[1]

[1] Brown, *Cross Talk*, 6.

SELECT BIBLIOGRAPHY

Ashley, Timothy R. *Numbers*. (Grand Rapids, MI: Eerdmans, 1993.)

Aulén, Gustaf, *Christus Victor: An Historical Study of the Three Main Types of the Idea of Atonement*, trans. A. G. Hebert (New York: Macmillan, 1951).

Averbeck, R. E., 'Sacrifices and Offerings', in *Dictionary of the Old Testament: Pentateuch*, (eds) T. Desmond Alexander and David W. Baker (Downers Grove, IL: InterVarsity Press, 2003), 706–33.

—'Tabernacle', in *Dictionary of the Old Testament: Pentateuch*, (eds) T. Desmond Alexander, and David W. Baker (Downers Grove, IL: InterVarsity Press, 2003), 807–27.

Bagnato, Robert A., 'Karl Barth's Personalizing of "Juridical Redemption".' *Anglican Theological Review* 49, no. 1 (1967), 45–69.

Baker, Mark D. and Joel B. Green, *Recovering the Scandal of the Cross: Atonement in New Testament and Contemporary Contexts* (Downers Grove, IL: InterVarsity Press, 2003).

Bakker, L. A. R., 'Jesus als Stellvertreter für unsere Sünden und sein Verhältnis zu Israel bei Karl Barth', *Zeitschrift für dialektische Theologie* 2 (1986), 39–59.

Balthasar, Hans Urs von, *Theo-Drama: Theological Dramatic Theory*, trans. Graham Harrison, Vol. 4: The Action (San Francisco, CA: Ignatius, 1988).

—*Mysterium Paschale: The Mystery of Easter*, trans. Aidan Nichols (San Francisco, CA: Ignatius Press, 1990).

—*The Theology of Karl Barth: Exposition and Interpretation*, trans. Edward T. Oakes (San Francisco, CA: Ignatius, 1992).

Barth, Karl, *Unterricht in der christlichen Religion*, ed. Heinrich Stoevesandt (Zürich: Theologischer Verlag, 1925–26).

—*Credo: A Presentation of the Chief Problems of Dogmatics with Reference to the Apostles' Creed* (London: Hodder & Stoughton, 1936).

—*This Christian Cause* (New York: Macmillan, 1941).

—*The Church and the War*, trans. Antonia H. Froendt (New York: Macmillan, 1944).

—*Dogmatik im Grundriss* (Zürich: Evangelischer Verlag, 1947).

—*Das Geschenk der Freiheit: Grundlegung evangelischer Ethik* (Zollikon-Zürich: Evangelischer verlag, 1953).

—*The Faith of the Church: A Commentary on the Apostle's Creed According to Calvin's Catechism*, trans. Gabriel A. Vahanian (New York: Meridian, 1958).

—*Dogmatics in Outline*, trans. G. T. Thompson (New York: Harper, 1959).

—*Anselm: Fides Quaerens Intellectum*, trans. Ian W. Robertson (New York: Meridian Books, 1960).

—*Community, State, and Church: Three Essays*, trans. H. M. Hall, G. Ronald Howe and Ronald Gregor Smith (Garden City, NY: Doubleday, 1960).

—*The Humanity of God*, trans. Thomas Wieser and John N. Thomas (Richmond, VA: WJK, 1960).

—*Deliverance to the Captives*, trans. Marguerite Wieser (New York: Harper & Row, 1961).

—*Evangelical Theology: An Introduction*, trans. Grover Foley (London: Weidenfeld and Nicolson, 1963).

—'Revelation', in *God in Action* (Manhasset, NY: Round Table Press, 1963), 3–19.

—*Karl Barth's Table Talk*, ed. John Drew Godsey (Edinburgh: Oliver and Boyd, 1963).

—*Letters, 1961–1968*, trans. Geoffrey William Bromiley, (eds) Jürgen Fangmeier and Hinrich Stoevesandt (Grand Rapids, MI: Eerdmans, 1981).

—*Wolfgang Amadeus Mozart*, trans. Clarence K. Pott (Grand Rapids, MI: Eerdmans, 1986).

—*Protestant Theology in the Nineteenth Century: Its Background and History*, trans. Brian Cozens and John Bowden (Grand Rapids, MI: Eerdmans, 2002).

Barth, Karl and Eduard Thurneysen, *Revolutionary Theology in the Making: Barth–Thurneysen Correspondence, 1914–1925*, trans. Geoffrey W. Bromiley (Richmond, VA: WJK, 1964).

Bauckham, Richard, *Jesus and the God of Israel: God Crucified and Other Studies on the New Testament's Christology of Divine Identity* (Grand Rapids, MI: Eerdmans, 2009).

Beale, G. K., *The Temple and the Church's Mission: A Biblical Theology of the Dwelling Place of God* (Downers Grove, IL: InterVarsity Press, 2004).

Beilby, James K. and Paul R. Eddy, (eds), *The Nature of the Atonement: Four Views* (Downers Grove, IL: IVP Academic, 2006).

Berkouwer, G. C., *The Triumph of Grace in the Theology of Karl Barth*, trans. Harry R. Boer (Grand Rapids, MI: Eerdmans, 1956).

Bettis, Joseph, 'Political Theology and Social Ethics: The Socialist Humanism of Karl Barth', in *Karl Barth and Radical Politics*, ed. by George Hunsinger (Philadelphia, PA: Westminster Press, 1976), 159–79.

Blocher, Henri, *Original Sin: Illuminating the Riddle* (Leicester: Apollos, 1997).

—'Biblical Metaphors and the Doctrine of the Atonement', *Journal of the Evangelical Theological Society* 47, no. 4 (2004), 629–45.

—'Atonement', in *Dictionary for Theological Interpretation of the Bible*, (eds) Kevin J. Vanhoozer, Craig G. Bartholomew, Daniel J. Treier and N. T. Wright (Grand Rapids, MI: Baker Academic, 2005), 72–6.

Bloesch, Donald G., *Jesus is Victor! Karl Barth's Doctrine of Salvation* (Nashville, TN: Abingdon, 1976).

Boersma, Hans, *Violence, Hospitality, and the Cross: Reappropriating the Atonement Tradition* (Grand Rapids, MI: Baker Academic, 2004).

Boff, Leonardo, *Passion of Christ, Passion of the World: The Facts, Their Interpretation, and Their Meaning Yesterday and Today* (Maryknoll, NY: Orbis, 1987).

Bravo, Carlos, 'Jesus of Nazareth, Christ the Liberator', in *Systematic Theology: Perspectives from Liberation Theology*, (eds) Jon Sobrino and Ignacio Ellacuría (Maryknoll, NY: Orbis, 1996), 106–23.

Brock, Rita Nakashima and Rebecca Ann Parker, *Proverbs of Ashes: Violence, Redemptive Suffering, and the Search for What Saves Us* (Boston, MA: Beacon Press, 2001).

Brown, Sally A. *Cross Talk: Preaching Redemption Here and Now* (Louisville, KY: WJK, 2008).

Brueggemann, Walter, *Theology of the Old Testament: Testimony, Dispute, Advocacy* (Minneapolis, MN: Fortress, 1997).

Brümmer, Vincent, *Atonement, Christology and the Trinity: Making Sense of Christian Doctrine* (Burlington, VT: Ashgate, 2005).

Busch, Eberhard, *Karl Barth: His Life from Letters and Autobiographical Texts*, trans. John Bowden (Philadelphia, PA: Fortress, 1976).

Carey, Holly J., *Jesus' Cry from the Cross: Towards a First-Century Understanding of the Intertextual Relationship Between Psalm 22 and the Narrative of Mark's Gospel.* (New York: T & T Clark, 2009).

Carson, D. A., 'The *SBJT* Forum: The Atonement Under Fire', *Southern Baptist Journal of Theology* 11, no. 2 (2007), 104–7.

Castelo, Daniel, *The Apathetic God: Exploring the Contemporary Relevance of Divine Impassibility* (Colorado Springs, CO: Paternoster, 2009).

Childs, Brevard S., *Introduction to the Old Testament as Scripture* (Philadelphia, PA: Fortress, 1979).

—*The Book of Exodus* (Philadelphia, PA: Westminster Press, 1974).

Christensen, Michael J. and Jeffery A. Wittung, *Partakers of the Divine Nature: The History and Development of Deificiation in the Christian Traditions* (Grand Rapids, MI: Baker Academic, 2007).

Clarke, W. Norris, *Explorations in Metaphysics: Being–God–Person* (Notre Dame, IN: University of Notre Dame Press, 1994).

Cochrane, Arthur C., *Reformed Confessions of the 16th Century* (Philadelphia, PA: Westminster Press, 1966).

Cole Graham A., *He Who Gives Life: The Doctrine of the Holy Spirit* (Wheaton, IL: Crossway, 2007).

—'Exodus 34, the Middoth and the Doctrine of God: The Importance of Biblical Theology to Evangelical Systematic Theology', *Southern Baptist Journal of Theology* 12, no. 3 (2008), 24–36.

—*God the Peacemaker* (Downers Grove, IL: InterVarsity Press, 2009).

Congar, Yves, *The Mystery of the Temple: Or the Manner of God's Presence to His Creatures from Genesis to Apocalypse*, trans. Reginald F. Trevett (London: Burns and Oates, 1962).

Cranfield, C. E. B., *The Gospel According to Saint Mark* (Cambridge: Cambridge University Press, 1963).

Crisp, Oliver D., 'On Barth's Denial of Universalism', *Themelios* 29, no. 1 (2003), 18–29.

Currie III, Thomas W., 'The Being and Act of God', in *Theology Beyond Christendom: Essays on the Centenary of the Birth of Karl Barth, May 10, 1886*, ed. John Thompson (Allison Park, PA: Pickwick, 1986), 1–12.

Davies, G. N., 'Tabernacle, Sanctuary', in *Dictionary of the Later New Testament and its Developments*, (eds) Ralph P. Martin and Peter H. Davids (Downers Grove, IL: InterVarsity Press, 1997), 1154–6.

Dawson, R. Dale, *The Resurrection in Karl Barth* (Burlington, VT: Ashgate, 2007).

Driscoll, Mark and Gerry Breshears, *Death by Love: Letters from the Cross* (Wheaton, IL: Crossway, 2008).

Drury, John L. 'The Priest Sacrificed in Our Place: Barth's Use of the Cultic Imagery of Hebrews in *Church Dogmatics* IV/1, §59.2', Paper presented at the Annual Barth Conference, Princeton Theological Seminary, NJ, 21–4 May 2006.

Dunn, James D. G., *The Partings of the Ways: Between Christianity and Judaism and Their Significance for the Character of Christianity* (London: SCM, 2006).

Fee, Gordon D. *The First Epistle to the Corinthians* (Grand Rapids, MI: Eerdmans, 1987).

Fergusson, David, 'Barth's Resurrection of the Dead: Further Reflections', *Scottish Journal of Theology* 56, no. 1 (2003), 65–72.

Fiddes, Paul S., *Past Event and Present Salvation: The Christian Idea of Atonement* (Louisville, KY: WJK, 1989).

Finlan, Stephen, *Options on Atonement in Christian Thought* (Collegeville, MN: Liturgical Press, 2007).

Finlan, Stephen and Vladimir Kharlamov, *Theōsis: Deification in Christian Theology* (Eugene, OR: Pickwick, 2006).

Geddert, Timothy J., *Watchwords: Mark 13 in Markan Eschatology* (Sheffield: Sheffield Academic Press, 1989).

Gerstenberger, E., 'עָזַב', in *Theological Dictionary of the Old Testament*, (eds) G. Johannes Botterweck and Helmer Ringgren (Grand Rapids, MI: Eerdmans, 1977), 584–92.

Girard, René, *Violence and the Sacred* (Baltimore, NJ: Johns Hopkins University Press, 1977).

—*I See Satan Fall Like Lightning* (Maryknoll, NY: Orbis, 2001).

Goldingay, John, *Psalms* (Grand Rapids, MI: Baker Academic, 2006).

Graham, Jeannine M., *Representation and Substitution in the Atonement Theologies of Dorothee Sölle, John Macquarrie, and Karl Barth* (New York: Peter Lang, 2005).

Gray, Timothy C. *The Temple in the Gospel of Mark: A Study in Its Narrative Role* (Tübingen: Mohr Siebeck, 2008).

Green, Clifford, 'Freedom for Humanity: Karl Barth and the Politics of the New World Order', in *For the Sake of the World: Karl Barth and the Future of Ecclesial Theology*, ed. George Hunsinger (Grand Rapids, MI: Eerdmans, 2004), 89–106.

Green, Joel B., 'Kaleidoscopic View', in *The Nature of the Atonement: Four Views*, (eds) James K. Beilby and Paul R. Eddy. (Downers Grove, IL: IVP Academic, 2006), 157–85.

Greggs, Tom, '"Jesus is Victor": Passing the Impasse of Barth on Universalism', *Scottish Journal of Theology* 60, no. 2 (2007), 196–212.

—*Barth, Origen, and Universal Salvation: Restoring Particularity* (Oxford: Oxford University Press, 2009).

Gunton, Colin E., *Becoming and Being: The Doctrine of God in Charles Hartshorne and Karl Barth* (Oxford: Oxford University Press, 1978).

—*The Actuality of Atonement: A Study of Metaphor, Rationality, and the Christian Tradition* (Grand Rapids, MI: Eerdmans, 1989).

—'Salvation', in *The Cambridge Companion to Karl Barth*, ed. J. B. Webster (New York: Cambridge University Press, 2000), 143–58.

—*Act and Being: Towards a Theology of the Divine Attributes* (Grand Rapids, MI: Eerdmans, 2003).

—*The Barth Lectures*, ed. Paul Brazier (New York: T & T Clark, 2007).

Gurtner, Daniel M., *The Torn Veil: Matthew's Exposition of the Death of Jesus* (New York: Cambridge University Press, 2007).

Gutiérrez, Gustavo, *A Theology of Liberation: History, Politics, and Salvation* (Maryknoll, NY: Orbis, 1973).

Hamilton, J. M., 'Divine Presence', in *Dictionary of the Old Testament: Wisdom, Poetry and Writings*, (eds) Tremper Longman and Peter Enns (Downers Grove, IL: IVP Academic, 2008), 116–20.

Hardin, Michael, 'Out of the Fog: New Horizons for Atonement Theory', in *Stricken by God? Nonviolent Identification and the Victory of Christ*, (eds) Brad Jersak and Michael Hardin (Grand Rapids, MI: Eerdmans, 2007).

Harnack, Adolf von, *What is Christianity?* (New York: Harper, 1957).

Hart, Trevor A., *Regarding Karl Barth: Essays Toward a Reading of His Theology* (Carlisle: Paternoster Press, 1999).

—'Revelation', in *The Cambridge Companion to Karl Barth*, ed. J. B. Webster (New York: Cambridge University Press, 2000), 37–56.

Hartley, J. E., *Leviticus*, (eds) Bruce M. Metzger, David A. Hubbard and Glenn W. Barker (Dallas, TX: Word Books, 1992).

—'Day of Atonement', in *Dictionary of the Old Testament: Pentateuch*, (eds) T. Desmond Alexander and David W. Baker (Downers Grove, IL: InterVarsity Press, 2003).

Hector, Kevin W., 'Election and the Trinity: How My Mind Has Changed', Paper presented at the American Academy of Religion, Chicago, IL, 31 October 2008.

—'Immutability, Necessity, and Trinity: Towards a Resolution of the Trinity and Election Controversy,' *Scottish Journal of Theology* 65:1, pp. 64–81).

Heim, S. Mark, *Saved from Sacrifice: A Theology of the Cross* (Grand Rapids, MI: Eerdmans, 2006).

Hengel, Martin, *Crucifixion in the Ancient World and the Folly of the Message of the Cross*, trans. John Bowden (Philadelphia, PA: Fortress, 1977).

Hieb, Nathan D., 'The Liberating Reconciliation of the Cross: Atonement for Sin and Liberation from Suffering in Karl Barth's "Theologia Crucis"', PhD diss., Princeton Theological Seminary, 2009.

Hill, Charles E. and Frank A. James (eds), *The Glory of the Atonement: Biblical, Historical and Practical Perspectives* (Downers Grove, IL: InterVarsity Press, 2004).

Holmes, Christopher R. J., *Revisiting the Doctrine of the Divine Attributes: In Dialogue with Karl Barth, Eberhard Jüngel and Wolf Krötke* (New York: Peter Lang, 2007).

Holmes, Stephen R. 'The Attributes of God', in *The Oxford Handbook of Systematic Theology*, (eds) J. B. Webster, Kathryn Tanner and Iain R. Torrance (Oxford: Oxford University Press, 2007).

Horst, J., 'μακροθυμία', in *Theological Dictionary of the New Testament*, (eds) Gerhard Kittel, Geoffrey William Bromiley and Gerhard Friedrich (Grand Rapids, MI: Eerdmans, 1964).

Hoskins, Paul M. *Jesus as the Fulfillment of the Temple in the Gospel of John* (Milton Keynes: Paternoster, 2006).

Hunsinger, George, *How to Read Karl Barth: The Shape of His Theology* (Oxford: Oxford University Press, 1991).

—*Disruptive Grace: Studies in the Theology of Karl Barth* (Grand Rapids, MI: Eerdmans, 2000).

—'Karl Barth's Christology: Its Basic Chalcedonian Character', in *The Cambridge Companion to Karl Barth*, ed. J. B. Webster (New York: Cambridge University Press, 2000), 127–42.

—'Election and the Trinity: Twenty-Five Theses on the Theology of Karl Barth', *Modern Theology* 24, no. 2 (2008), 179–98.

—'Justification and Justice: Toward an Evangelical Social Ethic'. In *What Is Justification About? Reformed Contributions to an Ecumenical Theme*, edited by Michael Weinrich, and John P. Burgess. Grand Rapids, MI: Eerdmans, 2009.

Jansen, John Frederick, *Calvin's Doctrine of the Work of Christ* (London: J. Clark, 1956).

Jehle, Frank, *Ever Against the Stream: The Politics of Karl Barth, 1906–1968* (Grand Rapids, MI: Eerdmans, 2002).

Jenson, Matt, *Gravity of Sin: Augustine, Luther and Barth on 'Homo Incurvatus in Se'* (New York: T & T Clark, 2006).

Jenson, Robert, 'On the Doctrine of the Atonement', *The Princeton Seminary Bulletin* 27, no. 2 (2006), 100–8.

Jenson, Robert W., *Alpha and Omega: A Study in the Theology of Karl Barth* (New York: Nelson, 1963).

Jersak, Brad and Michael Hardin (eds), *Stricken by God? Nonviolent Identification and the Victory of Christ* (Grand Rapids, MI: Eerdmans, 2007).

Jobes, Karen H., *1 Peter* (Grand Rapids, MI: Baker Academic, 2005).

Johnson, Adam, 'A Fuller Account: The Role of "Fittingness" in Thomas Aquinas' Development of the Doctrine of the Atonement', *International Journal of Systematic Theology* 12, no. 3 (2010), 302–18.

—'The Servant Lord: A Word of Caution Regarding the *munus triplex* in Karl Barth's Theology and the Church Today', *Scottish Journal of Theology* (Forthcoming).

Johnson, Luke Timothy, *Hebrews* (Louisville, KY: WJK, 2006).

Jones, Paul Dafydd, *The Humanity of Christ: Christology in Karl Barth's Church Dogmatics* (New York: T & T Clark, 2008).

Jorgenson, Allen, 'Karl Barth's Christological Treatment of Sin', *Scottish Journal of Theology* 54, no. 4 (2001), 439–62.

Jowers, Dennis W., 'The Reproach of Modalism: A Difficulty for Karl Barth's Doctrine of the Trinity', *Scottish Journal of Theology* 56, no. 2 (2003), 231–46.

Jüngel, Eberhard, 'What Does it Mean to Say, "God Is Love"?, in *Christ in Our Place: The Humanity of God in Christ for the Reconciliation of the World*, (eds) Trevor A. Hart and Daniel P. Thimell (Allison Park, PA: Pickwick, 1989), 294–312.

—*God's Being is in Becoming: The Trinitarian Being of God in the Theology of Karl Barth*, trans. J. B. Webster (Grand Rapids, MI: Eerdmans, 2001).

Kelsey, David H., 'Whatever Happened to the Doctrine of Sin?,' *Theology Today* 50, no. 2 (1993), 169–78.

Kilby, Karen, 'Is an Apophatic Trinitarianism Possible?', *International Journal of Systematic Theology* 12, no. 1 (2010), 65–77.

Kitamori, Kazo, *Theology of the Pain of God* (Richmond: John Knox Press, 1965).

Klappert, Bertold, *Die Auferweckung des Gekreuzigten: der Ansatz der Christologie Karl Barths im Zusammenhang der Christologie der Gegenwart* (Neukirchen: Neukirchener Verlag, 1974).

—*Versöhnung und Befreiung: Versuche, Karl Barth kontextuell zu verstehen* (Neukirchen: Neukirchener Verlag, 1994).

Kraus, C. Norman, *Jesus Christ Our Lord: Christology from a Disciple's Perspective* (Scottdale, PA: Herald Press, 1987).

Krötke, Wolf, *Sin and Nothingness in the Theology of Karl Barth*, trans. Philip G. Ziegler and Christina-Maria Bammel (Princeton, NJ: Princeton Theological Seminary, 2005.

Lauber, David, *Barth on the Descent into Hell: God, Atonement and the Christian Life* (Burlington, VT: Ashgate, 2004).

Lewis, Alan E., *Between Cross and Resurrection: A Theology of Holy Saturday* (Grand Rapids, MI: Eerdmans, 2001).

Lightfoot, J. B., *Saint Paul's Epistles to the Colossians and to Philemon* (London: Macmillan, 1916).

Love, Gregory Anderson, 'In Search of a Non-Violent Atonement Theory: Are Abelard and Girard a Help or a Problem?', in *Theology as Conversation: The Significance of Dialogue in Historical and Contemporary Theology*, ed. Bruce L. McCormack and Kimlyn J. Bender (Grand Rapids, MI: Eerdmans, 2009).

Marcus, Joel, *Mark* (New York: Doubleday, 2000).

Marshall, Bruce D., 'The Dereliction of Christ and the Impassibility of God', in *Divine Impassibility and the Mystery of Human Suffering*, (eds) James Keating and Thomas Joseph White (Grand Rapids, MI: Eerdmans, 2009).

Marshall, I. Howard, 'Church and Temple in the New Testament', *Tyndale Bulletin* 40, no. 2 (1989), 203–22.

Maurer, Ernstpeter, '"Für uns" An unserer Stelle hingerichtet: Die Herausforderung der Versöhnungslehre', *Zeitschrift für dialektische Theologie* 18 (2002), 190–210.

McCormack, Bruce L., *For Us and Our Salvation: Incarnation and Atonement in the Reformed Tradition*. Princeton, NJ: Princeton Theological Seminary, 1993.

—*Karl Barth's Critically Realistic Dialectical Theology: Its Genesis and Development, 1909–1936* (New York: Oxford University Press, 1995).

—'The Being of Holy Scripture is in Becoming', in *Evangelicals and Scripture: Tradition, Authority, and Hermeneutics*, (eds) Vincent Bacote, Laura C. Miguélez and Dennis L. Okholm (Downers Grove, IL: InterVarsity Press, 2004).

—'The Ontological Presuppositions of Barth's Doctrine of the Atonement', in *The Glory of the Atonement: Biblical, Historical and Practical Perspectives*, (eds) Roger R. Nicole, Charles E. Hill and Frank A. James (Downers Grove, IL: InterVarsity Press, 2004), 346–66.

—'The Actuality of God: Karl Barth in Conversation with Open Theism', in *Engaging the Doctrine of God: Contemporary Protestant Perspectives*, ed. Bruce L. McCormack (Grand Rapids, MI: Baker Academic, 2008).

—'Karl Barth's Historicized Christology: Just How "Chalcedonian" is it?', in *Orthodox and Modern: Studies in the Theology of Karl Barth* (Grand Rapids, MI: Baker Academic, 2008), 201–33.

—*Orthodox and Modern: Studies in the Theology of Karl Barth* (Grand Rapids, MI: Baker Academic, 2008).

—'Participation in God, Yes; Deification, No: Two Modern Protestant Responses to an Ancient Question', in *Orthodox and Modern: Studies in the Theology of Karl Barth* (Grand Rapids, MI: Baker Academic, 2008), 235–60.

—'God *Is* His Decision: The Jüngel–Gollwitzer "Debate" Revisited', in *Theology as Conversation: The Significance of Dialogue in Historical and Contemporary Theology*, (eds) Daniel L. Migliore, Bruce L. McCormack and Kimlyn J. Bender (Grand Rapids, MI: Eerdmans, 2009), 48–66.

—'"With Loud Cries and Tears": The Humanity of the Son in the Epistle to the Hebrews', in *The Epistle to the Hebrews and Christian Theology*, (eds) Richard Bauckham, Daniel R. Driver, Trevor A. Hart and Nathan MacDonald (Grand Rapids, MI: Eerdmans, 2009).

—'Election and the Trinity: Theses in Response to George Hunsinger', *Scottish Journal of Theology* 63, no. 2 (2010), 203–24.

McDowell, John C., 'Much Ado About Nothing: Karl Barth's Being Unable to Do Nothing About Nothing', *International Journal of Systematic Theology* 4, no. 3 (2002), 319–35.

McFarlane, Graham, 'Atonement, Creation and Trinity', in *The Atonement Debate: Papers From the London Symposium on the Theology of Atonement*, (eds) Derek Tidball, David Hilborn and Justin Thacker (Grand Rapids, MI: Zondervan, 2008).

McGrath, Alister E., 'The Moral Theory of the Atonement: An Historical and Theological Critique', *Scottish Journal of Theology* 38, no. 2 (1985), 205–20.

—'Karl Barth's Doctrine of Justification from an Evangelical Perspective', in *Karl Barth and Evangelical Theology* (Grand Rapids: Baker Academic, 2006), 172–90.

McIntyre, John, *The Shape of Soteriology: Studies in the Doctrine of the Death of Christ* (Edinburgh: T & T Clark, 1992).

McKnight, Scot, *A Community Called Atonement* (Nashville, TN: Abingdon Press, 2007).

Metzger, Paul Louis, *Trinitarian Soundings in Systematic Theology* (New York: T & T Clark, 2005).

Migliore, Daniel L., 'Sin and Self-Loss: Karl Barth and the Feminist Critique of Traditional Doctrines of Sin', in *Many Voices, One God*, (eds) George W. Stroup and Walter Brueggemann (Louisville, KY: WJK, 1998), 139–54.

—*Faith Seeking Understanding: An Introduction to Christian Theology* (Grand Rapids, MI: Eerdmans, 2004).

Molnar, Paul D., 'The Function of the Immanent Trinity in the Theology of Karl Barth: Implications for Today', *Scottish Journal of Theology* 42, no. 3 (1990), 367–99.

—*Divine Freedom and the Doctrine of the Immanent Trinity: In Dialogue with Karl Barth and Contemporary Theology* (New York: T & T Clark, 2005).

—'Can the Electing God be God Without Us? Some Implications of Bruce McCormack's Understanding of Barth's Doctrine of Election for the Doctrine of the Trinity', *Neue Zeitschrift für Systematische Theologie und Religionsphilosophie* 49, no. 2 (2007), 199–222.

—*Incarnation and Resurrection: Toward a Contemporary Understanding* (Grand Rapids, MI: Eerdmans, 2007).

Moltmann, Jürgen, 'The Motherly Father: Is Trinitarian Patripassianism Replacing Theological Patriarchalism?', in *God as Father*, (eds) Johannes-Baptist Metz, Edward Schillebeeckx and Marcus Lefébvre (New York: Seabury, 1981), 51–6.

—*The Trinity and the Kingdom: The Doctrine of God*, trans. Margaret Kohl (San Francisco, CA: Harper & Row, 1981).

—*The Crucified God: The Cross of Christ as the Foundation and Criticism of Christian Theology* (Minneapolis: Fortress, 1993).

Morris, Leon, *The Apostolic Preaching of the Cross* (London: Tyndale Press, 1955).

—*The Cross in the New Testament* (Grand Rapids, MI: Eerdmans, 1965).

Mueller, David L., *Foundation of Karl Barth's Doctrine of Reconciliation: Jesus Christ Crucified and Risen* (Lewiston, NY: Edwin Mellen, 1990).

Muller, Richard A., *Dictionary of Latin and Greek Theological Terms: Drawn Principally from Protestant Scholastic Theology* (Grand Rapids, MI: Baker Academic, 2006).

Neder, Adam, *Participation in Christ: An Entry into Karl Barth's Church Dogmatics* (Louisville, KY: WJK, 2009).

Nimmo, Paul T., *Being in Action: The Theological Shape of Barth's Ethical Vision* (New York: T & T Clark, 2007).

O'Brien, Peter Thomas, *The Letter to the Ephesians* (Grand Rapids, MI: Eerdmans, 1999).

Olson, Roger E., *The Mosaic of Christian Belief: Twenty Centuries of Unity and Diversity* (Downers Grove, IL: InterVarsity Press, 2002).

Overstreet, R. Larry, 'The Temple of God in the Book of Revelation', *Bibliotheca Sacra* 166 (2009), 446–62.

Ovey, Michael J., 'A Private Love? Karl Barth and the Triune God', in *Engaging with Barth: Contemporary Evangelical Critiques*, (eds) David Gibson and Daniel Strange (Nottingham: InterVarsity Press, 2008).

Packer, James I., 'What Did the Cross Achieve?: The Logic of Penal Substitution', *Tyndale Bulletin* 25 (1974), 3–45.

Park, Andrew Sung, *Triune Atonement: Christ's Healing for Sinners, Victims, and the Whole Creation* (Louisville, KY: WJK, 2009).

Peterson, Robert A., *Calvin and the Atonement* (Fearne, Scotland: Christian Focus Publications, 2008).

Pfleiderer, Georg, 'The Atonement', in *Trinitarian Soundings in Systematic Theology*, ed. Paul Louis Metzger (New York: T & T Clark, 2005), 127–38.

Plantinga Jr, Cornelius, 'The Threeness/Oneness Problem of the Trinity', *Calvin Theological Journal* 23, no. 1 (1998), 37–53.

Price, Robert B., 'Letters of the Divine Word: The Perfections of God in Karl Barth's *Church Dogmatics*', PhD diss., University of Aberdeen, 2007.

Propp, William H., *Exodus 19–40* (New York: Doubleday, 2006).

Rahner, Karl, *The Trinity*, trans. Joseph Donceel (New York: Herder and Herder, 1970).

Ramm, Bernard L., *After Fundamentalism: The Future of Evangelical Theology* (San Francisco, CA: Harper & Row, 1983).

Ray, Darby Kathleen, *Deceiving the Devil: Atonement, Abuse, and Ransom* (Cleveland, OH: Pilgrim Press, 1998).

Reesor, Rachel, 'Atonement: Mystery and Metaphorical Language', *Mennonite Quarterly Review* 68, no. 2 (1994), 209–18.

Roberts, Richard H., 'Barth's Doctrine of Time: Its Nature and Implications', in *Karl Barth*. Ithaca, (NY: Clarendon, 1979).

—*A Theology on its Way? Essays on Karl Barth* (Edinburgh: T & T Clark, 1991).

Ross, Allen P., *Holiness to the Lord* (Grand Rapids, MI: Baker Academic, 2002).

Ruddies, Hartmut, 'Christologie und Versöhnungslehre bei Karl Barth', *Zeitschrift für dialektische Theologie* 18 (2002), 174–89.

Sanders, Fred, *The Image of the Immanent Trinity: Rahner's Rule and the Theological Interpretation of Scripture* (New York: Peter Lang, 2005).

Schmiechen, Peter, *Saving Power: Theories of Atonement and Forms of the Church* (Grand Rapids, MI: Eerdmans, 2005).

Schrenk, Gottlob, 'ἱερόν', in *Theological Dictionary of the New Testament*, (eds) Gerhard Kittel, Geoffrey William Bromiley and Gerhard Friedrich (Grand Rapids, MI: Eerdmans, 1964).

Schwager, Raymund, 'Der Richter wird gerichtet: Zur Versöhnungslehre von Karl Barth', *Zeitschrift für katholische Theologie* 107, no. 1 (1985), 101–41.

—*Must There Be Scapegoats? Violence and Redemption in the Bible*, trans. Maria L. Assad (San Francisco, CA: Harper & Row, 1987).

Sherman, Robert, *King, Priest and Prophet: A Trinitarian Theology of Atonement* (Edinburgh: T & T Clark, 2004).

Shippey, Robert Clifford, 'The Suffering of God in Karl Barth's Doctrines of Election and Reconciliation', PhD diss., Southern Baptist Theological Seminary, 1991.

Sölle, Dorothee, *Christ the Representative: An Essay in Theology After the 'Death of God'* (London: SCM Press, 1967).

Sonderegger, Katherine, 'Barth and Feminism', in *The Cambridge Companion to Karl Barth*, ed. J. B. Webster (New York: Cambridge University Press, 2000).

Spence, Alan, *The Promise of Peace: A Unified Theory of Atonement* (New York: T & T Clark, 2006).

Stokes, David Lewis, 'Barth and the Atoning Narrative: The Figure of the Cross in the Church Dogmatics', PhD diss., Princeton Theological Seminary, 1989.

Stratis, Justin, 'Speculating About Divinity? God's Immanent Life and Actualistic Ontology', *International Journal of Systematic Theology* 12, no. 1 (2010), 20–32.

Stump, Eleonore, 'Presence and Omnipresence', in *Liberal Faith* (Notre Dame, IN: University of Notre Dame Press, 2008), 59–82.

Terry, Justyn, *The Justifying Judgement of God: A Reassessment of the Place of Judgment in the Saving Work of Christ* (Eugene, OR: Paternoster, 2007).

Thomas, Günter, 'Der für uns "gerichtete Richter". Kritische Erwägungen zu Karl Barths Versöhnungslehre', *Zeitschrift für dialektische Theologie* 18, no. 2 (2002), 211–25.

Thompson, John, *Christ in Perspective: Christological Perspectives in the Theology of Karl Barth* (Edinburgh: St Andrew Press, 1978).

—'Christology and Reconciliation in the Theology of Karl Barth', in *Christ in Our Place: The Humanity of God in Christ for the Reconciliation of the World*, (eds) James Torrance, Trevor A. Hart and Daniel P. Thimell (Allison Park, PA: Pickwick, 1990), 207–23.

Tidball, Derek, David Hilborn and Justin Thacker (eds), *The Atonement Debate: Papers From the London Symposium on the Theology of Atonement* (Grand Rapids, MI: Zondervan, 2008).

Torrance, Alan J., *Persons in Communion: An Essay on Trinitarian Description and Human Participation, with Special Reference to Volume One of Karl Barth's Church Dogmatics* (Edinburgh: T & T Clark, 1996).

—'The Trinity', in *The Cambridge Companion to Karl Barth*, ed. J. B. Webster (New York: Cambridge University Press, 2000).

Torrance, James, 'The Priesthood of Jesus', in *Essays in Christology for Karl Barth*, ed. T. H. L. Parker (London: Lutterworth Press, 1956).

Torrance, Thomas F., *Space, Time, and Resurrection* (Grand Rapids, MI: Eerdmans, 1976).

—*Karl Barth: Biblical and Evangelical Theologian* (Edinburgh: T & T Clark, 1990).

—*The Mediation of Christ* (Colorado Springs, CO: Helmers & Howard, 1992).

—*Atonement: The Person and Work of Christ*, ed. Robert Walker (Downers Grove, IL: InterVarsity Press, 2009).

Trelstad, Marit, *Cross Examinations: Readings on the Meaning of the Cross Today* (Minneapolis, MN: Fortress, 2006).

Van Buren, Paul M., *Christ in Our Place: The Substitutionary Character of Calvin's Doctrine of Reconciliation* (Edinburgh: Oliver and Boyd, 1957).

Vanhoozer, Kevin J., *Is There a Meaning in this Text? The Bible, the Reader, and the Morality of Literary Knowledge* (Grand Rapids, MI: Zondervan, 1998).

—'Introduction: The Love of God–Its Place, Meaning, and Function in Systematic Theology', in *Nothing Greater, Nothing Better: Theological Essays on the Love of God*, ed. Kevin J. Vanhoozer (Grand Rapids, MI: Eerdmans, 2001), 1–29.

—*First Theology: God, Scripture and Hermeneutics* (Downers Grove, IL: InterVarsity Press, 2002).

—'Atonement in Postmodernity: Guilt, Goats and Gifts', in *The Glory of the Atonement: Biblical, Historical and Practical Perspectives*, (eds) Charles E. Hill and Frank A. James (Downers Grove, IL: InterVarsity Press, 2004).

—*The Drama of Doctrine: A Canonical-Linguistic Approach to Christian Theology* (Louisville, KY: WJK, 2005).

Wainwright, Geoffrey, *For Our Salvation: Two Approaches to the Work of Christ* (Grand Rapids, MI: Eerdmans, 1997).

Ware, Bruce A., 'Christ's Atonement: A Work of the Trinity', in *Jesus in Trinitarian Perspective*, (eds) Fred Sanders and Klaus Issler (Nashville, TN: B & H Publishing Group, 2007).

Watson, Gordon, 'A Study in St Anselm's Soteriology and Karl Barth's Theological Method', *Scottish Journal of Theology* 42, no. 4 (1989), 493–512.

Weaver, J. Denny, *The Nonviolent Atonement* (Grand Rapids, MI: Eerdmans, 2001).

Webster, John, 'The Firmest Grasp of the Real: Barth on Original Sin', *Toronto Journal of Theology* 4, no. 1 (1988), 19–29.

—*Barth's Ethics of Reconciliation* (New York: Cambridge University Press, 1995).

—*Holiness* (London: SCM, 2003).

—*Holy Scripture: A Dogmatic Sketch* (New York: Cambridge University Press, 2003).

—'*Rector et iudex super omnia genera doctrinarum*? The Place of the Doctrine of Justification', in *What is Justification About? Reformed Contributions to an Ecumenical Theme*, (eds) Michael Weinrich and John P. Burgess (Grand Rapids, MI: Eerdmans, 2009).

—'Editorial', *International Journal of Systematic Theology* 12, no. 2 (2010), 116–17.

—'Trinity and Creation', *International Journal of Systematic Theology* 12, no. 1 (2010), 4–19.

Weingart, Richard E. *The Logic of Divine Love: A Critical Analysis of the Soteriology of Peter Abailard* (London: Clarendon, 1970).

Wendel, François, *Calvin: The Origins and Development of His Religious Thought* (New York: Harper & Row, 1963).

West, James E., 'Patience', in *The New Interpreter's Dictionary of the Bible*, (eds) Katherine Doob Sakenfeld, Samuel E. Balentine and Kah-Jin Jeffrey Kuan (Nashville, TN: Abingdon, 2006).

Whale, John Seldon, *Victor and Victim* (Cambridge: Cambridge University Press, 1960).

Williams, David T., 'Towards a Unified Theory of the Atonement', in *The Atonement Debate: Papers from the London Symposium on the Theology of Atonement*, (eds) Derek Tidball, David Hilborn and Justin Thacker (Grand Rapids, MI: Zondervan, 2008), 228–48.

Williams, Garry, 'Penal Substitution: A Response to Recent Criticisms', in *The Atonement Debate: Papers from the London Symposium on the Theology of Atonement*, (eds) Derek Tidball, David Hilborn and Justin Thacker (Grand Rapids, MI: Zondervan, 2008), 172–91.

Williams, Garry J., 'Karl Barth and the Doctrine of the Atonement', in *Engaging with Barth: Contemporary Evangelical Critiques*, (eds) David Gibson and Daniel Strange (Nottingham: InterVarsity Press, 2008), 232–72.

Williams, R. D., 'Barth on the Triune God', in *Karl Barth, Studies of His Theological Method*, ed. Stephen Sykes (New York: Oxford University Press, 1979), 147–93.

Williams, Thomas, 'Sin, Grace, and Redemption', in *The Cambridge Companion to Abelard*, (eds) Jeffrey E. Brower and Kevin Guilfoy (New York: Cambridge University Press, 2004), 258–78.

Wood, Laurence W., 'Defining the Modern Concept of Self-Revelation: Toward a Synthesis of Barth and Pannenberg', *Asbury Theological Journal* 41, no. 2 (1986), 85–105.

Wright, N. T., *The Epistles of Paul to the Colossians and to Philemon: An Introduction and Commentary* (Grand Rapids, MI: Eerdmans, 1988).

—*The Climax of the Covenant* (Minneapolis, MN: Fortress, 1992).

—*The New Testament and the People of God* (London: Fortress, 1992).

—*Jesus and the Victory of God* (Minneapolis, MN: Fortress, 1996).

Yocum, John, 'A Cry of Dereliction? Reconsidering a Recent Theological Commonplace', *International Journal of Systematic Theology* 7, no. 1 (2005), 72–80.

BIBLICAL INDEX

INDEX